COMMON BOUNDARIES

"*Common Boundaries* will quickly become a must-read book for researchers and students interested in environment, governance and property. A brilliant meditation on the origins of cooperation and a critical analysis of prospects for sustainability, this thought-provoking contribution pushes the boundaries of what we know and identifies future directions we must go."

Arun Agrawal, Samuel Trask Dana Professor,
School of Natural Resources and Environment, University of Michigan

"Michael Cox develops the concept of self-governance in the broadest possible way, from the individual to the planet and everything in between. *Common Boundaries* is both philosophically deep and immensely useful for anyone trying to evolve a better world."

David Sloan Wilson, President, ProSocial World,
and author of *This View of Life: Completing the Darwinian Revolution*

"Michael Cox has written a very readable account of the theory and practice of collective action as applied to environmental governance. Embedding his discussion in the framework provided by Garrett Hardin and especially Elinor Ostrom, he moves seamlessly from game theory to case studies, exploring various mechanisms, for example involving boundaries and property rights, that can lead to cooperation and collective action. The book will be of interest both to students across a wide spectrum, and to interested non-specialists."

Simon Levin, James S. McDonnell Distinguished University Professor
in Ecology and Evolutionary Biology, Princeton University

"In *Common Boundaries*, Michael Cox takes readers on a mountain-top journey to view the complex, interconnecting systems of knowledge by and through which we strive to live justly and sustainably with each other and the natural world. From that vantage point, aided by insightful case studies and an impressive array of interdisciplinary scholarship, Cox points a way forward in formulating environmental policies that are just, inclusive and impactful. This is an important book for experts and general audiences alike."

N. Bruce Duthu, Samson Occom Professor and Chair,
Department of Native American & Indigenous Studies, Dartmouth College

"Michael Cox's synthetic effort succeeds at offering an updated institutional theory of the diversity of environmental property rights. He does so by aptly weaving foundational concepts and empirical research on collective action, evolutionary biology, behavioral economics, environmental psychology, among others. The result is a theoretically innovative and policy-relevant contribution for students and practitioners seeking more nuanced approaches for environmental governance, better reflecting the diverse ways humans interact with a rapidly changing environment."

Xavier Basurto, Truman and Nellie Semans/Alex Brown
& Sons Professor, Duke University

"Michael Cox writes as if in conversation with the reader, explaining a wide span of time, theory and global examples, in a way that is readable, teachable and clear. *Common Boundaries* offers a vital resource to not only understand but shape, one of the most fundamental, yet layered, pivotal, yet taken for granted, forces of our lives."

Mehana Blaich Vaughan, Department of Natural Resources
and Environmental Management, University of Hawai'i at Mānoa

Common Boundaries

Common Boundaries

The Theory and Practice of Environmental
Property

Michael Cox

agenda
publishing

For Chris and for Ana

First edition published in 2024 by Agenda Publishing
Reprinted in paperback 2025

Agenda Publishing Limited
PO Box 185
Newcastle upon Tyne
NE20 2DH
www.agendapub.com

ISBN 978-1-78821-788-0

British Library Cataloguing-in-Publication Data
A catalogue record for this book is available from the British Library

Typeset by Newgen Publishing UK
Printed and bound in the UK by 4edge

EU GPSR authorised representative:
Logos Europe, 9 rue Nicolas Poussin, 17000 La Rochelle, France
contact@logoseurope.eu

Contents

CONTENTS

Acknowledgements

This book would not have been possible without the substantial influence of Elinor "Lin" Ostrom, which is seen on many of its pages. I have continued to benefit from a network of colleagues who I met during my time as Lin's PhD student at Indiana University, and I am grateful for this as well. I still miss Bloomington and the Ostrom Workshop where I began to find my professional place in the world.

This book grew out of 10 years of teaching a course on environmental governance at Dartmouth College, much of it inspired by Lin's work. I am grateful to my students in this course for their efforts to learn about the commons. I also want to thank Melody Burkins and the John Sloan Dickey Center for International Understanding at Dartmouth College for hosting a book review workshop, from which this work benefited immensely. Many thanks to my colleagues who attended this workshop to give me valuable feedback: J. T. Erbaugh, Forrest Fleischman, Maron Greenleaf, Courtney Hammond Wagner and Carey Nadell.

I have benefited from many conversations about content related to this book. Many of these discussions occurred during interviews I have conducted for the In Common Podcast. My thanks to all my interviewees; I appreciate the time and energy you have shared with me and our community of listeners. I am also grateful to David Sloan Wilson and Bruce Duthu for the time they have spent talking with me about how this work related to their own expertise. And many thanks to Rebecca Kohn for her editorial assistance, which greatly improved the readability of the book, and to Camilla Erskine at Agenda Publishing for engaging with me throughout this process.

And finally, thank you to Sarah for your patience and encouragement. It has been much appreciated. Here is the book.

Michael Cox

Introduction

It is not hard to find an article or book that calls for less reductionist approaches to environmental governance, and for a greater recognition of the complexities involved. We hear that we need to move beyond simplistic discourses that favour one solution over another based on our analytical framing and associated professional affiliations. Less addressed is the question, how do we do this? This book is my answer to this question. Specifically, in the following chapters I will explore the complexities of rights-based environmental governance. The approach is descriptive, asking about what we see in the world; and it is normative, asking why things are the way they are, and if they could be or should be different. I will explore different cultural perspectives on the idea of rights to the environment, and different rights-based policies such as protected areas and market-based policies. I will discuss multiple theories of environmental property and relate these theories to a range of cases to address an ongoing challenge facing the study of environment rights – this being a lack of synthesis across numerous cases and studies, each adding a brick to a house that no one can yet see.

In conducting this synthesis I have in mind the goal to help cultivate a new kind of environmental policy expert: someone who can make sense of a situation by connecting it at once to multiple concepts and cases; who can think of exceptions to a rule and often exceptions to these exceptions; who understands the importance of clarity as well as the unavoidability of ambiguity; and who is sensitized to the multiple aspects of human nature and their own position as an actor in the spaces they inhabit. We must combine these qualities to move us toward better outcomes for the planet and its people.

Seven brothers

Several years ago, I was in a motel in a coastal Dominican fishing village in the province of Monte Cristi, close to the Dominican/Haitian border. I heard a knock on the door. It was a local fisherman who was also a local leader, a man important to the work I was doing and to the work of my local partner, AgroFrontera. He wanted to show me something. I climbed onto his motorbike behind him, making sure not to burn myself on the exhaust pipe as I had the first time I rode a motorbike in the Dominican Republic. We zipped through the town towards the water, stopping at a small warehouse. Inside, a dozen Haitian men sat or stood on one side of the room. They didn't say anything, and I likely would not have understood them if they had; five years of primary school French does not prepare you to understand Haitian Creole (or in my experience, French). I felt uncomfortable – a white man suddenly in their presence, in an area where there are very few white people – and I wondered what they must have thought and felt. Maybe some of them attributed some authority to me that I did not have or feel. I thought they looked dejected and resigned, but the truth is I had no idea what they were thinking.

In the centre of the room were several Dominican men. At least one of these was a government official. They had apprehended the Haitians for fishing illegally in Dominican waters. My Dominican contact wanted me to see how much of a problem illegal Haitian fishing was, and to show me the fine mesh nets the Haitians used to catch small fish. Historically the Dominican government had not done much to support local fishers, leaving a hole that AgroFrontera had worked to fill by helping the fishers self-organize into fishing cooperatives. But AgroFrontera is a small organization of half a dozen people, so there are limits to how much they can do. Moreover, their primary expertise is in agronomy, which they practised with nearby rice farmers, and they had entered the fishing sector opportunistically, as they managed their own version of the NGO funding treadmill.

My contact was trying to organize the Dominicans in his village to better manage their fisheries, and a constant refrain we would hear from our partners and other Dominicans was that the Haitian fishers would come to Dominican waters and fish with fine-mesh nets, catching fish before they had a chance to grow and reproduce. And worse, they would break corals apart with small sledgehammers and rebar to extract worms that would be used as bait for hook and line fishing. Ironically, hook and line fishing would be considered responsible, if it were not for the use of these worms as bait.

It was likely that these Haitian fishers had been apprehended in an area off the coast called Cayos Siete Hermanos (seven brothers keys) Wildlife Refuge, so called because there are seven small islands that one can see off the coast on a clear day. Historically, this is a "paper park": you can find its boundaries on paper but there is little to no enforcement of any rules for environmental use within it. This area is not directly north of the Dominican Republic: it is directly north of Haiti. If Haitians in a nearby town go directly north, they will find themselves fishing "illegally" in Dominican waters. While the terrestrial boundary in the area travels mostly north to south, the marine border takes a left turn to move at a 45-degree angle northwest from the coast, including the wildlife refuge in Dominican territory. While this area is formally Dominican, informally, it is an international fisheries commons, and the two groups using it do not get along. It is a de facto open access property regime, with few controls limiting access and extraction. AgroFrontera has been working to organize fishing cooperatives in nearby Dominican fishing communities, with intermittent success.

Environmental property rights

By all accounts the fisheries where I have worked in the Dominican Republic and along the border are deteriorating as a result of poor and absent management. Dominican fishers feel that the Dominican state should help them, but the state, while claiming formal authority over marine resources, has been mostly absent (Cox *et al.* 2018). Watching this all unfold has been humbling as someone who is a certified expert in environmental governance. And this is not a large system; only a few hundred fishers are involved. It is relatively well-defined and the fish and the people are not crossing large distances. There are much larger environmental problems to address, from groundwater depletion to marine eutrophication to deforestation and climate change. How do we address these problems?

The answers to this question hinge on the central topic of this book: environmental property rights. These are social institutions that determine who can and who can't access and interact with the environment, and how. A "right" is a claim to an action or an outcome, and a "property" right is a kind of right where ownership over something is claimed. It is therefore a relationship between an owner and something that is owned. The claiming aspect of a right also implies that it represents a relationship between the claimer and other social actors (Bromley 1991). Finally, an "environmental" property right is a property right that involves ownership of some aspect of the natural environment, and therefore depends on us conceiving of parts of the world around us as ownable, and actively trying to implement ownership claims.

Writing this book has been a way of making sense of experiences like the one I just described, as well as the experiences of many others. A primary motivation for this book is the fact that the dominant theory of environmental property rights, for example as I learned it, is poorly integrated with many relevant disciplines, perspectives, ideas and experiences. In the first two sentences of their co-authored chapter on the economic and legal analysis of property rights, Ostrom and Cole (2012: 37) say the following:

> Property theory has not kept pace with the growth of empirical and historical data on property systems. Economists, legal scholars, and other social scientists continue to rely on simplistic, outmoded, and incomplete models that fail to capture the variety and complexity of property arrangements found throughout the world.

This book represents my attempt to address the challenge that Ostrom and Cole present with respect to rights to the environment. There is a wide diversity of such institutions in the world, and yet this diversity has not been fully documented and integrated into a coherent framework. And documenting this diversity is not merely an empirical exercise, but a normative one, because environmental rights influence outcomes that we care about. My goal is to provide readers not only with a thorough documentation of institutional diversity in this space, but to help them answer normative questions about rights: which approaches help us achieve the outcomes that we seek?

Consilience

To accomplish this goal, we need to make interdisciplinary connections. In the words of E. O. Wilson, we must strive for consilience, or a unity of understanding, to deal with our environmental problems (Wilson 1999). There are several ways to think about the importance of consilience. One is through the missing variable problem, which is a concept from statistical analysis that can be generalized to any causal claim about the impact of one factor on another. The issue here is that inferences about the impact of a supposed cause on an outcome may be biased by the influence of another factor that is left out of the analysis. A good example of this comes from the lobster fishery in the US state of Maine. This has been one of the most famous cases of successful environmental co-management, or joint governance between communities and a supportive government, with persistently high lobster catches being attributed to a series of important institutional innovations, several of which we will discuss later on (Acheson 2003). But this is not the whole story. As Steneck *et al.* (2011) describe, several other factors have contributed to maintaining the lobster population, including the fact that lobsters are effectively ranched as opposed to fished, with large amounts of herring and other fish being put in lobster traps. Other factors include the extirpation of cod, which had been a predator of lobster, and a changing climate with the Gulf of Maine warming faster than almost any other body of water on the planet, potentially supporting lobster populations there (Goode *et al.* 2019). Each of these factors may contribute to the high abundance of lobsters, meaning that we cannot necessarily give all the credit to the institutions that govern how lobsters are caught. The missing variable problem tells us that if we don't tell the whole story, we may be wrong about parts of the story that we do tell.

Another value of consilience is that we can do more with the concepts we have if we understand how they are related to many other concepts via what is called a network effect. In the previous section I provided a standard definition of environmental rights, but this is not all there is to it. I see environmental property rights as the hub in a network of concepts that we will explore to achieve a holistic understanding of their place in society and human–environment relationships. My goal in this book is to take readers on a walk through this network.

Too often, discourses of environmental rights have been dominated by the perspectives of law and economics, without consideration of other relevant disciplines. We see this in practice: the World Bank, whose work closely engages with environmental property rights, often hires economists, but rarely has positions open for anthropologists or sociologists. A range of theories from a diverse set of fields are applicable to the study of environmental rights, including cultural anthropology and human geography, Indigenous studies, behavioural economics and social psychology, evolutionary theory, ecosystems theory and restoration ecology, and the interdisciplinary study of the commons, which is my primary intellectual home. Achieving consilience means that while we consider arguments made by economists and legal scholars, we do so without privileging their claim to expertise in this area over others' perspectives. Understanding these different perspectives will help us avoid the "tunnel vision" of professionalization and expertise, from which we only see the world through a narrow lens that socially empowers while it analytically constrains.

The interdisciplinary nature of this work means that I am not an expert on much of the individual cases and perspectives that I will be incorporating into the text. My formal expertise when it comes to environmental property rights is fairly orthodox, or "Western", and I'll be referring to the traditional Western perspective throughout the book. I will be talking about customary and Indigenous practices and perspectives on environmental rights, while I am not a member of a resource-dependent community, and I am not an Indigenous person. The synthetic nature of this book means that we won't be able to dig into the complexities of individual cases as much as we might like, and we need to be aware of or trade-off between developing intra-case and intra-disciplinary understanding and inter-case and inter-disciplinary understanding.

Throughout the text I have striven to maintain awareness of my limitations and to refrain from forcing other points of view to accommodate my own perspective. With respect to my position as an outsider, particularly to the academic disciplines that I draw upon, I think the humility of the non-expert is an important strength that I will argue for, and try to embody, throughout the book. The point of interdisciplinarity is that there is no one perspective and an associated group that has privileged access to "the truth". The interdisciplinary approach I take also means that we will be engaging with concepts that one might not normally associate with environmental property rights, and that I will not be arguing for a unified theory of environmental property rights. Instead, I will consider a family of theoretical claims, and seek to connect them through a network of concepts.

The goal of this book is to help people who want to make sense of the environmental property rights arrangements that they find. And we want to make sense of real-world systems to honour their strengths and consider their problems. I want to help scholars and practitioners ask more helpful questions, and to be more self-aware of the assumptions they are making when they ask these questions. I don't think there is any one optimal way of engaging with the environment. If there is one lesson that I remember learning from my undergraduate degree in philosophy, it is that for any weighty principle we can think up to govern human behaviour, a clever person has thought of a reason why, or a situation where we would not want to follow that principle in practice. This can leave us without a sense of firm ground beneath our feet. But rather than insisting the ground adapt to our need for certainty, we will do better to adapt our outlook to shifting ground.

Plan for the book

The book is divided into three parts, each of which stands on its own, but with relationships to the others that I will draw out.

The first part develops the theory of collective action. This refers to a family of arguments about how and when humans can work together towards a common goal. The closest connection between the discourses of collective action and environmental property is seen through the theory of the tragedy of the commons, which predicts a lack of collective action to preserve shared resources in the absence of boundaries, or rights that constrain access. This is what I have been seeing in the Dominican Republic for the past 10 years.

Chapter 2 unpacks what we mean by boundaries and lays out my interpretation of the dominant theory of environmental property rights, which I call the theory of environmental reciprocity. In Chapter 3 we complement this with a discussion of the principles of kinship and reciprocity that, while closely integrated into the theory of cooperation, have historically not figured prominently in the literature on environmental rights. This is an important connection to make, for it provides us with another perspective to understand how the tragedy of the commons can be avoided through evolved kinship-based and reciprocal relationships with nature. Like boundaries, while psychologies of kinship and reciprocity are found among the fishers that I work with in the Dominican Republic, any application of these psychologies to the marine environment is largely absent.

Part II of the book goes further to document the diversity of property rights approaches by unpacking two questions: what does it mean to say one owns the environment, and what types of environmental principles and uses are used to establish such ownership? Different types of use of the environment also play a role in establishing ownership, and here the answers to the two questions overlap. Access, for example, is a fundamental right to physically enter a space, and repeated access is often used to establish one's right to the environment.

The most important idea with respect to the first question is probably the idea of bundle of rights (Schlager & Ostrom 1992). This represents the idea that there is no single way to own something. Instead, rights are distributed in semi-independent pieces. You may be able to access a property, but not physically change it or extract anything from it. You might be able to extract water from a river, but you cannot exchange this right with someone else without the approval of a local community. Another way to think about this is that rights come with restrictions. In the Dominican Republic, much of the discourse has been about what fishing gear should be allowed. It is illegal to fish with compressors (compressed tanks of air) as these are dangerous and increase fishing intensity. As I mentioned earlier, a central complaint that Dominicans have about Haitian fishers is the fine-mesh nets they use to catch small fish.

Turning to the second question, the allocation of environmental rights, in addition to occurring through use of the environment, can be based on many different criteria, including the dimensions of time and space and the principles of equity and efficiency. Often such principles conflict: as I mentioned before, the Siete Hermanos Wildlife Refuge is legally in Dominican water, and so nationality is used as an allocation principle by Dominicans. But what we will call the proximity principle (whoever is closest) would argue at least as much for the rights of Haitians.

In Part II we will address these two questions through a basic typology of rights that consists of use rights, control rights and exchange rights. Use rights are what they sound like, and there are several different ways we could directly use the environment. Control rights grant authority to design, allocate and enforce the rules associated with use grants. Exchange rights grant the authority to exchange one's rights to the environment. One final complexity is that we will distinguish between direct use and exchange rights, and entitlements, or the right to indirectly benefit from how the environment is used and how rights are exchanged. In Chapter 4, we tackle use and control rights, and in Chapter 5 we turn to exchange rights.

Part III unpacks the ideas of panaceas and property regimes. While the tragedy of the commons is the most often-cited problem that property rights address, an equally large problem is the tendency for groups to assume that a certain policy is best suited to solve this problem, overgeneralizing their preferred solution through simplifying assumptions. For example, during my time working with AgroFrontera, I have seen this small organization determine a go-to solution in working with the local fishing communities. Developing a preferred solution can provide some important psychological benefits for those involved by helping them feel efficacious. In Chapter 6, we unpack the relevant features and enabling conditions of policy panaceas.

Chapters 7 and 8 deal directly with the concept of property regimes. These have played an important role in the environmental rights discourse through arguments over which regime (mostly public, private or common) is best, and policy panaceas rely on assumptions about property regimes and the actors involved. There has been an evolution in the categories of actors that are commonly considered when talking about property regimes. Dominant economic discourses prefer a dichotomy of states and markets, which I disagree with because of two implications. One, that a market is social actor like a state, which it is not, and two, that anything non-state should be lumped into a vague "market" category, as if society is only about economic transactions. Following Ostrom's (1990) argument that communities are a viable owner of environmental property, a trichotomy of states, individuals, and communities has dominated a newer property regime discourse.

In Chapter 7 we explore the complicated relationship between individual and common property and the relative merits of each. In Chapter 8, we consider the importance of property regimes in explaining outcomes relative to other factors, such as how such regimes are implemented, and we explore the role of the state and its relationship to common property. We conclude the chapter by considering a relative newcomer to the environmental property regime space: nature itself.

Finally, Chapter 9 turns to the topic of market policies, which represent hybrid property regimes involving ownership by both resource users and governments. They also represent maybe the most dominant policy panaceas that we will discuss in this book. In this chapter we will discuss three types of market policies. The primary examples we will rely on come from catch shares in fishery policy and carbon markets in climate policy.

I conclude with some reflections on the nature of expertise needed to improve the discourse and practice of environmental property rights. Here I argue for a diagnostic approach to analysis that unpacks the relevant dimensions of a problem as well as the responses to it. I also unpack the types of attributes that experts and leaders need to promote better rights-based, environmental governance.

PART I

Collective action and groups

Our ability to work together or not has a dramatic impact on our ability to resolve any environmental problem. We therefore begin by exploring the concept of collective action, or cooperation. The theory of collective action has been developed in multiple independent disciplines. The perspective of evolutionary theory frames collective action as a mystery: why would individuals cooperate with each other when it is individually costly and publicly beneficial? In environmental studies, the failure to act collectively is associated with the tragedy of the commons, or environmental ruin.

The first chapter in this part deals with the tragedy of the commons as the dominant framing for environmental property rights. Here we will also interrogate the utility of this framing and consider others as well. Chapter 2 builds directly on Chapter 1 by asking how social and ecological boundaries can facilitate cooperation and address the tragedy of the commons. In this chapter we also consider the different types of boundaries that we see and what function they play. Finally, in Chapter 3 we turn to the primary mechanisms for cooperation among humans or any species: reciprocity and kinship. We will also see that the human psychologies of reciprocity and kinship can be used to motivate environmental stewardship and reframe the Western perspective on environmental property rights.

1

The tragedy of the commons

The fishers in the Dominican Republic are facing the potential collapse of their fishery. The dominant narrative for why this is happening is known as the tragedy of the commons, popularized by Garrett Hardin through an article of the same name (Hardin 1968), although Hardin attributed his inspiration to William Forster Lloyd, a British economist and historian. The tragedy of the commons is the single most common narrative used to motivate the implementation of environmental property rights. In this chapter we discuss how it has been used and how it relates to theories and models of cooperation. We will also explore the limits of the idea by considering what it leaves out: namely, inequalities of power and influence. We conclude by considering additional theories that need to be considered when describing the causes of environmental degradation that need to be accounted for by environmental institutions.

The famous scenario that Hardin got from Lloyd is the one that sticks with most with people who have read his work. It is an image of cows on a pasture, with each herdsman deciding how many cows to place on this pasture. This decision is based on two components. First, the individual benefit the herdsman receives from placing on additional cow on a pasture, and the collective cost to the group if overgrazing occurs – too many cows can overgraze a pasture and degrade it. This collective cost is commonly referred to as a negative externality. The meaning of the term is intuitive: it represents the fact that the costs imposed by an individual on a group are "external" to the individual's decision-making or are not accounted for. The problem, as Hardin sees it, is that if each herdsman follows their own individual interest, the collective interest will suffer. It is called a "tragedy" because everybody loses. This gap between the interest of individuals and the interests of the group is known as a collective action problem, and it is closely related to the free-rider problem, which represents the temptation that participants have to free-ride on the contributions of others towards providing group benefits.

Collective action problems represent the challenge of sustaining cooperation in a competitive world. They are beyond commonplace; they are the fundamental challenge of biological and social life (Wilson 2016). The presence of
collective action problems is the principal justification for governance: institutions, by which I mean formal rules and informal social norms, are supposedly
designed to reconcile such differences and motivate individuals to act more in
the public interest.

Games and the public good

Hardin's story is often criticized because it is highly simplified. For now, however, this simplification can help us understand the mechanics of the argument.
We can further unpack the tragedy of the commons narrative through the language of social dilemma games where players make decisions to cooperate or
defect. Before discussing several game models, it's important to remember that
these are just models, and the map is not the territory. Such models should be
seen less as descriptions of the world and more as intuition pumps (Dennett
2013). The importance of keeping this distinction clear will be reinforced in
Chapter 6 when we look at policy panaceas, which themselves are commonly
based on highly simplified governance models that are then conflated with
on-the-ground complexities.

By far the most famous game associated with collective action problems
is the prisoner's dilemma, so-called because of the story associated with the
game. This pictures two prisoners who are being interrogated, each of which
has the decision to confess (defect) or deny their guilt (cooperate). If one confesses and the other does not, the confessor receives a lighter sentence at the
expense of a longer sentence for the denier. But if both deny (cooperate), their
collective sentence length is shorter than if one confesses. This fits the criterion
then for the collective action concept that I just described if we interpret individual payoffs as self-interest and the joint payoff as the group interest.

An environmental scenario based on the parameters of this game is depicted
in Figure 1.1. Here, two fishers can each decide to cooperate (fish less) or defect
(fish more, threatening to deplete the resource). The most important thing to
know is that regardless of what either player does, it is individually advantageous for the other to defect based on the payoffs assigned to each decision,
thus the arrows point to mutual defection. This outcome is known as a Nash
equilibrium, which is defined as a situation in which no player has an incentive
to unilaterally change their strategy: they want to change together or not at all.
The result of this is intuitive: it is easier to avoid entering a situation of mutual
defection than it is to get out of one once you're in it.

Player 2

		Cooperate (fish less)	Defect (fish more)
Player 1	Cooperate (fish less)	2, 2 (4)	0, 3 (3)
	Defect (fish more)	3, 0 (3)	1, 1 (2)

Nash Equilibrium

Figure 1.1 The tragedy of the commons game (also referred to as the prisoner's dilemma) *Notes:* The numbers in the cells represent the payoffs for each player (first number is player one, second is player two). Higher numbers are better. Numbers in parentheses are the sum of individual payoffs, which is maximized by joint cooperation. These numbers don't have a concrete meaning and their absolute values don't matter; their significance is that they order the preferred outcomes for each player based on what the other player does. *Source:* Representation inspired by Ostrom, Gardner and Walker (1994).

There are other games that can be played. Figure 1.2 depicts a coordination game. The qualitative details in the figure are based on behaviours that I have seen during my studies of small-scale fisheries in the Dominican Republic. Here, many fishers free-dive, holding their breath and diving down to catch fish with spearguns. In the past 15 years, it has become increasingly common for fishers to use (formally illegal) compressors to store compressed air, which they can attach to a tube to breathe underwater. This allows fishers to dive deeper and fish longer. Doing this requires that a second fisher stay on the boat to manage the compressor while the diver fishes underwater. Thus, pairs of fishers must coordinate with each other to maximize their benefits. This is a theoretically easier problem to solve than the prisoner's dilemma, because of a second, cooperative Nash equilibrium. With the first game, regardless of what each player does in a given round, it is in the other player's best interest to defect in that round. Here, this is not the case: if you cooperate with me today, I should cooperate with you today. The shadow of future reciprocity is not required to incentivize cooperation.

Another lesson we should draw from this model is that cooperation or coordination is not synonymous with a broader public or environmental good. Compressors are illegal in the Dominican Republic because they enable

Player 2

Nash Equilibrium	Cooperate (compressor)	Defect (free-dive)
Cooperate (compressor)	2, 2 (4)	0, 1 (1)
Defect (free-dive)	1, 0 (1)	1, 1 (2)

Player 1

Nash Equilibrium

Figure 1.2 The coordination game
Notes: This game has two Nash equilibria: cooperate–cooperate, or defect–defect. Unlike the tragedy of the commons game described earlier, here cooperation is associated with fishing more.

further pressure on the natural environment. We should not conflate explanations of collective action with explanations of environmental conservation.

Asymmetries

The previous games were symmetric, in that each player is in an identical position to the other one. But some games are not symmetric, and their importance leads us to interrogate the concept of a group interest, or public good and the associated idea of collective action.

The primary way in which real-world situations depart from the tragedy of the commons scenario is through asymmetries of power and dependence. In many situations, some actors are upstream of downstream actors, and this changes the game that is being played. In irrigation systems, for example, we do not have a collective action problem with respect to the shared use of water, because upstream farmers are not dependent on the actions of downstream farmers: they can take as much water as they want and there is no opportunity for the downstream farmer to punish them by taking more water themselves. This scenario is modelled in Figure 1.3, where the upstream farmer has a choice to take more or less water, but the downstream farmer does not: they can only take what is left, which is modelled by them not having an additional column in the table to represent an option to defect

Downstream

		Take what is left
Upstream	Cooperate (take less water)	2, 2 (4)
	Defect (take more water)	3, 1 (4)

Figure 1.3 An asymmetric irrigation game
Notes: The four units of water translate into benefits. Regardless of what the upstream farmer does, the downstream farmer has no real choice, and no way to impact the benefits obtained by the upstream farmer.

or cooperate and thereby change the payoffs for the upstream player. In this situation it is hard to identify a group interest, which we must do to identify a collective action problem. The upstream farmers can take more to their own benefit, and there is not an easily discernible group interest. Unsurprisingly, experimental work has shown lower levels of prosocial behaviour in asymmetric games (Nockur *et al.* 2020).

The primary way in which this irrigation "game" is tied to a collective action situation is by connecting it to another game. The irrigation infrastructure, if it is to be built and maintained by the farmers themselves, is a public good that is required for anyone to withdraw water in the first place. If upstream farmers take too much water, downstream farmers may not help them with the provision of shared infrastructure (Janssen, Anderies & Cardenas 2011). This is then a collective action problem of producing shared infrastructure, and its presence helps to solve the asymmetric water use dilemma. It is maybe counterintuitive that the addition of a new problem helps at least some actors in the system. But this problem creates an interdependence that is the social glue for water sharing. When this is disrupted, the incentive for collective action is removed. Shivakoti and Ostrom (2002) describe an example in which the government of Nepal took over maintenance of irrigation infrastructure in a set of communities, which then performed more poorly afterwards, with the inference being that part of the reason for poor performance was the disruption of the interdependence between upstream and downstream farmers. This example highlights the importance of what has been called the ecology of games (or interconnected arenas of strategic behaviour) when trying to understand and intervene in a local governance regime (Lubell 2013).

Lansing (2012) describes a particularly interesting example of induced cooperation via interconnected games. In his examination of the Balinese Subak irrigation systems, Lansing introduces the problem of asymmetry, and then describes the "solution" that local farmers evolved over time through their response to the problem of pest control. All farmers face the challenge of pests who may eat their crops. And it turns out that in the Subak systems that Lansing studied, if farmers coordinate the fallowing of their fields, they create a resource constraint that limits pest populations across multiple fields. The cooperation required to implement this pest control strategy motivates upstream farmers to take less water than they might, cooperating with downstream farmers via the water asymmetric allocation game so that downstream farmers will cooperate with them in the pest control game. By recognizing this culturally evolved solution in their work, Lansing and his colleagues helped to reverse a series of top-down technical interventions in the Subaks, which included the use of pesticides to control pests that would evolve resistance to such pesticides, leading to a cycle of increased pesticide use in what is known as the pesticide treadmill (Wilson & Tisdell 2001).

Hierarchical versus balancing rights

Institutional asymmetry between upstream and downstream actors can also be created by hierarchical rights. Rights claims are often in conflict with each other. One's use of their land may have spillover effects that impact other landowners. For example, if a farmer uses pesticides on their land, this can have ecological impacts for the ecology on their neighbour's land. In many instances, governance of these spillovers relies on a "shed" concept (watershed, airshed, viewshed). For example, in Colorado new water users cannot appropriate water in a watershed that is already "fully appropriated", meaning that all of the water available has been accounted for as being taken by someone else. In cities, limitations on development are sometimes motivated by how they may influence the "viewshed" they are located in.

There are two approaches to address this type of issue. The first is that one set of rights can take precedence, and the other must adapt. The hierarchical model of rights is prominently used in western US water governance under the prior appropriation system: this system arranges rights-holders from senior to junior based on who started to use water first (more on the use of time to establish rights in Chapter 4). In times of drought, senior water rights-holders are to receive all their water before junior rights-holders receive any. Contrasting with this approach, much of environmental law has adopted a balancing rights approach when it comes to conflicts: if my behaviour affects your welfare, then we need to balance your need claims against mine. In contrast with prior appropriation, a balancing approach is used under the riparian rights regime in the eastern United States.

A hierarchical system like the prior appropriation regime in the western United States creates an institutional upstream-versus-downstream relationship. Senior water rights-holders are guaranteed their water before junior water-rights-holders. And like biophysical asymmetry, this diminishes the extent to which we can say there is a collective interest among senior and junior water-rights-holders within a prior appropriation system.

The balancing approach might seem preferable to prioritization, allowing as it does for multiple interests to be expressed and maybe a more holistic approach to governance that doesn't focus on just one thing and prioritize for that. But we might not want to always treat competing interests as fungible, which the balancing approach requires, if we think that one actor or group has a much greater claim than others do.

What is the public good?

As commonsense as it sounds, using the concept of a collective action problem is challenging, mostly because it requires defining what we mean by the interest of the individual and the interest of the group. The most obvious alternative to a collective action problem, which represents the potential for a win-win scenario, is a win-lose scenario, where one actor benefits at the cost of others. In the language of game theory, the question is whether or not we are in a "zero sum" or "non-zero sum" game. A zero-sum game is so called because the benefits to different players sum to zero, meaning that someone's win must be someone else's loss. Many sports involve a zero-sum game: one team or player wins, and the other team or player loses.

Calls for global cooperation to combat climate change often rely on the identification of a collective global interest (e.g., avoiding climate change). This is seen as an important framing to incentivize everyone to do something about the problem. But some authors have argued that climate change is not a tragedy of the commons (Mildenberger 2019). And to an extent I agree. Specifically, to the extent that climate change is disproportionately caused by a group of actors who are also disproportionately prepared to adapt to the consequences of climate change (Callahan & Mankin 2022), there is less of a global group interest in addressing it. An important complication of this argument, however, is that the damage from the processes that cause climate change also cause other more localized pollution problems (e.g., particulate matter, smog) that are more subject to the collective action framing and therefore may be more easily addressed in a way that is similar to the issue linkage of water use and irrigation infrastructure provision mentioned earlier.

Other models

The fundamental mechanism behind the tragedy of the commons is unaccounted for costs, or negative externalities as I mentioned earlier, and I think that unaccounted for costs and benefits are the source of all of our environmental problems. But within this framework, there are different nuances and models we should use to make sense of specific situations. To explore these, we need to unpack the role that time plays in environmental degradation. So far we have explored relationships across geographic space and social space (between individuals and groups). But time also plays an important role in the tragedy of the commons narrative, since the "group interest" that arises only arises over time with the eventual decline of the resource based on individual decisions. We can also think of the problem of asymmetry just described through time as well, if we imagine future generations as downstream actors to ourselves: actors whose welfare depends on our decisions but who cannot reciprocate with their own decisions.

Let's imagine what might be the response of a group of fishers who learn that they are depleting their fishery. One way to think about how they might respond is by treating the symptoms of their problem rather than dealing with its underlying drivers. This brings us to the concept known as shifting the burden (Senge 2010), which refers to the process of coping with the symptoms of a problem rather than adapting by dealing with its underlying drivers. Treating underlying drivers can get to the root of a problem and ultimately resolve it, but this is more costly and takes more time. Treating the symptoms of a problem creates a lag between environmental overuse and the impacts of such use.

I have seen this in my own work. In the Dominican Republic, for example, fishers in some of the villages historically fished closer to shore with spearguns and fins, holding their breath as they dive down to catch fish. This has increasingly changed in the past 10 years, with more and more fishers using compressors as I discussed earlier in this chapter. Because compressors allow fishers to breathe underwater, they can fish longer and fish in deeper waters further from the shore. And we believe that this has been a response of many fishers to the depletion of the part of the fishery closer to shore (Wilson, Pavlowich & Cox 2015; Cox *et al.* 2018).

I encountered a surprisingly similar situation in a very different place: the San Luis Valley of Colorado, where I worked with a group of colleagues from the University of Colorado, Boulder. Here, a group of irrigating farmers responded to a surface water drought in the 1950s by drilling individual wells to access underlying groundwater aquifers (Cody *et al.* 2015). This was particularly helpful to junior water users since, as mentioned earlier in this chapter, the regime of prior appropriation grants senior water users all the water they are entitled to before junior rights-holders get any. So access to an additional resource was particularly helpful to institutionally marginalized farmers.

The tragedy of the commons is relevant in each of these cases since it was an absence of use restrictions that led to depletion of the most nearshore area of the Dominican fishery, and the San Luis Valley farmers would go on to over-extract water from the underground aquifers due to a lack of limitations on use rights that has typified many groundwater systems, even when overlying surface waters are highly regulated. But it is not the whole story. Something else happening in each of these cases is the use of less collective, technical responses to avoid having to develop more collective political responses to adjust to increasing resource scarcity. In the language employed by Webster (2015) in her book, appropriately titled *Beyond the Tragedy in Global Fisheries*, these fishers and farmers created a profit disconnect; a disconnect between the declining state of the environment and the profits garnered by its users. This disconnect is what enables these farmers and fishers to "shift the burden" to the future, avoiding the underlying causes of their problems.

Another example of a technical solution that preserves a profit disconnect is found in depletion of cod stocks in the Atlantic. This depletion was partially caused by the increasing efficiency of fishing gear which was also used to cope with declining stocks, rather than fundamentally changing fishing behaviours (Kurlansky 2011). This is another kind of technology treadmill, similar to the pesticide treadmill I mentioned earlier. This situation was also enabled by the fact that the main metric used for the state of the fish stock were landings (amount of fish caught and landed at port) because these were easier to measure, and were more legible to governmental actors than the actual state of the stock. But the increased efficiency of fishing practices allowed landings to remain high compared to the declining state of the stock. This will be a central topic in Chapter 6.

The Dominican fisheries case in particular is a small-scale example of what is known as serial resource depletion, in which resource users go from one resource to the next, degrading as they go. In the case of the SLV farmers, they turned to groundwater when surface water became scarce, although this case is not a perfect fit to the serial depletion model because of the exogeneity of surface water declines (part of the reason for declining surface water was climate, which was out of the control of the farmers). In some cases, the use of diverse resources can be seen as a strength, increasing the resilience of resource users, but not when it is used primarily to avoid dealing with secular (non-periodic) resource declines.

This behaviour been seen elsewhere, such as in the global sea cucumber fishery (Anderson *et al.* 2011) and other international fisheries where the behaviour has been referred to as roving banditry (Berkes *et al.* 2006). One example Berkes *et al.* provide is the Gulf of Maine, where overfishing of cod, an apex predator, led to increasing populations of prey species including lobster and sea urchins. The authors describe the subsequent serial depletion of different sea urchin stocks across multiple fisheries around the world. Here we see serial depletion across and within species.

Examples of serial depletion by mobile actors have also been associated with land degradation. In his book on the history of the banana, Koeppel (2008) describes how multinational banana companies in Latin America established banana plantations in a plot of land until the quality of the soil degraded to a point where it could no longer support these plantations. The response of the companies was not to change their practices, but simply to move on to another plot of land. Serial resource depletion often involves both profit disconnects and what Webster (2015) calls power disconnects, or a scenario in which the costs of resource decline are distributed to less powerful groups. In many cases, powerful actors degrade a resource and then move on, leaving local communities and actors to suffer the consequences. This second factor closely relates to the asymmetry that I described earlier, with one (downstream) group being more exposed to the decisions made by others.

In sum, the tragedy of the commons is an important concept, but it is also an overly simplified model. Not all environmental problems are caused by collective action problems and a failed public interest, and an insistence on this framing can downplay the role that inequality and power play. Other models such as shifting the burden and serial resource depletion are equally important, and we will often find these models playing out in the same cases. But the idea of a collective action problem is still an important part of any diagnostic toolkit. In the next chapter, we discuss how property rights are used to set boundaries and preserve a group's common interest, and how such boundaries relate to the models of shifting the burden and serial resource depletion as well.

2

Boundaries

To further explore the tragedy of the commons and collective action, we turn to the topic of boundaries. Boundaries are critical for understanding what commons are and how collective action works. In the beginning of his depiction of the pasture and its herdsmen, Hardin (1968: 1244) asks the reader to "picture a pasture open to all". "Open to all" means an absence of boundaries that would limit access to the pasture. In *Governing the Commons*, Ostrom (1990) argued for the feasibility of community-based resource management by presenting a set of design principles that can help communities overcome collective action problems involved in managing shared resources. These principles are Ostrom's most famous theoretical contribution to the study of environmental policy and governance. I refer to these throughout this book and a version of them based on my own work (Cox, Arnold & Villamayor-Tomas 2010) is included in the Appendix. Ostrom's first principle (which is divided into two in the Appendix) calls for clear social boundaries around legitimate users to distinguish them from non-users, and for biophysical boundaries around community-owned resources. The combination of social boundaries that define who is in and who is out, and biophysical boundaries indicating which parts of the environment are accessible by those who are "in", is one way to define environmental property rights.

This chapter explores the importance of social boundaries as a key factor in promoting collective action by looking at the relationship between cooperation within groups and cooperation and conflict between groups. We will see that boundaries play the same role within the context of environmental property as they do in the context of collective action theory. The later parts of the chapter explore different types of boundaries and the roles they play. Here we first explore the difference between rigid and contextual boundaries, and we conclude the chapter with a discussion of general purpose versus special purpose boundaries as a way to understand the concept of common property, or the collective ownership of a resource by a group.

Within versus between group cooperation

In a paper by David Sloan Wilson, Elinor Ostrom and myself (Wilson, Ostrom & Cox 2013), we argued that Ostrom's principles were generalizable beyond the natural resource management scenario, and could be used to explain the ability of groups to maintain cooperation in the face of any collective action problem. Without the presence of an environmental resource, biophysical boundaries are less important; but social boundaries remain critical in any cooperative setting. Social boundaries are important for the development of cooperation within a group to prevent outsiders from free-riding on the benefits this cooperation brings.

To unpack this claim, we need to understand the relationship between cooperation within versus between groups. My discussion of this distinction is based on work by Wilson (2016), who has championed an explanation for how cooperation evolves in spite of collective action problems using a framework known as multilevel selection. This argues that while evolution promotes individual self-interest in humans, it also promotes group-interest. According to Wilson's model, while altruistic, prosocial behaviours are costly within a group, groups of cooperative actors will out-compete groups of selfish actors, and therefore individual-level altruism can be indirectly selected for. This is why highly cooperative species like ants and humans are so successful. The fact that humans have experienced evolutionary pressures at both the individual and the group level explains the tension between individual and group-level behaviours that human beings display, and how this tension is never entirely resolved.

This perspective helps us understand that competition between groups synergizes with cooperation within groups (see several empirical examples in Henrich 2020). The very idea of a collective action problem reflects this point: individual actors act in their self-interest because of the competition they face with other individuals. Cooperation at one level can undermine cooperation at higher levels. This is a critical limitation of local self-governance.

Humans have a suite of behaviours that they use to establish social boundaries, separating insiders from outsiders. The synergy between inclusion and exclusion reflects many of our worst instincts and tendencies to treat members of "out-groups" terribly, even while we may be acting ethically with members of our in-group. There is an in-group morality and another morality we reserve for out-groups (Greene 2013). Basurto *et al.* (2012: 606) describe an example of this in their discussion of the indigenous Seri fishing community of Punta Chueca in the Gulf of California, Mexico. The authors describe how this community did not start to conserve its resources until it faced an external threat:

> The presence of legally established property rights did not automatically result in the emergence of access controls for the Seri. It took them about 10 years from when they were granted marine tenure to the time when they started exercising access controls to the Infiernillo Channel. During this period they continued fishing down the food web … until the increasing encroachment of outsiders in Seri territory reminded them of the long history of domination attempts by Spaniard and Mexican – a strong incentive to overcome the costs of engaging in collective action towards the defense of their territory and resources. If history is a guide, the Seri are not a single cohesive social entity except when they are confronted with a common enemy. For the Seri, controlling access to their fishing grounds is also about defending the biophysical space that provides meaning to who they are as a distinctive social group.

These tensions are seen everywhere in life and literature. In her book, *Trick Mirror*, Jia Tolentino (2019: 22) reflects on the acerbic tone of internet discourse, saying that it

> partly reflects basic social physics. Having a mutual enemy is a quick way to make a friend – we learn this as early as elementary school – and politically, it's much easier to organize people against something than it is to unite them in an affirmative vision.

Human beings are highly sensitive to signals of in-group versus out-group membership. One of the most well-known descriptions of this is known as the "minimum group paradigm". It stands for the finding that human beings will use even arbitrary, otherwise meaningless markers to establish groups and foster in-group/out-group dynamics. This dynamic is acutely described in a book called *The Sneetches* by the well-known children's author, Dr Seuss, which tells the story of two almost identical groups, but one with stars on their bellies and the other without. This clearly arbitrary distinction serves as the basis for intergroup conflict through a lot of star-adding and removing to distinguish who is in and who is out of which group.

Humans are also sensitive to less arbitrary signs of difference. We are very sensitive to dialects used in the speech of other people and prefer to engage with others who have our same dialect (Henrich 2015) and it is worth pausing and considering this, because we do it so automatically that it is often invisible. Why should differences in, say, accents be so noticeable to us? Why do we perceive them in such a particular way, as identifying where someone is from and what group they are in or not in?

The synergy between intragroup cooperation and intergroup conflict explains patterns from the high levels of cooperation among sports teams to the ability of the United States to fundamentally transform its economy to meet the demands of engaging in the Second World War. As Henrich (2020: 120) describes, the historical scaling up of cooperative organizations such as the Roman Empire and modern states has depended in large part on intergroup conflict, and when intergroup conflict has lapsed, this has often led to the decline of states and societies. This synergy is thus a direct challenge to any kind of governance system. It means that to be inclusive is also to be exclusive: in order for humans to form bonds with each other, there need to be outsiders, or as Henrich (2020: 139) puts it: "Intergroup competition favors expanding the circle, but it's still a circle that places some people on the outside."

Large-scale cooperation is possible in part if we can maintain the presence of a threat to which we need to all unite against. Does this threat have to be human, or can humans unite against a common non-human threat? Our collective experience with the Covid-19 pandemic and with climate change, two massive-scale threats, so far serve as humbling lessons in this regard. Instead of serving as a threat that unites people across political, national or other identities, each has been cannibalized by our tribal instincts, serving as a marker of group membership based on whether or not one believes they are a threat or not.

The nature of cooperation and conflict

One could argue that this argument essentializes these traits in humans, viewing the relationship between intragroup cohesion and intergroup competition as universal and not artefacts of history and context. This relates to concerns about applying evolutionary thinking to social science and human society, which are often expressed as a criticism of Social Darwinism, or the justification of intergroup conflict and inequality as being "natural". Another way to express these concerns is to say that the multilevel selection perspective is overly deterministic because it does not account for the range of variation that we see across groups and across cultures.

The concern is legitimate, and there are several responses to it. First, humans do not have a single human "nature". Rather, like all species, humans are the result of an evolutionary process that has led to multiple natures, which are elicited based on our experiences and context, and lead us to be more proso-cial or more antisocial (Ryan & Deci 2018). We have numerous behavioural modules that can push us in conflicting directions. While we do have a poten-tially strong tendency for in-group bias and out-group othering, the strength of this tendency depends on how much it is activated by our social environ-ment. There are numerous examples, many of them dark, of leaders gather-ing support for themselves and their group by blaming their problems on an out-group. There is no way to make sense of this behaviour and its effective-ness without the relationship described above. This doesn't mean that we are doomed to intergroup conflict. But it is one of our "central tendencies" around which variation is observed.

Second, we shouldn't conflate "natural" with "good", which is to commit the naturalistic fallacy. Saying that there is a theoretically and empirically sup-ported synergy between intragroup cooperation and intergroup competition is not the same thing as saying that wars are okay because they help promote cooperation within warring countries (they do). At the limit, it is hard to imag-ine a world where we cannot recognize the potential for humans to follow their darker tendencies. Acknowledging them is not the same thing as sanctioning them; it is ideally the first step towards confronting them.

The theory of environmental reciprocity

Boundaries are important for maintaining collective action in two ways. One, by excluding outsiders, who can disrupt local norms and free-ride on the coop-erative efforts of group members; and two, by preventing group members from leaving. If costs of exit are high, then group members are dependent on their cooperative partners, since there are no other options (Ostrom 2007b). But if costs are low, then this can disrupt cooperation within a group. So, boundaries preventing some entry and exit are important for promoting cooperation.

My argument here is that boundaries play the same role within the context of human–environment relationships as they do in the context of collective action theory and in ways that directly reflect the two environmental chal-lenges brought up in the previous chapter: the tragedy of the commons and shifting the burden associated with serial resource depletion. Boundaries pro-mote collective action by helping ensure that cooperators engage with other cooperators, which in turn ensures that, over time, benefits of cooperation are returned to cooperators.

The importance of limits to entry and exit when applied to the relationship between a human actor and a natural resource is the same, except that we are describing the relationship between a social actor and the environment rather than between social actors. When barriers to exit are high, resource users do not have better alternatives and are dependent on a particular resource. If this is the case and a user can prevent others from using the resource, this user is more likely to engage with the same environment over time, which creates an incentive to invest in the environment now to secure benefits in the future. I use the word "invest" intentionally here, based on the following definition: "to make use of for future benefits or advantages" (Merriam-Webster). We consider two types of environmental investment in this book: stewardship and development, keeping in mind that while investment and development are sometimes used synonymously in everyday usage, I will use them differently. Stewardship and development are two different ways of using the environment, which we will unpack in Chapter 4. In short, barriers to exit and entry can incentivize either stewardship or development of the environment.

This is essentially the logic of reciprocity as commonly understood; if you take care of the land, it will take care of you. I refer to this interpretation, inspired by collective action theory, as the theory of environmental reciprocity because it is very much based on the logic of reciprocity, which we will discuss in more depth in the next chapter. This theory combines several others. First, the theory that outsiders must be excluded is commonly conceived in property rights discourses as a way to resolve the tragedy of the commons. Second, the theory that resource users are incentivized to steward the environment when exit costs are high has been expressed through the concept of resource dependence. Frey (2020) summarizes the empirical findings on the relationship between resource dependence and stewardship behaviour, observing that resource dependence has often been found to encourage resource stewardship, and that such dependence is more often found in common property arrangements (Nagendra 2007), since these help to secure community members against the risk of resource scarcity and uncertainty (see Chapter 7). The findings Frey discusses are not entirely in support of the resource dependence theory, with one important caveat being that under conditions of poverty, dependency may in fact lead to overuse of resources (Agrawal 2007). The importance of resource dependence also helps us to make sense of the phenomenon of serial resource depletion discussed at the end of Chapter 1: serial resource degraders are not dependent on any single resource, enabling them to serially degrade one after another.

How does this theory relate to property rights? For starters, limits to entry and exit are closely related to the two rights that are most prominently emphasized from a Western perspective: exclusion and alienation. Exclusion is a "gatekeeper" right (Verkuyten & Martinovic 2017): it stipulates that ownership means that I can exclude others from accessing what I own. Exclusion has long been seen as a central part of any property claim, putting it in a position of first among equals with respect to the rights an owner might have (Dagan 2011). Alienation means that one has the right to sell a property that one owns, and it is also traditionally thought of as constitutive of any property right (more on these rights in Chapter 5).

In one way, these rights are complementary. We are less likely to purchase something if we think that we cannot exclude others from the benefits of ownership (Degens 2021: 213). With respect to boundaries, however, these rights can play rather different roles. Exclusion plays the important function of preventing external actors from free-riding on the cooperative efforts of in-group members. Alienation often represents the disruption of a social boundary by allowing group members an opportunity to exit their social group.

The politics of exclusion and exit

The tragedy of the commons, as we discussed in the previous chapter, is not a purely technical problem, and the use of social boundaries to resolve it is not a purely technical solution. This is because social boundaries involve exclusion, which means that some people are left out of a group and the benefits that come with being in that group. How we feel about this likely depends on who is included and who is excluded.

A problematic aspect (among several, see Mildenberger 2019) of Garrett Hardin's work comes from how he discusses the topic of exclusion. In an article entitled "Living on a lifeboat", Hardin (1974: 562) argues in favour of an exclusionary "lifeboat ethics". His primary metaphor for the earth is that of a lifeboat, into which only so many people can fit, and he clearly thinks that poorer and larger populations pose a greater burden in this scenario. In this article he argues against the few helping the many:

> The 50 of us in the lifeboat see 100 others swimming in the water outside, asking for admission to the boat, or for handouts. How shall we respond to their calls? There are several possibilities. [...]
>
> Since the needs of all are the same, we take all the needy into our boat, making a total of 150 in a boat with a capacity of 60. The boat is swamped, and everyone drowns. Complete justice, complete catastrophe.

What Hardin does not recognize in this metaphor is that the impact that people have on the environment is proportional to their affluence, so that the average person from a wealthy country takes up much more "space" in the lifeboat than a poor person. We can't fit very many billionaires in a lifeboat. We also can't ignore the language of "us" and "others" that is being used here, with the "us" presumably referring to people like Hardin, and "others" to people not like him. This language can activate the dark side of our tribal instincts as I just discussed in the previous section.

Similarly, the issue of exit is not a purely technical issue either. We cannot simply prevent people from leaving their social groups because we want them to be resource dependent. During my time in New Mexico, I often heard about younger people not wanting to stay and be farmers like their parents and grandparents. The average farmer that I spoke with was at least middle-aged and most were older. And who am I to tell a young person to stay in rural New Mexico instead of heading to Albuquerque or Denver in search of better opportunities?

Contextual versus rigid boundaries

To deal with the tragedy of the commons, we need boundaries, the logic being that outsiders can come in and profit off the cooperative and conservational behaviours of insiders. If any outsider can be problematic from a social and ecological perspective, then we would expect to find rigid boundaries that prevent any infiltration. But this is not what we find. Instead, actual property rights systems in the world are often a tangle of complementary exclusion and inclusion and use for specific purposes, and we see more or less rigid boundaries across systems and sometimes within the same system.

Rigid boundaries do not change much over time and space. Contextual boundaries are subject to informal and sometimes ad hoc negotiations that change over time. Bollier and Helfrich (2019: 130–2) describe these as "semi-permeable membranes", borrowing a term from biological science, arguing that all functional barriers must be selectively porous. This distinction reflects a pattern that Acheson (2003) describes in his analysis of the lobster fishery in Maine. Here, Acheson distinguishes between "nucleated" and "perimeter-based" boundaries based on how much permeability is present. Nucleated boundaries, extending into the sea from coastal harbours, are based on a gradient: the closer you are to a fishing gang's harbour, the stronger the exclusionary norm is, and the farther away, the more you might get away with putting your traps in a harbour gang's territory. In the middle of the gradient, things are fuzzy; someone might be able to fish in an area or not, depending on their relationships with other fishers and ad hoc negotiations. This is distinct from the rigid perimeter-based regime that Acheson found surrounding the islands off the coast of Maine.

Acheson shows that the more rigid boundaries in the islands were enabled by their small group size (this being one of the primary drivers of collective action), physical isolation and high dependence on the resource, all of which makes it easier to maintain a sense of community and social capital. This has made it easier for island communities to maintain boundaries and exclude outsiders. The other part of this story is that both island and coastal communities have experienced external threats to incursion through new fishers, which as we have discussed earlier in this chapter, can promote in-group cooperation. Gelfand's (2018) work on "tight" versus "loose" cultures is also relevant here. Her main argument is that tighter, or more rigid, institutions are found in societies that have experienced external threats, such as violence or natural disasters, while looser cultures are found in places with less threat.

The proximity principle

The example provided by Acheson also demonstrates an important mechanism for allocating rights that I will call the proximity principle. While we more fully unpack different principles for allocating rights in Part II of the book, I want to explore this mechanism here as it relates so much to spatial boundaries. The proximity principle argues that your claim to exert ownership over a resource is strengthened when you own adjacent resources. In Acheson's example of the Maine lobster fishery, rights to fish are based on residence along the coast, with residence on islands being a particularly strong requirement for access to certain fishing grounds.

Proximity can be based on horizontal and vertical dimensions, and there is a long history of both. The *ad coelum* doctrine in ancient Roman and common law has long held that landowners are granted the rights to everything above and below their land. Most commonly this is used to allocate rights to underlying groundwater, minerals and fossil fuels, but it is also has been used to allocate rights to the overlying air column. In places where surface area is scarce, such as in large and expensive cities, proximity-based vertical rights become extremely valuable.

For an example of horizontal proximity we can return to the water rights context. While the principle of priority in time has dominated water policy in much of the western United States, the principle of proximity has dominated it in the eastern United States, with some western states including elements of both. For example, the doctrine of riparian rights dictates that those who own "appurtenant" land next to a body of water can claim at least use rights to this water. While this doctrine has historically held sway in the eastern United States, it was found to not work as well during the white settlement of the western United States where water is scarcer and there was little land next to a body of water. Here, if the right to use water was limited only to those owning land next to a body of water, few individuals would be able to make use of what water there was available. Separating water rights from land rights can be seen as an adaptation to biophysical circumstance, given the goals of settlement and development.

The proximity principle has also been applied to the land–sea interface. In fishing communities in the Dominican Republic where I have worked, for example, fishers claim exclusive access to those resources that are closest to their community. This is a communal version of the exclusive economic zones (EEZ) established by the 1982 United Nations Convention on the Law of the Sea that establish property rights for each country up to 200 miles off its coast (although "exclusive" is a bit disingenuous here since states, including developing countries, are required to either establish that they are fully exploiting their fishery resources or allow another state to do so). Another example is found in the coast of Maine, where obtaining permits that grant property rights to coastal shellfish are often limited to those who live in nearby towns (McGreavy *et al.* 2018). In cases such as this, the principle often represents a bridge between different property regimes as well, when privately owned land grants access and use privileges for a commonly or publicly owned body of water.

This principle is also used to claim rights over resources that grow out of or extend from owned resources (Heller & Salzman 2021). Crops grown by a farmer are rightly claimed to be theirs by most accounts, in part because they grew on the farmer's land. Heller and Salzman describe the interesting example of a supposedly universal rule that cow calves are allocated to the owners of their mothers. This is an interesting adaptation that helps the calves secure nourishment from their mothers, and is easier to monitor, since bovine maternity is much easier to measure than paternity.

There are several advantages to the proximity principle. It can potentially lower enforcement costs by assigning rights to those who already live near a common resource. It also can generate community cohesion and fight against external disturbances. "Absentee ownership", which we will discuss as a result of certain types of exchange rights in Chapters 5 and 9, is a growing phenomenon with rising inequality and mobile financial capital and has been argued to lead to a lack of social capital, sense of community, and alienation of locals from their environment.

These issues have played out extensively with the traditional Hispanic irrigation communities known as acequias in Taos, New Mexico. Historically, these communities had to depend on themselves for the enforcement of rules, and famously this was largely up to the mayordomo, or executive officer of each acequia. But additionally, each acequia member has an incentive to prevent others from taking water out of turn. A time-based property rights system goes hand-in-hand with a rotational distribution arrangement (people take turns). So, if I want to take water from a canal but there doesn't seem to be enough, this may tell me that someone upstream of me is taking water out of turn. I have heard stories about how this facilitated a measure of local self-enforcement among the acequias. However, the water has increasingly been separated from the land in acequia communities as wealthy people from California and else-where buy up property and the needed water rights. I mentioned earlier that this could be seen as an adaptation to the dry conditions in the west, but this is only an adaptation if our goal is to encourage development, which it has done. If our goals are community cohesion and low-cost enforcement, things look different.

The primary issue with spatial rights is that it can cause exclusion and rein-force inequalities by granting further rights based on existing rights; it repre-sents a strengthening of one group's rights potentially at the expense of others. This is not an easy or purely technical issue to resolve. Should the residents of Dearborn, Michigan, for example, be allowed to limit access to their parks to residents only (Armborst *et al.* 2017: 325)? As we have said before, how we view this exclusionary nature depends strongly on context. For example, a strength of the proximity principle is that it establishes a boundary, excluding outsiders from accessing a resource if they don't reside nearby and own other resources, usually land. If our perspective is of a resource-dependent community such as the acequias, exclusion is necessary, and violations of this exclusion can be seen as immoral. Threats to local communities have often come from the unbun-dling of rights and their forfeiture through market transactions. Many of us would react differently, however, if it was a community of resource users itself being excluded, which is happening, for example, along the coast of Maine, where wealthy individuals are buying up coastal properties, and then prevent-ing fishers from accessing their traditional shellfishing grounds (McGreavy *et al.* 2018). We now turn to a discussion of contextual boundaries as a way of finessing the double-edged sword of exclusion.

The value of contextual boundaries

In the previous section we characterized rigid boundaries as being a response to external threats, and rigid boundaries have other benefits as well. They are more often seen as being clearer and less complex than contextual bounda-ries. They are more legible to external actors, and therefore are preferred in formal governance. It is easy to find calls for clear boundaries in the commons and legal/economic literatures (Rose 2019). Clear boundaries establish exactly who owns what, which is needed both for collective action and for markets in goods. For schemes like payment for ecosystem services (PES) it is necessary to know who is impacting which aspects of the environment (e.g., keeping the trees in the forest for carbon storage) so that the appropriate payments can be made. Rigid, unchanging boundaries are simpler than contextual boundaries, and may clarify who is in and who is out. In their description of the incursion of export-driven, globalized sea cucumber markets into the state of Yap, Micronesia, Ferguson *et al.* (2022: 6) provide an example of the challenges of complexity and context:

> The large volumes of sea cucumbers being harvested in the small nearshore area of Yap alarmed local authorities. Violations of tenure rights were also of paramount concern; many of the fishers did not have rights to the areas where they were collecting. Yet due to the complexity of Yap's tenure system, as well as the customary deference owed to one another, it was difficult to prove or enforce individual cases of tenure violations.

In this case, the complexity of local tenure made it more difficult to prevent outsiders from using a resource, and this seems like an unavoidable trade-off when deciding whether a boundary is more fluid or rigid.

With this in mind, what can we say about the value of contextual boundaries? For one, we can say that they are not necessarily less clear than rigid boundaries. This is why I opted for the term "contextual"[1] rather than "fuzzy boundaries" as has been used elsewhere (Cox *et al.* 2010) since this literally means "unclear". While the need for clear boundaries is often mentioned as an important means to establish who owns what, it is not always clarified to whom boundaries should be made clear. It is true that more rigid boundaries, those that don't change based on informal negotiations, are going to be more formally legible, and this is arguably partly why states have preferred to sedentarize their populations in many places, as more mobile populations are harder for the state to "see" and therefore govern (Scott 1998; Niamir-Fuller 1999). We discuss the issue of legibility in depth in Chapter 6. Formal legibility is one thing, but contextual boundaries can be clear to those who abide by them without the need for external legibility.

The great advantage of contextual boundaries is that they are more flexible than rigid boundaries. The best-known examples of contextual environmental

---

1. My thanks to David Sloan Wilson for offering this term to describe this scenario.

boundaries come from the pastoral sector. Pastoralism is the cultural and economic practice of grazing livestock on fields (pastures), and through Hardin is the best-known image associated with the tragedy of the commons. Pastoralism is mostly found in environments where there is insufficient rain to support agriculture, and represents an adaptation to resource scarce environments. There are multiple components to this adaptive package (Henrich 2015), the first being the use of animals in the first place, as this is a way to store resources "on the hoof" (Agrawal 1993: 262).

Pastoralists around the world have worked to deal with the impact they have on the land, but they have done so not through adopting rigid boundaries, strictly demarcating where one group's pasture land ends and another's begins. Pastoralists frequently combine contextual boundaries and mobile lifeways to adapt to water-scarce environments. We can think about this in two steps. First, mobility is required to make sure that herdsmen can find enough land for their livestock to graze. Second, they must develop flexible social boundaries to navigate access to resources in different areas (Niamir-Fuller 1999).

This model is reminiscent of the nucleated boundaries described by Acheson (2003) in his discussion of the Maine lobster fishery. In her study of African pastoralism, Niamir-Fuller (1999) describes how each pastoralist group has a relatively rigid home base, surrounded by its grazing lands, the boundaries of which are more fluid. Groups then negotiate with each other for reciprocal access to each other's grazing lands in what amounts to intergroup cooperation. Niamir-Fuller (1999: 117) further argues that such arrangements are often illegible to external actors, demonstrating a theme we will further develop in Chapter 6:

> The inclusive (or porous) nature of transhumant tenure institutions has often been misread as evidence for the lack of institutions governing resource access – for example, a resource open to all. Such conclusions confuse a lack of rigid exclusion (a defined membership) with the lack of exclusionary powers. In fact, outsiders can only use resources with the permission of the group with usufruct rights.

Finally, this strategy of resilience to disturbance through diversity of access is not limited to mobile actors. As Shipton (2009) describes, the Luo people of western Kenya often own several plots of land with different characteristics to diversify their agricultural portfolios as it were. As we will discuss in Chapter 7, we should also be sensitive to the overinterpretation of supposedly adaptive traits. Shipton, for example, also observes that some farmers prefer to have additional plots of land as a way to get away from their friends and family for a bit.

What is "the commons"?

There is a contradiction to resolve here. I argued earlier that rigid boundaries can be seen as a response to scarcity, but here we see contextual boundaries as an adaptation to a resource-scarce environment. A response to this can be taken from Moritz *et al.* (2018: 12861), who argue that a condition for successful contextual boundaries, is "a low potential for exploitation competition", which is in part facilitated by the mobility of the pastoralists to move about from place to place and not all compete for the same patch of land. So, while the overall environment is more scarce, due to the relatively light touch that humans have on this environment, the logic of collective action problems and the tragedy of the commons is not necessarily the most appropriate one. It may be more appropriate to frame this as the "tragedy of the anticommons" (Heller 1998). This represents the possibility that the environment and other resources may be underused and underprovided as a result of an excess of property rights that thwart such use and provision. In our context, such underuse could result from a preponderance of rigid boundaries.

These observations force us to reflect on what we think we mean by "the commons". To me, a commons is a shared resource that can be subdivided into common-pool resources such as fish and forests, which are exhaustible, and public goods such as knowledge and institutions, which are not. Both are shared because it is difficult to exclude people from their use and benefit. So common-pool resources are supposedly defined because their use is subtractable, (they can be used up), and non-excludible (they are shared). But not all so-called common-pool resources have these properties, as these depend on the relationship between a resource and its environment. Calling a part of the environment a common-pool resource is as much a statement about how that resource is used as it is a statement about that resource (Bromley 1992; Hinkel *et al.* 2015; Bollier & Helfrich 2019: 234–6). Technology, for example, has continually improved our ability to have a greater impact on the environment, effectively creating more subtractability, and assuming that the environment is inherently subtractable is making an assumption about our relationship with that environment. This is a more relational than essentialist argument, defining concepts by their relationships with others rather than in isolation. It is worth noting that Western analytic thinkers tend to be more essentialist than relational (Henrich 2020).

The supposed subtractability of natural resources represents an assumption that use of the environment is necessary a win–lose (humans win, the environment loses). But whether or not this relationship is a win–lose depends not just on the nature of the resource, but on its relationship with human users. If use also means stewardship, as is argued for many traditional and Indigenous management systems, then these assumptions don't hold (Berkes 2018).

I believe this discussion also helps us distinguish the behaviour of mobile pastoralists with the more destructive serial depletion behaviours described at the end of the previous chapter. Pastoralists are not serially depleting resources; they are engaging in reciprocal relationships with each other to access additional resources as needed. Like many factors, the effects of mobility can be highly varied.

I have seen this issue at work during my fieldwork in in Taos, New Mexico, when I was there studying a group of acequia irrigation communities for my PhD dissertation. These communities are the descendants of the original Spanish colonists who travelled up along the Rio Grande starting around 1600. These settlers brought with them their traditional water management practices, which still stand as one of the best-preserved examples of community-based natural resource management in the country.

Taos is a hard place to make it as a farmer. It sits at roughly 7,000 feet above sea level, and there is little rain to support agriculture. Instead, the system is dependent on snowmelt from the nearby Sangre de Cristo mountains. Water flows from these mountains every spring through seven ephemeral streams and ultimately into the Rio Grande River to the west.

The early acequia communities faced upstream–downstream conflict around water use. They had to decide how to manage their water, and how to cooperate to build the needed irrigation infrastructure to convey this water. These communities have historically relied on unlined, earthen ditches to convey water to their fields. This has been criticized as being inefficient, as the water percolates below ground and is presumably lost from the system. Except when it isn't. Hydrological research has shown that this water can recharge shallow aquifers and become available to other farmers downstream of those who used it as irrigation water (Fernald & Guldan 2006; Fernald, Baker & Guldan 2007). This has the potential to ameliorate upstream–downstream conflict. And if we line these ditches for the sake of a particular definition of efficiency, we remove this potential advantage.

Excludability or non-excludability is also not an entirely inherent quality of a commons; it also depends on the type of technology available and how the environment is being used. For some time in the western United States, fences with barbed wire have been the standard way to exclude outsiders from using pasture lands, but before its invention by J. F. Glidden in 1874, more open access conditions were prevalent ("the law of the open range"), which benefited white ranchers and was more in line with the mobile native American peoples (99% Invisible 2015). The invention of this exclusionary device enabled the closure of the pasture commons and the victory of the farmers over the ranchers, two groups that had been in tension over the use of arid lands in the western United States. This was the preferred outcome by the United States government, which like many central governments, prefers more sedentary and therefore more governable subjects (Scott 1998). The introduction of barbed wire also led to the massive decline of American buffalo herds and the way of life for many Native American tribes.

A more recent example, described in a *New York Times* article (Howe 2022), also comes from the American west, where hunters and recreationists have historically been excluded from much supposedly public land because it was surrounded by private land which acted as a boundary, preventing access. Some landowners saw such public lands as an extension of their own land, reflecting the proximity principle discussed earlier.

This situation was exposed through a new app called OnX, which is described as "Google Maps for hunters", and included property boundaries throughout the country, helping hunters know where they could legally hunt and where they couldn't. It also included topography that would help a hunter decide where the best spots to hunt would be. This app has increased access to public lands and the wildlife on them by making this knowledge cheaply accessible, and therefore made it harder for nearby private landowners to exclude hunters from hunting near their land. With the maps, hunters are able to navigate around private property to access public property, sometimes by "corner crossing", stepping from one public square on a checkerboard of land to another and between two private parcels.

I am arguing here against a perspective called essentialism, that views the properties of people and objects as being inherent in themselves. The opposite of this can be called holism, which focuses on the connection between objects and how these impact the characteristics of each within a larger system. Holism views properties as being more relational than essential. In departing from essentialism, I think we can go too far. There are qualities of the environment that are less dependent on their social context. Even in the Taos example just mentioned, we see the importance of water being a mobile resource, creating the potential for asymmetric conflict (Schlager, Blomquist & Tang 1994). In their discussion of the sea cucumber trade that we have briefly touched on, Ferguson *et al.* (2022: 2) provide another example of the importance of inherent qualities of a resource: "Sea cucumbers are particularly vulnerable to overfishing because they are easy to collect and store, grow slowly, and reproduce through broadcast spawning, a strategy that relies on high densities for reproduction to be successful." The use of such a species is more likely to be more subtractable. And in general, a resource that is more renewable will be less subtractable.

Turning to excludability, there are aspects of this that turn on inherent properties of a commons. This property correlates closely to the phase of matter that we are talking about: resources associated with the solid phase are the most easily divided and owned, followed by the liquid phase and then the gaseous phase. And this is largely because of the increased mobility and decreased visibility of the liquid and gaseous phases. Land itself is arguably the most easily managed. In comparison, water is highly mobile, making it hard to claim ownership over, just as highly mobile human actors are harder to govern. Air is harder still to control and therefore own, although like water, it is often claimed to be owned through the proximity principle when landowners claim rights over the overlying air column.

Usufruct rights

In one of the quotations of Niamir-Fuller in our discussion of pastoralists, she mentions that they exercise usufruct rights to each other's land. A usufruct right is a right to use ("usus") or otherwise benefit from ("fructus") the property of someone else. In general, they are more temporary than normal rights, and the types of use are generally confined to withdraw with some limited development that does not damage the property allowed in some situations; alienation, or sale of property is not allowed, although subleasing may be (see Part II for a discussion of the elements of the environmental bundle of rights). Usufruct rights are ubiquitous, including any kind of leasing arrangement, for example, in which a lessee is granted usufruct rights of the lessor.

Usufruct rights are particularly prevalent in the environmental context. Often, the granter of rights is a state entity, which claims formal ownership over natural resources, granting specific use rights and benefit entitlements to private actors. This has occurred, for example, between the United States government and some Native American tribes such as the Chippewa, who claimed usufruct rights to their historic lands after they lost such lands in a treaty with the US federal government. In Cuba, the national government granted usufruct rights to peasant farmers to develop agricultural fields on abandoned state-owned lands as a means to combat food poverty resulting from international embargos the country faced (Mesa-Lago & González-Corzo 2021), and throughout Latin America, agrarian reforms that distributed land to rural peasants tended to grant them usufruct rights (Albertus 2021).

As contextual boundaries, usufruct rights can grant additional flexibility, as the transaction costs of lease-type arrangements are often lower. They can also represent substantial imbalances of power, as they do in the two examples just mentioned. How we feel about this likely depends on the identity of the actors involved. We might be fine with it if, in the case of the rights of nature movement, it is argued that humanity should be thought of as having only usufruct rights to the environmental, which is owned by nature herself (Talbot-Jones 2017). (See Chapter 8 for a discussion of the rights of nature movement.)

The concept represents a distinction between two social classes: those who own and those who do not own but can use or otherwise benefit from. In the pastoral example described above, this is less the case, as there is a reciprocal exchange of usufruct rights between different groups to each other's territories over time.

Conclusion

It's important to not think that either rigid or contextual boundaries are better. Like the various types of property regimes we will discuss in Part II, we often find a mix of more rigid and contextual boundaries in the same system. Niamir-Fuller (1999), for example, discusses how pastoralist communities employ a mix of relatively fixed to flexible boundaries, with more rigid boundaries at a geographic core, surrounded by more fluid boundaries at the outside of a group's territory. I argued earlier that this sounds like Acheson's (2003) idea of a nucleated boundary, with a strong core contained within a more flexible periphery.

These first two chapters have discussed some of the foundational arguments about environmental property rights and expanded upon them. A throughline in both chapters is that politics and power matter; not all environmental problems are the result of a failure to support a collective interest, and insisting on such a collective interests can hide the fact that many of our environmental problems are associated with clear winners and losers. Similarly, boundaries as a solution to the tragedy of the commons are inherently exclusionary and political, although not necessarily as rigidly exclusionary as one might think.

This discussion leads to the main focus of Chapter 6 in Part III: policy panaceas, or policy solutions that are overgeneralized and artificially depoliticized. In the rest of Part III we unpack the topic of property regimes, which themselves have served as the basis for environmental policy panaceas (e.g., assumptions that individual property is best). Chapter 7 includes a discussion of the relationship between individual and common property which builds directly on our discussions from these first two chapters. Readers who want to move directly from our discussion of boundaries to explore the relationship between individual versus collective boundaries, which is what we mean by individual and common property, can proceed there if they wish.

For now, however, we have one more chapter to dive further into the theory of collective action and its relationship to environmental rights. The most important concepts in these chapters are kinship and reciprocity, the two foundational mechanisms for cooperation in any species. We have already seen the importance of reciprocity in the theory of environmental reciprocity, and in Niamir-Fuller's discussion of the negotiations between pastoralists groups for ad hoc access to each other's grazing lands. Kinship and reciprocity are both fundamental ways in which humans cooperate and grant access to nature. Beyond this, some communities have also applied to our relationships with nature, which fundamentally changes what it means to have rights to nature.

3

Kinship, reciprocity and intrinsic value

In the previous chapter, we discussed how intergroup competition promotes within-group cooperation. But this is not the only thing needed for cooperation; we must also consider mechanisms that develop and maintain cooperation within groups. The two most well-established mechanisms for enabling cooperation across all species are kinship and reciprocity. We have already touched on reciprocity in the previous chapter.

A large scientific controversy persists over whether intergroup competition and the selection of cooperation at the level of groups, as discussed in Chapter 2, or reciprocity and kinship are the primary factors that enable cooperation. As an outsider to the academic communities involved, my interpretation is that this controversy is in part due to the very same tribal instincts we discussed in Chapter 2: often the easiest way to identify yourself as belonging to a group is to clarify that you don't like "them" and what they're doing and thinking. In his discussion of the mathematical equivalence between group selection and kinship-based selection, Wilson (2016) – arguably the primary proponent of group-based selection through his multilevel selection framework – has argued that these mechanisms do not need to be seen as mutually exclusive. My interpretation is that cooperation requires the identification of an in-group to ensure that the costs of cooperation are recouped, and that kinship and reciprocity are the two primary mechanisms for this identification. In this chapter, we discuss each of these as mechanisms for establishing and maintaining cooperation, as a means for establishing property rights, and as a way to fundamentally change how we view nature and environmental rights to nature.

Kinship and reciprocity closely relate to the distinction between intrinsic and extrinsic values. Intrinsic values come from the inside, and need no external reinforcement; extrinsic values are only instrumental, and without external reinforcement, will fade. The dominant Western discourse about property rights and public policy has mostly neglected intrinsic value. This is in part due to an abridged understanding of the nature of human actors as only responding to extrinsic incentives (Bowles 2016). I believe that another reason for this is that certain aspects of intrinsic motivation are harder to implement at scale, which is an inherent goal of any public policy. Feelings of kinship and reciprocity in particular are specific to an individual person or object, as we will explore further.

In this chapter we will explore kinship and reciprocity as mechanisms for cooperation and the allocation of property rights. We will also explore how they can represent intrinsic value, and how the psychologies of each can be applied not just to other people but to other species and the environment, with implications for how we view environmental property rights.

Kinship

The most fundamental altruistic, kinship-based relationship is rooted in the unconditional love and support that parents commonly bestow on their children. This relationship most embodies the defining feature of kinship-based relationships, the intrinsic value that they involve: kin are valued for their own sake, not just for their instrumental or extrinsic value. Because of this close relationship there is a special word for the way in which kinship is used to grant property rights: inheritance. The right to bequeath one's property to one's heirs is an important right to have (Kilic, Moylan & Koolwal 2021). In Bali, as in many places, farmland is only inherited by sons, sometimes by only the oldest son (Lansing 2012). This has the significant consequence of creating and reinforcing inequality in ownership, in many cases disenfranchising women. Kinship serves to facilitate and limit access more broadly as well. Basurto (2005: 649), for example, observes that among the Seri fishers of Mexico, cooperation is almost entirely limited to "immediate kin: parents and siblings". Basurto also describes a norm whereby non-Seri who marry a Seri member are granted fishing rights. This reflects the role that marriage has historically played to bridge intergroup barriers to cooperation (Henrich 2020).

The centrality of parent–offspring relations can be understood from the evolutionary point of view. Kin-based cooperation is based on the perspective of "seeing like a gene". Altruistic behaviour is at least partially genetically determined, and altruistic genes will be favoured to evolve based on the ratio of the individual costs to the altruist individual to the benefits of those who are helped. Altruistic behaviours will evolve based on what is referred to as kin selection if $Br > C$, where B = benefits to receivers, C = costs to the altruist, and r is the coefficient of relatedness between the altruist and those who are helped

(Hamilton 1964). This coefficient represents the probability that another individual will also carry the same altruistic gene, thus conferring an evolutionary advantage to the gene that is contributing to altruist behaviour. If r = 0.5, as in the case of children and parents or between siblings, it means that the gene will be favoured by behaviours with at least twice the benefits versus the costs. For cousins, the benefits must be eight times greater than the costs. We can see from this that the probability of altruistic (and therefore costly) behaviours evolving through kin selection radically decreases as we move more than one or two genetic steps away from ourselves.

Humans are unusual in the extent to which they invest in their offspring, and we are unusual in the extent to which we extend our kinship-based psychology beyond our offspring to our siblings and cousins, and to unrelated individuals, which allows us to be more cooperative than we would be if we were limited by the math described in the previous paragraph. Cultural anthropologists have documented the ubiquity of cultural kinship, or "fictive kin": the treatment of non-genetically related individuals as if they were kin (Sahlins 2011: 3).

Christakis (2019: 134) describes an evolutionary interpretation of cultural kinship, by which the same psychological mechanism that evolved to incentivize parental care of offspring has been subsequently applied to other relationships:

> It seems that, across evolutionary time, humans evolved to love their offspring first, then their mates, and then to feel affection for their biological kin, then their affinal kin (their in-laws), and then their friends and groups. I wonder sometimes if we are in the middle of a long-timescale transition to becoming a species that feels attachment to ever larger numbers of people.

This is a hopeful, even aspirational hypothesis. Christakis is describing a process whereby an initial (pre)adaptation is leveraged for further benefit. In evolutionary parlance, this is known as exaptation, and this idea will play a large role in how we understand the relationship that people can have with their local environment as well.

Reciprocity

Just as humans have a psychological module for kinship psychology, we also have evolved psychological mechanisms to engage in reciprocity: I help you if you help me. Between the extremes of supposedly pure extrinsic and intrinsic valuation, we can think of situations where we are not entirely intrinsically motivated, but we still have a sense of obligation towards our partner in a relationship. This is the domain of reciprocity. This is often conflated with a situation where no such sense of obligation is present at all, which is purely extrinsic, when we only view a partner in a relationship through what they can do for us.

Like kinship, reciprocity mediates access to natural resources. This occurs through pastoralists' use of contextual boundaries, offering each other access to their grazing lands in reciprocal arrangements. And kinship and reciprocity can work together to determine group membership and access, as Brewer (2012: 389) describes in the case of fishing rights in the Maine lobster fishery, where

> Individuals from long-established local families are virtually guaranteed entry rights to the lobster fishery, particularly if close kin are fishing at the time. Men without local kin can often gain entry privileges by marrying into a fishing family and establishing exchange relationships with their in-laws.

The mechanism of reciprocity is similar to kin selection: for altruistic behaviours to evolve, they need to provide benefits that are greater than the costs. In this context we can apply Hamilton's same formula as a heuristic, redefining the benefits and costs to be both specific to the altruist, and the coefficient of relatedness (the probability of two individuals sharing the same altruistic gene) as a coefficient of reciprocity, or the probability that altruistic behaviour is reciprocated, providing benefits back to cooperators to cover their costs. For a given set of costs and benefits then the key is this probability. And how is this probability increased? There are several models that have been proposed based on the ways in which individuals engage with each other (Nowak 2006; Kurzban, Burton-Chellew & West 2015). For us, the models that are most relevant are direct reciprocity and indirect reciprocity.

Direct reciprocity

In direct reciprocity, the benefits provided to a cooperator are derived from the actors who they are cooperating with when those actors reciprocally cooperate themselves. The most relevant finding from research on direct reciprocity is the role that the shadow of the future plays in influencing each participant's decisions (Nowak 2006). In experimental research on two-way cooperative games like the prisoner's dilemma game discussed in Chapter 1, it has been shown that games that are played over multiple rounds help to sustain more cooperation than is found in single-round games, because each participant's behaviour in future rounds becomes a part of the other participant's calculus. This calculus is the theoretical basis for the theory of environmental reciprocity discussed in the previous chapter. The key argument is that investment in the environment is motivated by a long-term, reciprocal relationship with that environment, which is enabled in part by property rights arrangements.

So far, our discussion of reciprocity has been extrinsic, and the tit-for-tat arrangement of reciprocity can feel instrumental. But there are several ways in which our reciprocal psychology expresses intrinsic value. First, even in the absence of repeated interactions, humans have a tendency to act altruistically towards partners in public goods-oriented games (Henrich 2015). Second, as Tooby and Cosmides (1996: 139) argue, we have a tendency to internalize the value of partners in repeated exchange interactions:

> It seems to be a pervasive expression of human psychology that people in repeated contact feel the need to rapidly transform relationships that began in commercial transactions into something "more" with signs that indicate the relationship is no longer simply of contingent exchange, but of friendship.

A good example of this phenomenon comes from Basurto *et al.*'s (2020) examination of the relationships between fishers and fish buyers at several study sites in Mexico. We will discuss this arrangement, known as a patron–client relationship, further in Chapter 5. The authors describe how what starts as exclusively exchange relationships can blur over time into the provision of mutual assistance and aid. Another example comes from a podcast interview I had with the scholar and activist Raul Pacheco-Vega. During our conversation, Pacheco-Vega (2020: np) described how households would develop relationships with waste pickers who came to collect their waste over time:

> Households develop a relationship with their waste pickers. In that sense they become protective of their health, and protective of their rights … this repeated interaction between the households and the waste pickers, with time, they develop an informal arrangement, that is collaborative between the household and the waste picker.

Repeated interactions allow for mutual extrinsic gain, but they also allow each partner to humanize the other one and develop a feeling of caring for their well-being independent of their instrumental value.

Indirect reciprocity

There is also a more indirect version of reciprocity that is based on more diffuse networks of interactions. With indirect reciprocity, the benefits of helping others are not based on an exchange partner, but on the reputation one garners in a community and the rewards that other people bestow on someone who has shown themselves to be trustworthy. In the anthropological literature this behaviour is often referred to as a "gift economy", or an economy based less on direct, reciprocal exchanges and more diffuse networks of gift-giving (Mauss 2016). Gift economies change what it means to say that you "own" something, as ownership becomes more temporary. Temporary ownership is important in order to maintain the flow of a gift through a community, and this flow is important from a cooperative standpoint: once a gift stops moving, it stops reinforcing social ties through trust and indirect reciprocity. Hyde (2019: 4) describes a rule that is used in some gift economies that states that "One man's gift … must not be another man's capital". If a household receives a goat, they can view this as a resource unit to be consumed, say as part of a collective feast, or passed on, or as capital from which to derive ongoing benefits (more on this distinction in Part II). Using the goat as capital, say by producing milk, can be seen as a violation of norms requiring the continued flow of a gift.

A famous example of a gift economy as described by Mauss and other anthropologists comes from the Māori of Aotearoa, or New Zealand. Reflecting the temporary nature of ownership in this culture, the "Māori make a fundamental distinction between ownership and what is considered temporary possession by using two versions of the possessive particle – either *tō* and *tā* in this case" (Hēnare 2018: 456). English has no such distinction. Spanish – the only other language I know well enough to mention here – does this for the verb "to be" with the verbs "ser" and "estar".

Indirect reciprocity helps to improve the cohesion of a group. And who is in the group? Hyde (2019: 22–3) describes how, in the case of the Māori this group includes the forest:

> when hunters return from the forest with birds they have killed, they give a portion of the kill to the priests, who, in turn, cook the birds at a sacred fire. The priests eat a few of them and then prepare a sort of talisman, the mauri, which is the physical embodiment of the forest hau. This mauri is a gift the priests give back to the forest, where, as a Māori sage once explained to an Englishman, it "causes the birds to be abundant …, that they may be slain and taken by man". […]
>
> There are three gifts in this hunting ritual: the forest gives to the hunters, the hunters to the priests, and the priests to the forest. At the

end, the gift moves from the third party back to the first. The ceremony that the priests perform is called whangai hau, which means "nourishing hau," feeding the spirit.

There are several points to emphasize here that will start to take us to the most important arguments to be made in this chapter. First, we need to be careful in interpreting the Māori words *hau* and *mauri* in the quotation above. *Hau* is generally understood to be "a spiritual force impelling behaviour – an ethic of reciprocity" (Nicholson 2019: 138). But as Nicholson argues, there has been a problematic trend of non-Māori scholars interpreting Māori concepts as if they were unitary, with only one meaning, arguably to make them legible to an outside audience. But these terms can mean a great many things, as native speakers in any language are generally aware of for terms in their own language.

Second, this brief example relates to the feeling that Christakis expressed earlier; of an ever-widening circle of reciprocity and intrinsic value. One problem with such a quasi-evolutionary perspective is that it disregards the fact that such a widening has in fact often occurred in indigenous cultures. How this widened circle relates to environmental property rights is the subject of the rest of this chapter.

Allocating rights: food sharing

The food sharing behaviours of some groups combine multiple components discussed so far in this chapter. An example comes from the Mbuti people of Eastern Zaire (Ichikawa 1981). For a part of their diet, they depend on honey that must be obtained through climbing trees to reach hives 30 metres above the ground. As Ichikawa (1981: 58) describes,

> When a Mbuti finds out a beehive he breaks the underbushes around the tree with the beehive, or slash a piece of bark, to make a finder's mark (*bunde*). A beehive thus marked is regarded to belong to the finder and no one else can collect the honey without the permission of the 'owner'.

So we start with individual property in this case.

Ichikawa (1981: 63) further elaborates on the honey-sharing practices of the Mbuti:

> honey belongs to its finder. However, part from the rare occasion that only a little honey is available, Mbuti usually do not consume their

honey by themselves. Anyone that accompanies the owner to the honey collecting site takes his portion. Honey brought back to the camp is always distributed to some members of the camp. To the Mbuti honey is the food which should be shared with others. Honey is more than food which supplies nutrition. It plays an important role in the social life of the Mbuti.

Most of the honey of higher quality … is wrapped with Maranthaceae leaves and carried back to the camp. These packs of honey are distributed to other camp members in an informal way. Visitors, affinal relatives and family members take the share more often, but honey is distributed also to other members of different bands. This type of distribution is best expressed by the term "general reciprocity" … although they give honey to other persons with the expectation of its return, they never do so based on the strict calculation of the amount given and taken. Rather, this distribution is based on the vague assumption that the frequent distribution has the overall levelling effect on the amount given and taken in the long run.

Multiple mechanisms are at play here. We start with the initial claim to the honey by the person who collects it, but then there is a distribution to other gatherers who are also seen to contribute to this outcome. This is a form of direct reciprocity. Then we have a more indirect form of reciprocity, whereby the honey is shared with a broader community as a mechanism for maintaining social cohesion. And this reflects another more indirect way in which common property can serve as an adaptation to scarcity and concomitant risk; by preserving social cohesion of a group of interdependent actors. The food sharing practices of the Mbuti and other hunter-gatherers have been interpreted as a risk mitigation strategy (Bahuchet 1990). Sharing with others is a way to ensure that if one does not find food in the future, they will reciprocate by sharing their food. Like indirect reciprocity, this is a kind of giving without the expectation of immediate return. Tooby and Cosmides (1996) present a similar argument in their evolutionary explanation for human friendship: it is based on this kind of delayed reciprocity: a friend is someone who one cares about intrinsically. And why is this important? Because, as the authors argue, the importance of a friend is that they will help us precisely when we are unable to reciprocate their support. This then relates to the final part of the quote and the idea of "general reciprocity" between groups, which represents a less strict form of reciprocity and is similar to what Bollier and Helfrich (2019) call "gentle reciprocity", not requiring a strict accounting of tit for tat.

Intrinsic motivation and holistic management

The real value of intrinsic value is the care that is bestowed. Intrinsically valuing something means literal "caregiving", a term that is the United States refers to the care given to children by "caretakers". And the value of care is that it is holistic; it takes the time to see the interconnected parts of a person, or as we will discuss, an ecosystem. The value of a parent's unconditional love for their child may seem obvious, given a child's inability to support itself. But why does it matter that there is a sense of unconditionality, or intrinsic value? Researchers have found that a child must feel "seen" by their parent, and be recognized for who they are, in all their pieces (and we all have many pieces, which we will discuss in Chapter 7). A severe lack of such respectful recognition can leave a child feeling (and being) fragmented, unable to integrate of all of their parts and experiences (Van der Kolk 2015).

In the book *Compassionomics* by Trzeciak and Mazzarelli (2019), the authors describe a "crisis of compassion" (or lack of compassion), by healthcare professionals, document the costs for patients, and argue that a lack of compassion stems in part from the shift from intrinsic to extrinsic motivation on the part of healthcare professionals, meaning that patients are seen less as whole people and more through a narrow lens as patients or even more simply, a list of symptoms. When we are intrinsically motivated, it is more natural for us to see each other as whole people and to care for clients, make them feel seen, and create a process of co-production, whereby services are co-produced by service provider and receiver, rather than a more asymmetrical, expert-oriented service delivery model. To an intrinsically motivated service provider, a client is seen as a partner. When we are extrinsically motivated, we reduce a client's problems to emotionally flat, analytical archetypes, and expedite formal processes to check this box or that and move on.

Such simplification is not always a bad thing: there are many relationships in our lives that arguably should stay instrumental, and of course we cannot afford to become intrinsically invested in all the people that we encounter. Similarly, there are some tasks are more "algorithmic", straightforward and not requiring creativity or complex thinking, and these do not necessarily need intrinsic motivation (Pink 2011). But when we are in the role of providing services to individuals, and the challenges such individuals are facing are the result of a complex history of interactions among their different parts, then the task is concomitantly more complex and a more intrinsically motivated, holistic perspective is warranted.

This relationship applies to our pursuit of interdisciplinary consilience as well, which I discussed in the introduction to this book. In my experience, much of interdisciplinary engagement is extrinsically motivated, (e.g., to obtain a grant), but this approach often leads to what I call the "baton model" of interdisciplinarity, with one discipline simply handing its results off to another without true engagement or integration. In pursuing the interdisciplinary synthesis in this book, I have needed to rely on my own intrinsic motivation, although this sometimes needed to be tempered by the extrinsic need to ultimately finish the book!

It is hard to miss the fact that intrinsic motivation and its consequences, including holistic engagement and well-being, can be contagious, or transitive: the more intrinsically motivated we are in our interactions with others, the more we are able to meet their own basic needs as well, helping them pass the benefits on, as it were. This points us towards applying the same set of considerations to service providers as we do to recipients, or to government officials as we do to community members. If the selection process that determines who can succeed as a particular type of service provider (for example, who gets into medical school) is highly controlling and thwarts basic needs, this process will lead to poorer outcomes for those that they are trying to support (Ryan & Deci 2018).

A common denominator in some of this work is the idea of basic human needs. Ryan and Deci have pioneered a research programme on self-determination theory (SDT), arguing that human beings have three basic needs: autonomy, or self-integration, efficacy, and belonging. From the SDT perspective, autonomy is not just about freedom from external constraint, or what has been called negative liberty. Autonomy is about a coherence between one's sense of self and one's actions, and therefore requires that one has an established sense of self. This is dependent on a supportive parental and later social environment, which has been called positive liberty. Efficacy is the feeling that one can impact one's environment and is particularly important with respect to the ability to accomplish goals autonomously, or goals that one values. Belonging is the feeling that one can relate to other people within a group; that one's identity is valued. Ryan and Deci argue that when our basic needs are satisfied, we are more prosocial and cooperative, which to me reflects the transitivity of intrinsic motivation. This theory then adds to our ongoing discussion of the ways in which human beings can act collectively. We started with a discussion of the importance of boundaries and here we have a second set of psychological factors.

Other research has argued that satisfying these needs can also lead to pro-environmental behaviour and environmental stewardship. Based on a survey of recreational users of protected areas in the Appalachian United States, Landon *et al.* (2021) conclude that our attachment to place is based on direct experiences with that place, and that this is mediated by the extent to which those experiences satisfy the three basic needs of autonomy, relatedness and efficacy. Wang, Fielding and Dean (2022) offer a summary of the application of psychological ownership to the context of our relationship with nature. They posit a near-identical list of basic needs and similarly argue that when these are met through an engagement with the environment, they lead to a psychology of environmental ownership. The authors also argue that the ways in which these needs are satisfied are through investing labour or other resources into the environment (which as we will discuss is one of the most commonly used ways of establishing environmental rights), exerting some amount of influence, and obtaining knowledge about the environment. Each of these will tend to accumulate over time, and one of the most consistent findings from the literature on place attachment, along with it motivating stewardship, is that it increases with the amount of time someone is in a place (Lewicka 2011), although this is not a universal finding (Trimbach, Fleming & Biedenweg 2022). Notice the similarity to the observation we made earlier about reciprocal relationships between people – that extrinsic exchange relationships repeated over time can be internalized as intrinsically valuable by the participants.

To conclude, we are starting a new discourse on the factors that can incentivize stewardship that complement our discussion from the previous chapter. There, the theory of environmental reciprocity is based entirely on extrinsic motivation; there is no idea of internalized norms or values or basic needs in that theory. A part of that theory is the idea of place dependence, or the instrumental importance of a place to a person that raises the costs of exit. Here we are dealing with an intrinsic analogue, which has gone by several names in the literature, but which I shall refer to with the term place attachment.

Kinship and reciprocity with nature

How does place attachment manifest? A big part of the answer to this is through the psychologies of kinship and reciprocity. Earlier I referred to Christakis' argument that our kinship psychology has been exapted, extending beyond those genetically related to us, in order to further promote larger-scale social integration. I believe that this is also how we can interpret the relationships that many people have with their local environment. My interpretation is that in many such some places, cultural exaptation has occurred, in which our kinship psychology and reciprocity psychology are leveraged to improve the relationship that we have with nature by allowing us to view nature as a reciprocal partner and as kin.

Through these psychologies we can develop a sense of nature's intrinsic value, and a desire to care for it and respect it. Actions taken from this perspective are what I would define as stewardship, which I have used somewhat loosely as a concept up to this point but now want to be more precise about. For me, the most vital ingredient to stewardship is care, and care means that we engage with something more intrinsically, with its own interest in mind. There can be degrees to which this intrinsic value is internalized, but it at least includes an interest in caring for the future state of that which is stewarded, and at most it means that we soften our demands for reciprocity and engage more holistically, taking account of complex relationships that we see in nature (or each other). We now turn to several examples of intrinsically motivated environmental stewardship.

Salmon boy

Our first example of environmental kinship comes from the Native peoples of Alaska. Here, Carothers *et al.* (2021: 19), citing work by Langdon (2007) have observed that:

> Across Indigenous cultures of Alaska, there is a foundational importance of spirituality, respectful and reciprocal relationships between people and other beings, and active management of ecosystems … We see similarity across Indigenous cultures of Alaska who view salmon as nonhuman kin who return to give themselves to people.

Here we see our kin and reciprocal psychologies being applied to our relationship with the natural world. Langdon (2007: 240–1) describes these dynamics through the relationship between salmon and the Tlingit people and the Tlingit story of salmon boy, which he learned of during his own fieldwork:

> A young boy is hungry and asks his mother for some food. She directs him to the remaining small amount of dried fish. The piece he selects has mold on it, and he throws it down in disgust. His mother reprimands him for his behaviour. He leaves the house, wearing a copper necklace, and goes down to the beach to check his bird snare. He slips and falls into the water but is saved from drowning by the salmon people, who take him to live with them in their village … there the boy sees that salmon are people, and the salmon chief teaches him many things about how to treat salmon.

Langdon continues to describe the return of salmon boy in the form of a salmon, which culminates in his being reunited with his family, and taking the role of a teacher about the ways to respectfully treat salmon:

> From this mythic charter, Tlingits acquire a number of concepts about salmon: that they are persons like themselves, that they feel and make choices, that they attend to human action and communication, that they require respectful treatment, and that they will not return if they are not treated with respect.

A strong part of this narrative is the need to steward the salmon and treat them respectfully, without waste. We can see here our reciprocity and kinship psychologies being marshalled to favour environmental stewardship through the telling of a mythical story that is also referred to by Langdon as the Tlingits' covenant with the salmon.

Kuleana

This way of viewing human–environment relationships is so distinct from the Western approach that it can feel jarring to apply the concept of property here, which can come with substantial cultural baggage. Are there terms that can express the idea of rights and responsibilities as coexisting and being expressed through the psychologies of kinship and reciprocity? An example of one such word comes from a terrific book by Mehana Blaich Vaughan (2018) called *Kaiāulu: Gathering Tides*. In this book Vaughan describes the Native Hawaiian relationship to the environment. An important term within Hawaiian culture is *kuleana*, meaning both rights and responsibilities that are based on long-standing relationships with the environment. Vaughan describes how *kuleana* represents the inseparability of rights to the environment and obligations to it, and how maintenance of a healthy environment is important for maintaining rights to it. Vaughan's work illustrates several important ideas that we have discussed so far; the importance of understanding a concept as part of a net-work of ideas, as I briefly mentioned with the Māori concept of the *hau*; the specificity of stewardship as a relationship that develops over time; and the transitivity of intrinsic value.

As it was used before Western contact, *kuleana* referred to plots of land granted to individual Hawaiians and their families by ruling chiefs and chief-esses, who were seen to be holding the land in trust for the akua, or gods (Vaughan 2018: 89). Individual and family *kuleana* titles were effectively usu-fruct rights, granting the rights to use the land for certain purposes while ultimate ownership resided elsewhere. More formal land titles were instituted by King Kamehameha, granting *kuleana* land and sea plots through the Kuleana Act, to make traditional tenure more legible to Westerners. This process was followed by further Western incursion and waves of dispossession that Hawaiians have faced in part because of the ignorance of common property within US property law.

Kuleana is one among many important Hawaiian terms that Vaughan uses to describe reciprocal and kinship-based human–environment relationships and a blending of human–nature identity. Some of these terms refer to other species, such as the term *ʻaumākua*, meaning a personal or familiar deity that often takes the form of specific species or even individuals, as Vaughan (2018: 19) describes:

> For many Hawaiian fishing families … sharks are ʻaumākua, embodiments of ancestors who serve as guardians for their descendants. Multiple species, both marine and terrestrial, were considered ʻaumākua, such as honu (turtles), manta rays, and pueo (owls). ʻAumākua were not just any animal of a given species, but particular individuals, many named, who embodied the spirits of recently or long-departed ancestors. The belief that departed relatives become a part of marine ecosystems within their home area encapsulates the idea of families' connection to place.
>
> Sharks are described helping people in reciprocal relationships. In some places, the grandparents of today's fisher men and women fed ʻaumākua sharks in rivers or nearshore waters. Fishermen fed sharks a share of their catch, tossing some of the harvest to a particular shark who would in turn help herd fish into nets.

This personification of non-target species reflects the indirect reciprocity psychology described earlier. Fish and other catch species are thought of as *Mea ʻOla*, or sentient beings, who "choose whether or not to be caught" (Vaughan 2018: 21), reflecting again a reciprocal framing of fisher–prey relationships.

Vaughan describes the significance of other Hawaiian terms that demonstrate the importance of attachment to place:

> The word *kahu* means 'keeper' and refers to the action of caring and nurturing. This term is commonly used to describe the individual or family who cares for a particular *ʻaina*, especially sacred areas throughout Hawaʻi. Kuleana associated with fishing includes the responsibility to *malama*, (take care of) fishing spots before harvesting them. Use

of natural resources relies on building relationships with specific harvesting areas and gathering in a way that cultivates their continued
abundance.   (Vaughan 2018: 34)

Values that apply more generally to behaviour in all places, such as
mālama 'āina (take care of the land) are important, but lack relationship and reciprocity with a specific place.   (Vaughan 2018: 47)

We have seen this specificity in our discussion of kinship and reciprocity earlier in this chapter; these are not psychologies that are applied at random, but
are developed within the context of specific relationships. Finally, Vaughan
describes traditional Hawaiian fishing practices that reflect many of the items
that Berkes *et al.* (2006) list as being characteristic of holistic indigenous management: cultivating habitat for and accounting for the reproductive needs of
marine species and rotating harvesting areas. She also describes how seaweed
is tended to and used both as a source of nutrition and seen as an important "foundation of a healthy marine ecosystem" (Vaughan 2018: 43). And
I believe this finding resonates with the transitive nature of intrinsic motivation I described earlier. Vaughan is describing individuals who can compe-
tently engage with the natural environment with a sense of autonomy, or that
one's actions with the environment are meeting one's values, and in the context
of a supportive social system.

Sacred groves

I want to offer a final example of intrinsic human–nature relations before con-
cluding the chapter. I learned of this example during a research project on
the role that religion can play in natural resource management. Specifically,
we were analysing the role of religion in local natural resource management.
Our question was, could religious beliefs and values help to implement important governance functions associated with Ostrom's design principles, such
as establishing social and ecological boundaries? To answer this question we
conducted a meta-analysis of the relevant literatures (Cox, Villamayor-Tomas
& Hartberg 2014). We found many cases where a local religion does play a
large role in resource management, and the most common context we found
occurred in the use of forests, conceived as sacred groves. We haven't talked
about the idea of being "sacred" so far, but it is one of the most important
terms used for expressing a deeply intrinsic value held for a person or place.
Something that is sacred evokes strong emotions of reverence, and is closely
associated with one's individual and collective sense of self. A sacred grove

is a patch of forest that is experienced in this way, and because of this sacred groves have played important conservation roles for many years (Gadgil 2018). Brockington, Duffy and Igoe (2008) make the important observation in this context that sacred groves are the original, community-based "protected area". We will discuss protected areas as a formal conservation mechanism further in Chapter 8.

In our research, we found 21 cases of sacred groves in Africa and 19 in India. The countries with the most cases in our dataset were India with 10, Indonesia with five, and China and Zimbabwe with four each. In these cases, it is common for segments of a forest to be demarcated with sacred landmarks, which help set biophysical boundaries. In some cases, it is believed that aspects of nature such as trees or wildlife contain the spirits of ancestors, distinguishing them as either sources of intrinsic, kinship-based value to be protected, or sources of social vigilance that monitor local communities to make sure they comply with environmental norms.

One of the most prominent writers and actors advocating for sacred groves has been Madhav Gadgil, an Indian ecologist who studied the ecology and conservation of forests in the Western Ghats of India. Gadgil (2018: n.p.) expresses his own attachment to this area and how he came to develop a research programme there. His work has helped confront assumptions that institutions like sacred groves are only "lingering elements of nature worship prevalent in all supposedly primitive societies; they had no secular functions but persisted purely because of superstition". Instead, Gadgil has shown that sacred groves in the Western Ghats have both extrinsic and intrinsic value for the people living there, and that these people also feel a sense of reciprocal obligation to nature in exchange for the benefits they receive from the environment.

Conclusion

In this chapter we have dealt with two closely related ideas: reciprocity and kinship as mechanisms for social and ecological cooperation, and the distinction between intrinsic and extrinsic value. I have also argued for a stronger appreciation for intrinsic value in our relationships with each other and our natural world. A challenging question about intrinsic value is, where does it come from? And the answer to some extent is, itself; when people feel cared for, they are better caregivers themselves.

I believe the ideas expressed in this chapter are profound. We can spend much of our lives feeling burnt out, or unattached to people and places, without fully realizing that our most basic needs are not being met. We can feel fragmented, unable to integrate our experiences and move forward with a sense of purpose and autonomy. In my own culture there is no use for the word "sacred"; it is seen as something "other", or a part of a religious package that is eyed with scepticism if not cynicism. But without intrinsic value there is no meaning; extrinsic value can increase the efficiency of our activities, but it cannot tell us where we should be so efficiently speeding off to.

This all said, the conclusion here is not that we need to have maximum intrinsic value and minimum extrinsic value in our lives. This is a new optimization problem; indeed the idea that we need to optimize our lives (for what?) is a very extrinsic-oriented framing. Intrinsic value is costly and inefficient, and sometimes this is the point; my intrinsic interest in integrating multiple paths of thought has been the engine in driving this book forward. At the same time, if I only cared about intrinsic value, I would never finish this book! The two values are not necessarily negatively associated with each other; as we have discussed, intrinsic value grows over time with people and places that are initially valued instrumentally. The conclusion here is that we need to develop an awareness of the sources of our own values, be they intrinsic or extrinsic, and decide how we feel about them.

Another dichotomy I want to resist here is Western versus non-Western, although I have fallen back on this a bit so far. The examples provided fall largely outside of the Western view of environmental property rights. But there are examples of the sentiments just described coming from Western thinkers. Maybe the most famous example here is Aldo Leopold's (2020: 192) idea of a land ethic, which he expresses in this book *A Sand County Almanac*: "In short, a land ethic changes the role of Homo sapiens from conqueror of the land-community to plain member and citizen of it. It implies respect for his fellow-members, and also respect for the community as such."

This passage strongly resonates with the sentiments expressed earlier in this chapter of a widening circle of care. And we similarly see sentiments of obligation in the "Lockean proviso", named after the famous English philosopher John Locke, which argued that property claims should extend only insofar as they do not deprive others from having enough for themselves (Bollier & Helfrich 2019). This reflects a comment made by Vaughan that the traditional Hawaiian system emphasizes only taking from the environment until one has enough, and not more.

Having explored collective action and its relationship to environmental property rights, in the rest of the book we will move into a discussion of types of property rights arrangements, many of which are often framed as solutions to the tragedy of the commons. And as we will see, implementing solutions brings with it a whole new set of issues to address.

PART II

Bundles of rights

I have stated that a primary goal of this book is to document the institutional diversity of environmental property rights. In this section of the book, we have this goal squarely in mind. We will be unpacking what we might mean when we talk about ownership of the environment and the concept of a bundle of rights that I mentioned in the introduction. This section builds most directly on our previous discussions of specific rights, namely exclusion and alienation, as well as principles for rights allocation such as the proximity principle from Chapter 2. We also will maintain our collective action framing and consider its applicability when understanding the challenges associated with the design, allocation and enforcement of rights.

I think one of the reasons why we don't always dive into the tricky details of what exactly it means to own something is because it requires more analytical grunt work, and we cannot as easily make policy pronouncements based on these details. My hope for this section is that it helps the reader understand the diversity of arrangements that we might be referring to when we loosely talk about property rights or "rights-based" policies. Saying that property rights are important is just the beginning, even if it is often treated as a conclusion.

To motivate this discussion, let's return to the situation in the Dominican fisheries that I described in Chapter 1. The fishers in the Dominican Republic have been depleting their local resources, in part because the fishery is nearly open access with few constraints on use. If I'm in one of the fishing villages where my local partners work, and I tell the fishers that we should develop a system of environmental property rights to better manage the declining fishery, there are points that would need to be clarified. First, some fishers might argue that certain types of fishing should not be allowed, such as use of the compressors mentioned in Chapter 1, since these enable greater fishing pressure, and are also dangerous to use. Gear restrictions are an example of expressing environmental use rights.

These are rights to directly engage with the environment for one's benefit. There are several ways we will consider that someone could use the environment: access, extraction (or emission), development and stewardship. The Dominican fishers in my scenario may also want to clarify whether rights to fish can be traded and under what conditions, and whether the right to sell the fish should be regulated. This is an equally important question: exchange is a form of reciprocity and can lead to substantial social gain. But it can also lead to the alienation of historic resource rights from customary resource users.

To further unpack use rights and exchange rights, we need to distinguish between resource systems and resource units (Ostrom, Gardner & Walker 1994). A resource system is a set of interconnected parts that work together to support a stream of benefits to resource users. The use rights we are discussing are rights to use a resource system, and one of the main use rights we will discuss, extraction, refers to the right to withdraw a resource unit from a resource system (taking fish from a fishery). Resource units are the consumable parts of a resource system. A good non-environmental example of this distinction is the difference between owning the copyright to a book and owning a physical book: one provides a stream of benefits, the other is a tangible object.

The boundaries between resource systems and units can be fuzzy. For example, is a cow a resource unit to be consumed or exchanged, or a source of a stream of benefits in the form of milk or reproduction (Hinkel *et al.* 2015)? Like the commons, the identity of a resource as a unit or system is not entirely inherent; rather it is a function of human use. And treating a resource as capital to produce a stream of benefits or a unit to be further exchanged or consumed can have significant social impacts. Hyde (2019: 4) mentions a principle among gift-giving cultures that "one man's gift … must not become another man's capital" as it can disrupt the indirect reciprocity of circular exchange that we discussed in Chapter 3. To demonstrate this, Hyde (2019) cites the work of Wendy James who studied the sharing practices of the Uduk in northeast Africa. James (1970: 81) found that among the Uduk "any wealth transferred from one subclan to another, whether animals, grain or money, is in the nature of a *gift*, and should be consumed, not invested for growth".

In this book we are mostly talking about rights to resource systems, with an exception being exchange rights, where we have also touched on the exchange of physical gifts as a form of indirect reciprocity. The distinction between units and resources helps to clarify the multiple roles that exchange rights can have. Trading in benefit streams is more fundamental than trading in tangible goods.

Because of this I refer to the quality of rights to an environmental system such as a forest being exchangeable as the right of alienation, further clarifying a term that we have mentioned before.

Returning to my hypothetical scenario in a Dominican fishing village, another point that would need to be clarified is, who is going to design, allocate and enforce the new property regime that we would set up? Is it up to the fishing community itself, and if so, who in the community? Here we are talking about control rights (Sikor, He & Lestrelin 2017). A control right grants its owner the authority to design, allocate and enforce the rules associated with use and exchange rights. Some control rights point to a specific use right. Exclusion, for example, is the right to control the right to access a resource, and management rights confer authority over the expression of other use rights, most significantly, extraction and development.

Here I need to explain my use of the terms "use" and "control" rights in this framework. The taxonomy is based on foundational work by Schlager and Ostrom (1992) who used the terms "operational" for use and "collective-choice" for control. "Collective-choice" is an overly idealistic term, evoking a group decision-making process. Such decisions are not necessarily made collectively, and so the term can be misleading as a description of the world. The terms I use are based on work by Sikor, He and Lestrelin (2017) who updated the framework of Schlager and Ostrom. While I largely agree with the analysis of Sikor *et al.*, I also do not follow their new taxonomy to the letter.

Next, also we need to consider more indirect and often informal ways in which rights can be allocated and benefits of environmental use and exchange obtained (Ribot & Peluso 2003). Any of the rights we discuss in this section can be allocated more directly or indirectly. We tend to be more aware of direct rights allocations that occur with formal rules, but indirect allocations matter just as much. Ribot's (1998) analysis of the Senegalese charcoal sector provides an example of this. In rural Senegal, migrant Fulbe woodcutters called "surga" are hired by patrons to cut wood with permission from local chiefs. Ribot (1998: 324) describes how non-Fulbe face several barriers to entering the charcoal sector, including not knowing how to build, operate and maintain charcoal kilns, and not having relationships with charcoal buyers who could also provide them subsistence loans. Similarly, Leach, Mearns and Scoones (1999: 235) describe the importance of social capital and household negotiations in facilitating access to an economically significant leaf and to markets in this leaf for women in forest-using communities in Ghana. These women also must work to establish and maintain relationships with market buyers so that they can ultimately benefit from their harvesting.

There are many examples of informal and indirect rights allocations. In the example of food sharing in Chapter 3, for example, the physical ability to climb trees is a requirement for accessing beehives and harvesting honey. Similarly, in the Dominican Republic the dominant way of fishing in some communities, spearfishing, requires substantial physical skill and strength. Or on the coast of Maine, I was once told that women are often excluded from participating as users of coastal shellfisheries because they find it harder to find someone to mentor them, and a shellfisher needs mentorship to accumulate enough knowledge to fish effectively. Finally, Stoll *et al.* (2019) describe how elsewhere in Maine the bureaucratic requirements to obtain an aquaculture licence have likely served as a barrier to fishermen to transition from the wild catch sector to the aquaculture sector. An important reason to be aware of indirect rights allocations is that it helps us understand the importance of inequality. Some people have resources that enable them to exercise certain rights and obtain certain benefits, and others do not.

Building on this perspective, we need add to our typology of rights to recognize that there are also indirect ways of benefiting from the environment. Returning to the Dominican case, we could ask if the fishers want to try to improve the status of their fisheries by fishing less and adopting alternative livelihoods via an ecotourism scheme, through which tourists would pay fishers to take them to local reefs and islands? Another option might be for an external organization to pay the fishers to fish less, the way that some farmers are paid to farm less. This would be a type of public goods market that we will discuss in Chapter 9, and it would provide what we will call a use entitlement, or a guarantee of financial benefits to fishers based on how a resource is used (or not used). A direct use right is a claim to use the environment, whereas a use entitlement is a claim to benefits based on use. And just as there are use entitlements, there are exchange entitlements. The ecotourism programme could also create benefits indirectly, bestowing exchange entitlements through which the fishers would be financially compensated for their role in the programme.

There are thus three core types of rights: use, exchange and control. For both use and exchange, we further subdivide these into direct rights and (indirect) entitlements (Figure II.1). Finally, for each type of right we can ask if they are allocated more or less directly. In Chapter 4, we will discuss control rights and use rights. In Chapter 5 we dive into the subject of exchange rights. My goal for this section is to help us better appreciate the diversity of arrangements we might be referring to when we loosely talk about the importance of rights-based governance approaches.

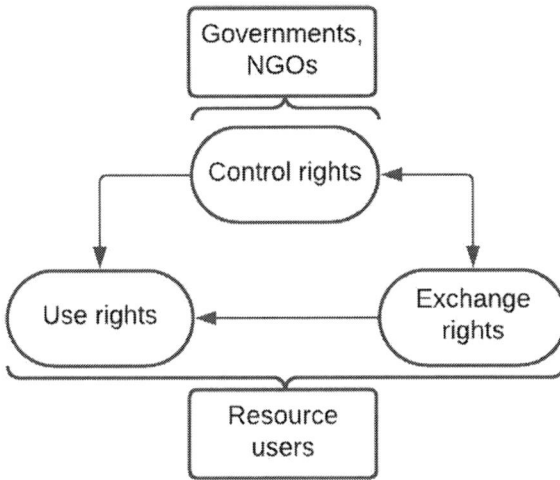

Figure II.1 A framework of environmental rights

Notes: An arrow pointing from one class of rights to another indicates that the first group describes activities that influence the second group. Control rights determine use rights as well as exchange rights, and exchange rights relate to the trade of primarily use rights, but some control rights can be exchanged as well. The figure also indicates which actors tend to have which types of rights.

Source: After Sikor *et al.* (2017).

4

Control and use rights

In this chapter we unpack the bundle of rights concept by exploring three categories of rights: direct use, use entitlements and control. Theoretically we could explore the idea of control entitlements, but we will leave that for another day. We begin by building on our collective action framing from Chapter 1 by discussing the nature of control rights (institutional design, allocation and enforcement) as public goods. A well designed environmental property regime isn't free: someone has to design it and implement it, and others will have incentives to free-ride on costly governance activities.

From here, the majority of the chapter focuses on use rights. In Chapter 2, we questioned a common framing of the commons as being subtractable: if someone uses a forest, this means someone else cannot. But as we saw, this depends on what we mean by "use". Thus how we understand environmental use has implications for how we frame the main challenges to be addressed by environmental rights. A common theme we will see is that use of the environment is a common way to also establish ownership (e.g., squatting is a way of establishing access rights), which itself is an allocation right. In this way, use and allocation rights intersect. We conclude the chapter with a discussion of use entitlements, or the indirect benefits that actors can claim based on how the environment is used by themselves or someone else.

Design, allocation and enforcement as public goods

The control rights of institutional design and enforcement confer power and responsibility. The development and enforcement of rules to enact use rights can be thought of as public goods: they may benefit a whole group, but are costly to provide. Thinking again of the Dominican fishing village, if the fishers could agree to a set of rules about fishing rights and obtain some degree of compliance, they could all benefit from a sustainable fishery. But who is going to make the effort to achieve this? The provision of enforced social institutions is a second-order collective action problem since individuals have an incentive to free-ride on the efforts of others to craft and enforce institutions. Previously we have discussed first-order collective action problems, such as the problem of overusing a shared resource. Resolving such problems requires rules and norms. Designing and enforcing rules and norms is a second-order collective action problem.

Enforcement, which I define as the combination of monitoring for rule violations and sanctioning offenders, might not sound like it is necessarily a public good. Much so-called enforcement can be oppressive and unjust, particularly if is done by one group onto another. Within a group, however, we also need to recognize the possibility of altruistic punishment as part of intragroup self-enforcement. This refers to the fact that punishing someone for a violation of a norm imposes costs on the one doing the sanctioning, yet benefits a larger group. For example, when someone in a group continually violates an important norm, such as not doing their share of work on a group project, but no one speaks up to stop them, we are grateful when someone does speak up (so we can free-ride on their efforts). Many people exhibit what is called strong reciprocity, or the tendency to both cooperate with norm followers and punish violators. The ability to self-enforce rules is one of the most well-established factors in promoting cooperation in experimental contexts. DeCaro, Janssen and Lee (2015), for example, provide experimental evidence that a group's ability to vote on which rules it will use and its ability to enforce these rules have synergistically positive effects on cooperation and rule compliance by its members.

It is important to mention another one of Ostrom's design principles here: graduated sanctions. Often the words "sanction" and "punishment" conjure up an image of a harsh penalty. And if we are thinking about deterrence from a so-called rational, cost–benefit perspective, we might conclude that we do want to have harsh penalties so that the costs of rule violation outweigh the benefits. To the contrary, in many cases sanctions are proportional to the severity or repetition of the offense, striking a balance between deterrence and maintaining social capital in a group. Starting with less severe sanctions also imposes lower enforcement costs on sanctioners, allowing for a more diffuse sanctioning process by more group members. At the lower end, there is a fuzzy boundary between a sanction and an advisement, with an enforcement procedure starting with a notification that a violation has been detected. My favourite example of graduated sanctioning comes from Acheson's (2003: 49–50) description of the enforcement protocols of Maine lobstermen:

> When a person or a group decides to defend "their" fishing territory against incursion, they will usually warn the interloper. Sometimes,

the interloper is threatened verbally or abused in some way, but more usually there is some molestation of his gear. Sometimes two half hitches of rope are tied around the spindles of the offending traps; in others, bottles are left in the trap with notes; sometimes the heads in the traps are cut out; in still other cases, the traps are pulled, the legal-sized lobsters are taken out, and the doors of the trap are cut off. In other instances, buoys of the offending traps are tied together. In many cases, interlopers will move their traps when pointedly warned in this way. If the violation continues, the defenders may decide not to take further action, or they may decide to sanction the interloper further. When they decide further action is warranted, they almost always will destroy the offending traps.

We should recall here that it was Acheson who made the distinction between coastal "nucleated" and island "perimeter" boundaries that we discussed in Chapter 2, with nucleated boundaries being more contextual and perimeter being more rigid. And there is a connection between contextual boundaries and graduated sanctions to highlight here; the closer a fisherman is to the nucleus of another gang's territory, the more likely the fisher is to receive a harsh penalty (Acheson 2003: 56). This contrasts with the enforcement of perimeter-based boundaries (Acheson 2003: 58):

One of the primary characteristics of perimeter-defended areas is the strong defense of the island's boundaries. Interlopers placing traps within the borders of such areas are almost certain to lose traps very quickly to the harbor gangs owning these areas, who traditionally have shown little tolerance for those who violate their boundaries.

Graduated sanctions can similarly be seen as a departure from rigid boundaries. Ideally, graduated enforcement represents a system that can bend without breaking.

Direct use rights

Direct use rights are the core of our discussion of rights bundles. It is direct use of the environment that motivated our discussion of the tragedy of the commons in Chapter 1, and all of the scenarios we discuss in this book involve direct use of the environment, so we need to understand what use can mean. There are four ways that we will talk about how someone might use a resource system:

1. *Access*: physically moving through or occupying a space.
2. *Stock and flow*: taking resource units out of the environment via extraction or putting pollutants into the environment via emission.
3. *Development*: adding physical infrastructure to a resource system.
4. *Stewardship*: caring for a resource.

Access is a precursor right, since none of the other rights can be exercised without it, unless we are talking about emissions rights, but this is not a large part of our discussion until Chapter 9 when we discuss carbon markets. Development is commonly thought of as more invasive than extraction, but not necessarily, as both extraction and development can take the form of environmental stewardship. Finally, in Chapter 2 we discussed the theory of environmental reciprocity, which argued that barriers to exit and entry incentivize investment in the environment, with investment being defined as either development or stewardship.

Access

We saw the importance of access in Chapter 2 when we discussed the difference between rigid and contextual boundaries, which are about mediating access. Access is important for its own sake, and because as it enables further use of the environment. Because it is so fundamental to life and livelihood, preventing access is also one of the strictest impediments that can be imposed on people, physically preventing their movement through space. Many of history's worst abuses of humanity have occurred through the oppressive removal of access rights, from which all else follows. The creation of the Native American reservation system and the Bantustan and the homeland system in apartheid-era South Africa are important examples.

We might usually think of access and other use rights being allocated directly, say via a sign that says "KEEP OUT". And certainly there are many examples of direct exclusion. When we visit a public park, it is often explicitly stated that we are allowed to physically move through highly prescribed parts of the space and maybe engage with existing physical infrastructure (e.g., sit on a park bench) but not take away materials or make any lasting changes. This limitation is part of what defines the idea of a park to many people. Outside of such well-defined scenarios, however, access to the environment and the benefits it produces can be more informal and indirect.

For example, if you ever wanted to take a subway train to the neighbourhood of Georgetown in Washington, DC, or the Pacific Heights neighbourhood of San Francisco, both in the United States, you will have discovered that you cannot. Wealthier areas in many cities are often less accessible, partly because they are simply higher up, and partly because public transportation options have been strategically limited. And sometimes, the presence of a road itself can represent a barrier to access. In a book aptly entitled *The Arsenal of Exclusion and Inclusion*, for example, Armborst *et al.* (2017) describe a street in Baltimore, Maryland, that serves to effectively divide a wealthier neighbourhood from a poorer one. The street is wide, there are not many pedestrian crossings, and what few side-streets attach to the main street from the wealthy neighbourhood are mostly one-way, leading out to the street but not in. Elsewhere in the book the authors describe many ways in which access is limited and supported, often, but not necessarily, with the aid of a formal rule or regulation. I think it is particularly important to emphasize the ubiquity of indirect allocations of access rights because, as I mentioned in the beginning of this section, from access, all else follows.

Stock and flow rights

Stock and flow rights are about adding or subtracting from environmental stocks through extraction or emission. In this book we are primarily, but not exclusively, talking about resource extraction, with the main exception being our discussion of emission rights in carbon markets in Chapter 9. Here we start with a discussion of how extraction is often used as a means of establishing ownership before diving into the different ways in which an extraction right can be expressed. Thus, while we have stopped talking about control rights directly, we are continuing to unpack these by discussing how the exercise of rights themselves can be claims to such rights.

Use as allocation and the role of time

Extraction, sometimes referred to more lightly as appropriation, involves taking resource units out of the environment. It is one of the most common ways to use the environment, and along with access is one of the most common ways to establish ownership. Most commonly this is about ownership over the resource unit that is extracted (e.g., lumber, fish), which we saw in the example of ownership over collected honey by the Mbuti of Eastern Zaire. There the primary logic for ownership claims are the capital inputs (time, energy, equipment) expended to extract a resource and this is one of the dominant ways in which ownership is established (Heller & Salzman 2021). We will call this the capital inputs principle of rights allocation, and I think it is often the underlying logic for the use of extraction activities to establish extraction rights over resource units.

Extraction can also be used to establish rights over the resource system, using extraction to establish further extraction rights. And this requires a decision rule for evaluating competing claims based on use by different actors. The most common answer to this question is to prioritize rights based on who started to use a resource first. The doctrine of prior appropriation I mentioned in Chapter 1 is an obvious example of this, allocating extraction rights to those who are first to take water from a natural waterbody.

Historically, the idea of priority ("prior-ity") has always been closely associated with the idea of being prior in time. "First in time, first in right", which I call the priority principle, may be the single most fundamental principle underlying environmental property claims. It is arguably universal. It states that whoever claims ownership over the environment first has the most senior claim to it, granting what political theorists refer to as an historical right (Verkuyten & Martinovic 2017). This principle is the basis for much informal social order. For example, the concept of a line that people stand and wait in is based on this principle. At least within our own groups, we view this principle as embodying a sense of fairness.

Historical rights can be established intergenerationally as well through inheritance. In his discussion of the Luo people of western Kenya, Shipton (2009: 115) describes the importance of historical rights, where the right being used to establish ownership is physical development (clearing brush):

> In and around Luo country, one is a first-class citizen if one belongs where one is by virtue of being a Luo first arriver or a descendent of one who was (it also helps to be a senior male). If one can demonstrate that one's patrilineal ancestors cleared a place of wild brush for first settlement, or cleared it of members of Maasai, Nandi, or other ethnic groups deemed enemies – one enjoys the states of … master … of the land.

We see in this description the interconnection between the priority principle and other aspects of identity (gender), and we see the ever-present in-group versus out-group at play here as well.

The idea of early events being more valued also applies to the development of the rules governing use. Rules that are established earlier have precedence over those that are established later. It is most formally established in the practice of "common law", which is a body of law established by judges in specific court cases. In this system, precedence plays an important role in determining future decisions, and this is arguably its defining feature. This also applies to the difference between control rights and use rights, since the former are established earlier; future rules and norms are established in response to existing rules and norms, creating an institutional path dependence. And because control rights are often established before use rights, these tend to be more resistant to change.

While the priority principle is fundamental, it is not the only principle related to time that governs the allocation of use rights. We also value continued use of a resource up to the present. Someone may have started to use a resource a long time ago, but if they are no longer using this resource, this lessens their claim to it. This is reflected in the prior appropriation regimes of many US western states. In order to maintain a water right under this regime, a user must actively divert water and put it to what is referred to as "beneficial use". If someone does not actively use their water for five years they may forfeit their rights, and this is seen as a way of preventing speculative ownership claims (Smith 2019: 190).

It is important to remember that neutral-sounding principles can be applied differently based on in-groups versus out-groups. Throughout human history, environmental resources have commonly been taken by force, with this being justified after the fact. There may be principles for allocating rights, but these are often only applied to members of an in-group, to the exclusion of legitimate claims made by other groups. Duthu (2008), for example, describes how the "discovery doctrine", which is a version of the priority principle, was applied during the white colonization of what would become the United States. This principle was only applied within the Christian culture and was used to dispossess Native Americans, who ought to have been prioritized by this principle, but were excluded in part because their priority was based not on actual first use, but when their homelands were recognized under US federal law (Duthu, personal communication).

Using extraction as a principle for allocating extraction as a right can have implications for resource use behaviours. This is demonstrated by the "rule of capture". This principle governs the allocation of oil rights in the United States and several other countries (Daintith 2010), as well as the use of groundwater in the state of Texas. It states that the first person to extract oil that lies below their land can lay claim to the resource system, or the underlying oil field. As such it exerts elements of both time and space, the latter via the *ad coelum* principle mentioned earlier. This is also an example of indirect rights allocation, as the rule indirectly requires that extraction technology is available to establish rights because this is needed to appropriate oil.

The rule of capture is "technology seeking", argued to promote innovations in extraction by granting rights to those who are able to find resources that become increasingly scarce. It effectively creates an arms race in extraction technologies. In instances where we want to spur innovation, this can be a good thing. Harvey, Orvis and Rissman (2018) for example argue for the importance of rules that encourage actors to innovate new technologies in the area of energy policy. But as Daintith (2010) describes, many have criticized the rule of capture for creating a "race to the bottom" of the oil wells themselves and to the detriment of cooperation and environmental stewardship and efficient resource use, as users are incentivized to grab what is under their land before others do, potentially leading to a tragedy of the commons, widespread speculation and wasted non-renewable resources. Daintith (2010: 415–16) also comments on the challenges posed by the national preference for individual property in the United States, which has subdivided land ownership and created greater potential for the actions of one actor to have negative consequences for their neighbours.

Limitations have sometimes been placed on resource extraction rights in the oil sector based on the correlative rights doctrine, which argues that resource users have an obligation to avoid damaging the resource and the interests of other users, but Daintith argues that this has not had a strong effect on oil governance in the United States. What has been more successful is a process known as unitization, whereby a group of landowners formally agree to jointly manage their fossil resources, in a manner that to me resembles the model of community-based natural resource management that we will discuss in Chapter 8. Unitization is not a panacea, as knowledge about underlying reservoirs is imperfect and its distribution heterogeneous, and in the United States it must be scaffolded on top of a system that defaults to prioritizing individual rights.

Finally, Daintith (2010: 302) argues "that the rule of capture has actually been strengthened by the creation of the massive regulatory apparatus it engendered, because that regulation has been constructed on a property right foundation of which capture forms part". This is another example of path dependence, occurring when a dominant institutional design must be adapted to even as its negative effects are dealt with.

Inputs and outputs

In the fisheries governance literature, there is a common distinction made between rules pertaining to inputs versus outputs, with input rules prescribing the type and amount of capital inputs put towards fishing, and output being about the type and amount of fish caught.[1] This dimension is closely related to another, this being the difference between qualitative rules about how fishing is done, and quantitative rules about how much fishing is done. We can think of these two dimensions creating a 2 × 2 table of combinations, which we will discuss in this section. A qualitative input rule, for example, could describe the types of fishing gear that are allowed or prohibited, as we have seen in the Dominican fisheries that formally prohibit the use of compressors. A quantitative input rule might describe how much time fishers are allowed to fish. A qualitative output right might prohibit the catch of pregnant females, or restrict the catch of females as reproductive bottlenecks, which is commonly done in the licensing of hunting permits in the United States. A quantitative output rule would simply describe how many fish are allowed to be caught.

Different types of governance have taken different approaches to these dimensions. Acheson and Wilson (1996: 582) analysed 36 fishing systems, comparing seven scientific fisheries management cases with 29 community-based management cases, and found that

> all of the rules and practices used in the 29 tribal and peasant societies … regulate "how" fishing is done. That is, they limit location, time, stage of life of the target species, or technology. None limit the amount of various species that can be caught. Use of quotas – the single most important concept and tool of scientific management – is conspicuous by its absence.

In our terminology, the authors are saying that state-centric governance uses more quantitative output, while local communities use more qualitative input and output rules. There are several potential reasons for this pattern to consider. One is that rules about how much fish are caught are more legible to external governmental actors, and so would tend to be favoured by them (more on legibility in Chapter 6). Quantitative approaches offer a sense of certainty as well about how much of a resource is where. Many central planners and bureaucrats feel it is necessary to have an idea of how much of a resource remains so that we can calibrate our extraction accordingly. A prominent example of this thinking is the "maximum sustainable yield" framework (MSY), most prominent in the fisheries sector but also historically prominent in the forestry sector and in some groundwater contexts. This approach models the dynamics

---

1. A third category, outcome rules, is also used to specify the quantity of a stock that is allowed to or required to be in the environment.

of a fish population and calculates the optimum rate of harvest that can be sustained over time. Applying a quantitative output rule to a resource requires knowledge of the state of the resource, so that aggregate levels of extraction can be set and adjusted appropriately. It is thus usually more technologically and scientifically intensive.

While holding a potential advantage in terms of formal legibility, a critique of the MSY approach in particular has been its historic ignorance of ecological interactions and the potential for ecological disturbances. And as we will discuss in Chapter 6, we need to ask, legibility for whom? An informational advantage of qualitative rules used by communities, according to Acheson and Wilson (1996: 583), is they involve "moderate information and enforcement costs, resulting in the development of effective institutions". Qualitative rules are often more easily measured and enforced by the communities who adopt them.

While the work by Acheson and Wilson (1996) is a helpful starting point, we should view the pattern they describe as a central tendency, and not a hard rule, meaning that we should also be interested in the variation around this central tendency. And indeed there are many exceptions to the broad trend that Acheson and Wilson describe. States, for example, also use input rules. An example of a quantitative input rule comes from the Maine lobster fishery, which specifies that lobstermen can only put so many lobster traps in the water.[2] In pollution cases it is common for states to set technological standards. A reason for this may be that inputs may be as formally legible as outputs, and both more legible than outcomes. An example of this comes from the case of development aid practices, which often focus on measurable inputs such as money spent and outputs such as trainings and workshops when outcomes are more diffused and lagged (Muller 2018: 156).

Turning to communities, they also use quantitative rules in their own ways. One example of this comes from the Native Hawaiians who have an environmental principle to only take until you have "enough" (Vaughan 2018), which is a kind of soft quantitative rule. Another example comes from the acequia irrigation communities of New Mexico, where it is common for water rights to be distributed in units of time, with individuals taking turns, rather than in strict amounts of water. This is a quantitative input rule. In the case of the acequias, this can be seen in part as an adaptation to scarcity: measuring whether someone is using water for two hours at a certain time is easier than measuring precisely how much water they are taking, which you need to do

---

2. In describing this rule, Brewer (2012: 394) makes the observation that the new trap limits became internalized as a new norm, with fishermen who had used fewer traps now increasing their numbers to this norm.

if you express rights in terms of amounts of water. Expressing rights in units of time can have an additional adaptive function in low-technology contexts. If there is less water for an acequia because of a drought, everyone automatically uses less water because there is less water available to them during their allotted time.

An obvious disadvantage of time-based rights here is that they cannot be used to guarantee that certain amounts of a resource are used in the amount of time allotted, and a lack of precision and control is seen as a general disadvantage of input rules. An example of this has played out in the fisheries sector. Here, many governance systems have used temporal bans, or open and closed fishing seasons. Banning fishing during a specific period can be ecologically appropriate if done during a critical life stage of a target species. On the other hand, the use of closed and open seasons has been criticized for creating perverse incentives to fish more intensively when it is allowed, creating "fishing derbies". Van der Voo (2016: 32) describes this situation in the Alaska crab sector, also mentioning that this has happened in many other places where temporal bans were put in place:

> Thus every time a crabbing season opened, and for ever-shortening lengths of time, fishermen rushed to the water like seafaring cowboys, no matter the weather, gunning to catch more crab than the next guy. Most boats fished so hard that crab seasons for some species were as short as three days. The fishing was correspondingly rough. Boats piled ambitiously high with pots capsized and people drowned.

An important difference between this situation and the acequias of New Mexico is the amount of capitalization, or physical infrastructure developed, and the concomitant extractability of the resource. Acequia members can't physically try to take much more water during the several hours allotted to them, so there is no "race for water". But the temporal fishing bans combine with extensive over-capitalization (too many boats) in many fisheries to create a race to fish. An interesting example of the trade-offs involved here comes from the Vessel Days Scheme for skipjack tuna agreed to by eight Pacific island states. This scheme uses a quantitative input rule that restricts fishing effort to so many vessel days, creating what we will call in Chapter 9 a tradeable environmental allowance, but for input rights where most policies use output rights (Havice 2013). This type of scheme then has the potential advantage adapting to scarcity like the acequias, but is also vulnerable to "effort creep" if improvements in fishing technologies allow for more efficient catch per day or more technically, catch per unit effort.

Quantitative output rules can also vary in terms of their adaptability to change. They can be expressed in absolute amounts, such as a certain amount of water or fish taken or emissions produced, or as a proportion of a cap on extraction or emission. The good thing about a proportion is that rights adjust automatically if the overall cap is adjusted, approximating this advantage of time-based rights I described earlier in the case of the New Mexico acequias. Most fish catch share programmes, which we will discuss in depth in Chapter 9, distribute individual fishing quotas proportionately to an overall cap to allow for adjustment. The New Zealand catch share programme initially allocated rights in absolute amounts and had to buy back rights when they wanted to make curtailments, and eventually switched to a proportional rights system (Holland 2022).

A lack of this type of automatic adjustment has been seen in some systems that express rights in units of water, such as the Colorado river compact. The compact divvied out amounts of water to seven western states based on an estimation of how much water would be available, but it turned out that this estimation was based on an unusually wet period that hasn't been repeated since, leading to shortages in the amounts allocated. To avoid this, the Colorado compact could have divided up water in proportional amounts, based on how much is available in a given year.

Finally, the distinctions made in this section to clarify how stock and flow rights can be expressed are not necessarily limited to such rights. "How" rules in particular are very much relevant for the next two sets of direct use rights we will consider: physical development and stewardship. Indeed, granting or denying such rights is very much a decision about how the environment is to be used.

Physical development

Physical development is a more intensive way to use a resource system than extraction, although sometimes development is required for extraction of certain resources (e.g., fossil fuels). By development I mean the right to change "the goods and services provided by the resource"[3] (Galik & Jagger 2015: 77). This

---

3. Galik and Jagger describe this as the right of "alteration" and distinguish it as a more extreme version of the similar sounding right of "management", introduced by Schlager and Ostrom (1992), on whose work they are building. I believe that Schlager and Ostrom, in defining management as "The right to regulate internal use patterns and transform the resource by making improvements", are defining two rights at once. The first half is about managing the behaviour of other actors, and the second is about what I am calling development. I refer to Galik and Jagger above because I find their single definition to be most clear, and because when I hear "management", I mostly think of the first half of the definition from Schlager and Ostrom.

can include "clearing forested land for agriculture, planting trees on marginal pastureland, or impounding a waterway and inundating associated low-lying areas in the name of hydroelectricity generation" (Galik & Jagger 2015: 78). My own use of development here includes a gradient of interventions, from the application of fertilizers or pesticides, which themselves can have significant impacts depending on application levels and their intensity, to fundamental changes such as ploughing or clearing a field and growing a single crop on it, to intensive mining activities.

Development, like extraction, is also used to establish ownership, as we saw in Shipton's example of the Luo people who use brush clearing in this way. Using physical development to establish land rights has also played an important role in conflicts between Native Americans and white settler culture, and indigenous and Western perspectives more generally. Cronon (2011: 56) describes this situation when comparing the property arrangements of the native Americans in colonial New England with those of the white settlers. From the perspective of many white settlers, the Native Americans had not claimed the land because they had not "improved" it through physical development. The Native Americans relied on high levels of mobility similar to the pastoralists described earlier, and Cronon describes how this system was often invisible to and not valued by the white settlers.

At least a part of the logic behind the use of physical development as a basis for resource claims is the same as it is for extraction – it requires capital inputs: if I worked on something, then it is mine (Heller & Salzman 2021). Earlier we referred to this as the capital inputs principle of rights allocation. Additionally, the use of inputs as a means of establishing rights is also an important mechanism for maintaining cooperation. Proportioning benefits to inputs is described in one of Ostrom's (1990) principles, this being that there should exist a proportionality of costs and benefits, such that those who help more with the provision of public goods are able to internalize those benefits at least to some extent. Returning to the acequias example from my work in New Mexico, we see a common rule from many community-based irrigation systems, this being that to obtain rights to water, farmers must contribute to maintaining the physical infrastructure that acts as a public good to convey way to each farmer's field. This principle helps to establish a network of reciprocal interactions among participants among the acequias and other similar systems: to obtain benefits, you need to contribute to the public good. Depending on the nature of the costs, these can help integrate a community. In more recent times, this has been replaced by a more transactional arrangement, whereby acequia farmers often pay to have someone else do the labour for them. This is part of a broader integration of the acequias into market-based arrangements, which arguably has undercut their social cohesion.

Like the limitations we discussed on extraction rights (e.g., to only use certain fishing gear), limitations on development rights are commonplace. One example is conservation easements, an entitlement-based policy that we will discuss later in this chapter. An issue that often arises in the context of such limits on development rights is NIMBYism, or Not In My Backyard. Many people, for example, who are otherwise in favour of, say, the development of renewable energy infrastructure, nevertheless don't want this development to be happening in their "backyard". Perhaps somewhat perversely, arguments against the development of renewable energy infrastructure have often been based on environmental laws.

Stewardship

In Chapter 3, I defined stewardship as being about care: something is stewarded when it is cared for. Based on the work of Vaughan (2018) and others, we can think of use as stewardship as another category of environmental use here. This evokes the "use as stewardship" approach that is absent from the Western framing of environmental rights, which mostly sees rights as decoupled from obligations to what is owned. In the communities that Vaughan describes, stewardship of the land is seen as an important factor in establishing and maintaining rights and is inseparable from the way in which people use the environment. Beyond the context described by Vaughan, it is commonly understood that when a space appears cared for, it is also claimed by someone. When there is a sense that someone cares about a park or a city neighbourhood enough to put time into caring for it, the landscape is perceived differently.

Stewardship can be seen as a lens to apply to the other rights we have discussed. Vaughan, for example, describes an ethic of respect for the environment and taking until you have "enough", and not more, which we can interpret as a soft quantitative rule as discussed earlier. The other aspect of stewardship is about "how" to use a resource, and we can think of this as changing what we think it means to develop the environment, beyond simply displacing natural processes with physical infrastructure. As Vaughan described, the activities of the Hawaiian fishers involve actively cultivating habitat.

Use entitlements

In addition to the direct use rights we have been discussing, people can also possess indirect use rights (Sikor, He & Lestrelin 2017), such as the right to benefit from how the environment is used or not used. We have already heard of this in our discussion of usufruct rights, the second half of which ("fructus") refers to the right to benefit from property owned by someone else. Following Bromley and Hodge (1990) I use the term use entitlements rather than indirect use right, because it more reflects how this term is used elsewhere (Sen 1982) – as an indication of the benefits that one is entitled or empowered to receive. I will use this term for indirect rights throughout.

Like other rights, entitlements can be more or less formally allocated. The honey sharing practices of the Mbuti of Eastern Zaire that we discussed in Chapter 3 is an example of informal entitlements. Ichikawa (1981) describes how the individuals who gather the honey share it with their kin and communities, and we can view this as enacting an entitlement arrangement. There are also more formal models that grant entitlements to non-users and non-managers. In the United States, a well-known example is the limited liability corporation, or LLC, which creates a shareholder class that benefits from the actions of the corporate managers.

In our context an important organizational model that creates a separate class of non-user beneficiaries are trusts, in which a trustee manages a resource for a beneficiary. In the forestry sector, for example, there has been a transition from more vertically integrated companies that owned both the land and infrastructure such as paper mills to the current situation, where timber investment management organizations (TIMOs) and real estate investment trusts (REITs) manage land for a set of investors who have entitlements to the benefits via land management. This transition has changed how such organizations view and manage their land, as they are no longer optimizing for timber production, but for financial return for a set of investors in a given plot of land. This has raised concerns about the sustainability of such a framework, although some work has shown that the implications are not necessarily negative (Gunnoe, Bailey & Ameyaw 2018). Still, an observation that we will return to is that the separation of users and managers and beneficiaries creates a class of people whose interests are seen as the primary goal of use and management, and who do not have any direct interaction with the environment, which, based on our discussion in Chapter 3, we would predict would lower intrinsic values for this environment.

There are many land trusts in the United States and elsewhere, and a primary activity of many of them is to create what are known as conservation easements, which may provide entitlement benefits to landowners through tax breaks in exchange for forgoing development rights to their lands. In the state of Vermont there is also a "current use" programme, which taxes land (less) based on its current use value rather than its market exchange value and is often used by farmers who then forego rights to develop their land lest they lose their favourable status. Many other US states have similar programmes to promote the provision of ecosystem services (Kilgore *et al.* 2018). And a final example of a land conservation-oriented entitlement programme is the US federal Conservation Reserve programme, which pays farmers to stop farming on vulnerable land and to plant environmentally friendly species. This is an example of a payment for ecosystem services policy, which we will discuss in greater depth in Chapter 9.

Conclusion

Let's return to my hypothetical scenario in the Dominican fishing village. It should be clear now that telling the fishers that a property rights regime should be implemented to help them with their overfishing problem is just the start of a complicated conversation. Who will volunteer to do the work to craft the rules that should be followed, and who will enforce these rules? And what principles should we use to allocate rights, say based on whether or not someone started fishing long ago, or by inheriting fishing rights from a parent, using kinship as a form of allocation as described in Chapter 3. Moving to use rights, we would need to address whether there should be restrictions on the use of certain fishing gears, and we should consider how these restrictions might indirectly allocate rights more to some than others, say if we only allowed fishers to free-dive, which is physically quite demanding. And finally, some fishers would likely be interested in developing new sources of livelihood entirely, developing the inchoate ecotourism sector in the area, and deriving entitlement-based benefits from the fishery that way. And we aren't done unpacking the complexity of rights bundles yet. In the next chapter, we dive into a whole other set of questions about if and how rights should be exchanged.

5

Exchange rights

Exchange, most broadly, is the act of carrying out our psychology of reciprocity. I give you this, you give me that, or in the case of indirect reciprocity, I give you this so someone else will give me that. Because exchange is a form of cooperation, we can view it as the source of social benefit. Ideally, in the case of direct reciprocity, an exchange produces a win-win outcome between the partners involved, because each partner values what they receive more than what they give up. The potential magic here is that social value is created out of nothing, simply by reallocating resources. This simple, imagined scenario drives a lot of policy discourse and decision-making through phrases like "let the market decide". What does this mean exactly, and how does exchange of environmental rights promote the public good, or not?

In the previous chapter, we unpacked what it means to use the environment, both directly and indirectly. In this chapter we do the same for exchange: what does it mean to trade in environmental rights? To begin, we continue the discussion of entitlements from the end of the last chapter by discussing the role of exchange entitlements. We do so through the lens of what is referred to as a patron-client relationship, which will have us question a win-win, cooperative framing of exchange.

From here, much of the chapter deals with arguments related to exchange and its relationship to efficiency. Efficiency is the primary theoretical motivation for several market-based environmental policies we will discuss in Chapter 9, so it is worth spending some time grappling with the background. We start by engaging with a dominant discourse that argues that markets promote efficient allocations of resources. To unpack this argument, we explore the relationship between efficiency and equity, which can also be seen as an important allocational principle. After this we explore the relationship between efficiency and stewardship, and explore a hypothesis that efficient markets tend to discount broader social and environmental impacts of exchange. Building on this discussion, we consider the argument that alienation, even if it does not necessarily incentivize stewardship, might incentivize development. We conclude the chapter with a discussion of the difference between market exchange value and use value.

Exchange entitlements

In Chapter 1 we questioned the apolitical framing of collective action and the tragedy of the commons, and a part of this framing was based on the assumption of win-win outcomes. This same critique applies to the assumption of win-win outcomes for exchanges. If we are talking about two actors involved in direct exchange, it is often the case that one actor may feel disadvantaged or worse, coerced. And as we discussed in Chapter 2, cooperation within a group often involves antagonism between groups; just because an exchange benefits the parties involved does not mean these benefits scale to other actors. In economics this is expressed as an externality. A negative externality, for example, is a cost associated with a transaction (e.g., the pollution required to produce a car that is sold) that is not internalized by those involved in this transaction.

The entitlement rights associated with exchanges further demonstrate this concern. Just as we did for use rights, we can make a distinction between direct exchange rights and indirect exchange entitlements. Direct exchange rights grant an actor the right to trade what they own. Indirect exchange rights, or exchange entitlements, distribute costs and benefits of exchanges to those directly or indirectly involved in an exchange. This concept is another way of teasing apart who has what rights and privileges. In Malawi, for example, Kilic, Moylan and Koolwal (2021) find that women have fewer exchange entitlements than men when it comes to controlling the money obtained through the sale or rental of household property.

Exchanges do not necessarily benefit those with the closest relationship to the environment. It is often the opposite: those who exercise access and extraction rights are those with the weakest entitlements with respect to the sale of the goods associated with their activities. And when the sale of goods is the primary source of benefit of resource extraction, exchange entitlements largely determine use entitlements: the person who benefits from environmental use is the person who benefits from market exchange. An example of this pattern comes from the charcoal commodity chain of Senegal that we discussed earlier. Here, charcoal merchants garner most of the benefits of exchange by collusively fixing the price, leaving little left for the woodcutters or the local villagers or chiefs (Ribot 1998: 327). In this case a collective action problem is solved by one group (the merchants) by increasing what is for them a public good (market price for charcoal) at the expense of another group.

The relationship between a resource user and a market intermediary is often a good example of a patron–client relationship, which occurs when a wealthier patron loans resources to a client who then repays them with labour and loyalty. In the context of natural resource use, these resources often include physical capital for natural resource harvesting and usufruct extraction rights. A common archetype for such relationships in this context is a market intermediary who uses their power to benefit more from market sales than does the client, who is the more direct resource user.

Patron–client relationships have been studied extensively in the small-scale fisheries sector. Most commonly, a fisher takes on a debt to a fish buyer to obtain the means to fish, and then must catch fish in order to repay the debt. In this literature, we see a similar concern to that expressed in the last chapter with use entitlements: that exchange entitlements create a class of actors whose interests heavily influence the use of natural resources, but who are at least one step removed from direct engagement with the resources themselves. Miñarro et al. (2016: 73), for example, compare the fishing behaviours of fishers who work with patrons to those who do not in the Spermonde Archipelago of Indonesia, and find that fishers who belong to a patron–client system "use less diversified gears and increase their focus on commercial fishing" with negative environmental consequences.

Also in the small-scale fishing sector, Basurto et al. (2020: 14) compare the distribution of benefits that result from the patron–client model with the most common alternative, that fishers work within a fisher cooperative, and find that fishers working within the patron–client system "receive less benefits from fishing" and are "particularly vulnerable to exploitation because they are often in debt to the fish buyer and have no access to collective-choice arenas shaping their working conditions".

The authors use "collective-choice" where I am using "control", to describe a lack of control rights for fishers under the patron–client model. This is an important way in which the fishers are disempowered under this model. At the same time, Basurto et al. (2020) caution against assuming that every patron–client relationship must play out the same way. The patron–client model is a simplified model of a social relationship, just like a collective action problem. And similarly, we should avoid using such a model to apply the same interpretation to every situation. There are several other ways to interpret this type of relationship. First, we can interpret this as a principal–agent relationship, which steers us towards the perspective of the patron. In this relationship, a principal contracts with an agent to carry out activities and accomplish certain outcomes for them. The most common example of a principal–agent relationship is an employer and an employee. This relationship creates a problem for the principal, who cannot easily access information about the agent's activities, otherwise known as information asymmetry, and knows that their interests are not necessarily aligned.

Patron–client models can also represent reciprocal win-wins in some cases. Johnson (2010: 269), for example, argues that in the Indian fishing community of Junagadh, patron–client relationships "provide fishers an insurance mechanism to cope with periods during the year when catches are low or absent while ensuring a stable resource stream for fish buyers". In the small-scale fisheries sector in Zanzibar, Tanzania, there is a diversity of patron–client relationships, depending on the identities of those involved, and "the fisher-trader link is not as one-sided as previously presented. In fact, it has a more symbiotic exchange deeply nested in a broader trading and social system" (Drury O'Neill & Crona 2017: 196).

Additionally, what starts as purely economic relationships can grow to involve intrinsic value of one exchange partner for another, as I mentioned in Chapter 3. According to Drury O'Neill and Crona (2017: 199),

> Surveys show that actors in the market place nurture relations above and beyond mere sales transactions and these appear to be important for the functioning of the marketplace. The most commonly mentioned non-sales related relations in this study were linked to various forms of assistance.

O'Neill and Crona also find that the nature of patron–client relationships varies with the gender of the participants and whether they are in primarily rural or urban spaces. They also argue that part of the reason that gender-based variation in experiences can be underestimated is because men are so often much more visible in public spaces such as the fisheries sector, and a standard patron–client model has often presumed that it involves two males.

The study of these types of relationships represents an important move forward in the study of resource governance. As Basurto *et al.* (2020) argue in their comparison of the patron–client and cooperative models, too much of the study of local resource governance has focused on the geographic confines of individual cases, not examining the relationships between resource users in a case and the relationships they have with external actors and processes. We need to understand how various social arenas are connected. The distinction between use rights and control rights is in fact the most commonly explored example of this, with some social arenas revolving around the use of control rights to craft rules associated with use rights.

Efficiency and equity

We have framed exchange as a form of reciprocity and therefore as a source of social benefit, at least for the parties involved. The dominant discourse about the public benefit of markets argues that exchange relationships facilitate a more global public good. The patron saint of this view is Adam Smith with his invisible hand, which steers self-interest towards the global good through exchange. The main concept that is used to encapsulate this argument is efficiency. If economics were a religion, and I think some aspects of academic disciplines are, then the market would be its central deity, bringing efficiency to the people. As economics has come to dominate policy circles, it has brought with it focus on efficiency as the most important policy goal, and markets as a primary tool to achieve this goal (Berman 2022). "The market" is often anthropomorphized, carrying out actions that normally are reserved for mere mortals. In economic parlance we often refer to markets as being "free", meaning free of external imposition or constraint. This coincides with them being characterized as the decentralized alternative to state governance, which is presumed to be more top-down. Attaching adjectives and verbs to markets that we would normally reserve for social agents is misleading, for markets are not actors at all, but systems of exchange between actors.

We have seen arguments related to efficiency before when we discussed the relationship between individual and common property. Here, individual property was seen to be more efficient (productive) because it didn't suffer from the collective action problems that common property can involve. We questioned this narrative to an extent based on observations that common property can serve as an adaptation to scarcity, and that we should not assume that individual actors are necessarily capable of acting in their own self-interest to promote efficient use of their own resources.

But all of this is begging the question: what does efficiency mean? It is often contrasted with equity with the following language: "While efficiency is a relatively objective measure, equity is far from straightforward and is more subjective" (Daigneault, Greenhalgh & Samarasinghe 2017: 450). And there is an element of efficiency that is "objective" in the sense of not being subject to multiple perspectives. Efficiency means maximizing the ratio of a numerator over a denominator: getting more for less. More efficient processes put more stuff in the numerator and/or less stuff in the denominator. Once we decide what counts as "stuff", the process amounts to an objective counting exercise (Stone 1997). The intuition about exchange and efficiency is based on the scenario described earlier: if two partners exchange things that lead to each of them receiving something they want more than what they gave up, then we have more social value for the same amount of stuff.

There is nothing inherently good or bad about efficiency; it all depends on what stuff we are talking about and how we feel about that stuff. Efficiency is also a relational term: when we say that something is efficient, we are implicitly comparing it to something else that is less efficient. So, any efficiency claim is implicitly based on some counterfactual, even if that counterfactual is left unsaid. The main problem we run into with efficiency is treating it as a politically neutral metric (Stone 1997). We can be fooled into doing so if we forget about the initial decision to decide what goes into the numerator and the denominator, after which it is a technical counting exercise. But deciding what goes into each bucket is unavoidably political.

Stone (1997) mentions several questions that need to be asked about any definition of efficiency: who has the right to decide on the definition of efficiency? How do the outputs and inputs of the calculation impact the costs and benefits to different groups? How do we count the opportunity costs of not implementing some other policy? While efficiency is an important idea, what stuff and whose benefits and costs get to be put on either side of the ledger is open to debate, and often it is the most measurable stuff that gets counted.

Efficiency for whom?

Efficiency is disguised as a political neutral concept through the idea of allocative efficiency as framed by the discipline of neoclassical economics. On its own, allocative efficiency is in some ways an inarguably useful concept: who wouldn't want to put resources towards their best use? Within neoclassical economics, allocative efficiency has come to mostly mean putting resources "into producing the goods and services that consumers valued most highly, at the lowest sustainable prices", as Berman (2022: 72) describes it in her discussion of the dominance of efficiency and economic thinking in US policy.

The idea that markets promote economic efficiency is one version of a broader argument that exchange promotes the public good. Probably the most famous work that promoted the idea that markets work for the common good is Adam Smith's *The Wealth of Nations*. This argument has been popularized within the field of economics (Berman 2022). And there is some wisdom in the standard economic policy framework. Through the language of market failures, it acknowledges that there are conditions under which markets do not produce efficient outcomes, and these make sense in the light of our discussion of intragroup cooperation and intergroup competition from Chapter 2. One of the most prominent market failures is a lack of competition in the form of monopolies that can charge excessive prices. And a monopoly is nothing more than a group of producers who have realized that a public good they all share is the price of the goods they sell. This is a collective action problem faced by any producers of economic commodities: as they increase supply, the price of their goods will drop. And individually, they might want to respond to a price drop by increasing supply, but on the aggregate, this further decreases the market price. This is why there are government programmes designed to curtail production or set minimum prices for some commodities. So a monopoly is an example of successful collective action, but within a group that then imposes costs on other groups. So the concept of a monopoly represents a distinction between the interests of a group and other groups and a larger society.

To me the most important type of market failure is a term we have seen before: externalities. In a market context, these are costs and benefits associated with an exchange that are not accounted for by the participants in that exchange. Common environmental externalities include the degradation of natural resources and emission of pollutants that are associated with the manufacture of physical goods. Externalities fit with our discussion of intragroup versus intergroup cooperation from Chapter 2 as well. There, we observed that cooperation within a group can exacerbate relationships between groups, meaning that we cannot assume that local cooperation leads to the global good. An externality is another way of saying this same thing: it acknowledges that even if a transaction is a win-win for those involved (which it may not be), it can impose costs on other people outside of the "group" of transacting partners.

While I think externalities are an important concept, I disagree with the common framing of externalities as being exceptions to the rule. From our collective action perspective, there is an unavoidable tendency for groups of cooperators to impose costs on each other, and as such we should expect externalities to be ubiquitous. Put differently, there is no theoretical or empirical reason to extrapolate from the reciprocal benefits of exchange to the idea that markets automatically support a broader public good.

The idea of allocative efficiency also implies that the denominator of efficiency is the satisfaction of consumer preferences: markets are seen as allocatively efficient because they direct resources towards the most valuable uses as defined by the amount of money buyers are willing to pay for the things they buy, with the lowest costs if firms compete with each other and therefore cannot charge monopolistic prices. Defining the numerator through the expression of consumer behaviour depends on a conflation of exchange and use value: from this perspective, there is no separate judgement as to the use value of a purchased object other than what someone is willing to pay for it.

Willingness to pay is a direct function of ability to pay, which itself is a function of wealth and income, which themselves are distributed unequally. The stronger connection there is between willingness to pay and wealth and income, therefore, the more allocative efficiency becomes a technical-sounding endorsement of the current distribution of wealth and income, and the less efficiency and equity can be seen as independent factors. The current distribution is then implied to be the technically correct distribution of wealth and income, an impression that is reinforced by words like "redistribution" (in, say, "redistributive policy"), which itself represents a wilful ignorance of past political events and inequalities that led to our current distribution of resources. But there is no original, apolitical, amoral distribution after which everything else is "redistributive". Another way to put this is that what is allocatively efficient is defined only for a given distribution of endowments in a society. Change the distribution, and we change what is judged to be allocatively efficient. If we question the equity of the distribution, we are also questioning what is judged to be allocatively efficient, and we can only maintain that allocative efficiency is politically agnostic if we insist that the current distribution itself is somehow optimal, or at least politically uncontroversial.

Equity

I have just argued that efficiency and equity are not independent factors. What relationship do they then have? The use of terms like redistributive policy implies a negative relationship: we can spend money to redistribute resources, and these expenses lower efficiency. While I resist this framing, there are cases where efficiency and equity are negatively associated with each other. In Chapter 9, for example, we will discuss the catch share policies in the fisheries sector, which are promoted to improve the efficiency of catching fish through a market in rights to fish. And this they may well do, but this has often come at the cost of increasingly unequal distributions of fishing rights within catch share regimes. And in general, economies of scale can mean that more unequal distributions of resources can increase efficiency if those with the resources can use them more economically, although Albertus (2021) argues that this pattern is overplayed in the agricultural sector.

While I disagree with arguments that efficiency is objective while equity is not, we also shouldn't view equity as an unproblematic alternative to efficiency. Stone (1997) questions this outcome in the same way she does efficiency. Similar questions arise: who gets to decide what it means to be equitable? Whose benefits and costs are counted when we make such a decision? Are we concerned with equity among members of a group, or also between groups? Referring to the previous chapter, what uses of the environment should we prioritize and conclude as the "fairest" basis for ownership claims? And is it fair to prioritize the rights of those who started using a resource first? Definitions of equity are often expressed with proportions: they argue that a distribution of rights (or anything else) should be proportional to something else. A fair outcome could be to distribute resources in proportion to how much value they have, with a common argument being that everyone has equal moral value. This takes us to the idea of equality, which we will explore through the distinction between distributive justice and procedural justice. These have been argued to function similarly to our basic needs that I described earlier, and may overlap with them theoretically. Van Prooijen (2009), for example, shows that people's estimation of a procedure as being fair or not is predicted by whether or not it supported their basic need for autonomy. Thus, elements of equity may have an inherent value through the well-being they support.

An example of a policy designed to increase distributive justice through equality of outcomes are the agrarian and land reforms that have taken place largely in Latin America as well as in parts of Africa and Asia, spurred in part by theoretical arguments that increased inequality hurt development, and that increased equality could improve rural livelihoods and welfare (Albertus 2021). Unfortunately, as Albertus documents, these policies have often left a "property rights gap" between what the policies promise and what resulted. The conclusion that Albertus comes to is that these gaps are largely the result of government officials working to keep rural landowners dependent on the government for the security of their land tenure.

Working to maintain equality of endowments is both important and challenging because of cumulative advantage, which is a form of path dependence, whereby initial gains are used to widen the gap between the haves and the have-nots. One way in which cumulative advantage can occur is through the accumulation of rights based on already having other rights. The proximity principle, described in Chapter 2 as justifying the use of one resource based on the ownership of another, can be thought of as a special, spatial example of a broader principle: that rights should be granted based on other rights that are held. The most common example of this is based on rights granted to those who own land. Voting rights, for example, have often been limited to those who own land, translating the inequalities of land distribution into inequalities of formal political power, translating a distributive injustice into a procedure injustice. The right to vote is often a control right, or the right to influence the rules that one will be subject to.

Another avenue by which distributive injustice translates to procedural injustice comes through the actions of more powerful individuals to bend formal rules and processes to their own interests, even if these were meant to promote the public interest (Bagley 2019). And the more inequality there is, the more this will warp a sense of a common interest, in part also because wealthier individuals are able to buffer themselves from the effects of their actions, as we described in Chapter 1 in our discussion of social asymmetries.

One response to cumulative advantage is to not base allocational decisions on any factor associated with the individuals competing for rights. This is also known as a lottery. Common examples of lottery-based allocation in the United States are in the distribution of wildlife hunting licences and licences to fish for certain species such as scallops (Stoll *et al.* 2019). Leaving allocation to chance might sound like it's not a principle at all, but the lack of a principle, since it allocates rights not based on any metric that varies among potential users. But this is precisely the principle that the fishers of Alanya, Turkey use to allocate fishing grounds within a common fishery, as described by Berkes (1986), and popularized by Ostrom (1990) as one of the cases of successful community-based management that she describes. Arguably an equally important part of this regime is the rotation of sites each day, such that everyone ultimately is able to take a turn accessing the best sites.

A lottery-based system has the benefit of avoiding concerns of injustice that can arise from the use of a more directed principle. It avoids some potential gaming of more metric-driven arrangements by more powerful actors, such as the case where actors increase their appropriation of a resource such as a fishery when they are aware that an individual transferable quota system will be implemented that will allocate rights based on historic use. A lottery-based system also incurs fewer allocation costs than other systems that are imposed from the top-down, such as prior appropriation, which require documenting exactly who started using a resource first, often decades to centuries ago. It is not based on current resource endowments, and therefore may reinforce existing inequalities less.

The primary disadvantage of lottery-based allocations is that often we do believe that the other allocational principles should be respected. And this is more likely the case if the potential rights owners are heterogeneous in how well they satisfy such principles (Libecap 2007). An example of this comes from Vaughan's discussion of the formalization of Native Hawaiian resource rights by the state of Hawaii. She describes a tension between the state's approach, which aimed to treat everyone equally with respect to fishing rights, including folks not from traditional Hawaiian communities, and the Native Hawaiians' preference to privilege their own use, as well the rights of elders in their communities when it came to accessing certain resources. None of us would be happy if our own property was suddenly put up for a lottery, even if we were included in this lottery, because we think we have done more to deserve these things than other people have (this also reflects the endowment effect, whereby people value resources in their possession more than those they do not possess). Returning to the Alanya example, the lottery was perceived as fair because it was only made available to fishers from the community, a fairly homogenous group.

Efficiency, transaction costs and unbundling

So far we have considered the relationship between exchange and efficiency and equity. Now we turn to stewardship. For some, alienation, like exclusion, is necessary for the stewardship of the environment (Anderson & Libecap 2014). This can be interpreted as two different arguments – one, that alienation could be necessary to promote stewardship, and the other that it is sufficient. A cause is necessary if an outcome cannot be achieved without it; a cause is sufficient if its presence guarantees that an outcome is achieved. Environmental property rights, for example, can be viewed as necessary but insufficient ingredients for addressing the tragedy of the commons. We need them, but they are often not enough.

To claim necessity of alienation for stewardship would be to argue that stewardship is not seen in any culture without well-articulated markets in resource rights. This is not the case, as we documented in Chapter 3. What about sufficiency? There are two ways in which alienation could positively influence stewardship behaviour: by impacting the incentives of a current owner from what they would be if alienation weren't possible, and by serving as an allocation mechanism, distributing resources to those who are more likely to steward them. Insofar as the exchange value of a resource system reflects how much we steward it to an extent that compensates us for the opportunity costs of stewardship, then yes, this can encourage us to steward the resource.

These opportunity costs increasingly come in the form of foregone sale of natural resource products, or resource units, as we have called them. Stewardship behaviour here then depends on whether or not the market values the sustainability of a resource system more than it values the resource units extracted from that system. And in many cases, it values extraction over stewardship. Markets have allowed us to scale up our social organization to a global level. But the sale of environmental goods, or natural resource units, over long distances is a dominant factor in the degradation of the environment around the world. Long distance markets are one of the enabling factors that Berkes *et al.* (2006) include in their description of roving banditry, whereby actors serially deplete one resource and then the next. Ferguson *et al.* (2022) refer to serial environmental degradation to satisfy international resource markets as the tragedy of the commodity, establishing this pattern as an alternative interpretation to the traditional tragedy of the commons framing. Much of the social and environmental degradation that we see (or don't see) is fed by markets that are selling to increasingly distant buyers who don't have to witness or suffer from the degradation that they fuel. There are many examples of the impacts that markets have on collective action and resource use in local communities. Several studies have found, for example, that proximity to markets predicts natural resource degradation (Agrawal & Yadama 1997; Cinner *et al.* 2013).

We can partly make sense of these outcomes through the concepts of externalities as described earlier and transaction costs, or the costs of developing and enforcing exchange agreements. From the transaction cost perspective, an efficient market is one with few transaction costs: we are maximizing the amount of trading happening per the costs of creating and enforcing such trades. From this perspective, the most important policy goal is to minimize transaction costs involved in making market exchanges and maximize the number of (presumably win-win) exchanges. But minimizing transaction costs means maximizing the number of unaccounted-for externalities, since accounting for such externalities is costly. Efficient markets, from this perspective, are designed to efficiently externalize the costs of trade.

To explore this issue further, let's return to the regime of prior appropriation that governs water use in the western United States. It is often said that "water flows uphill to money" in this part of the country (Reisner 1986), and during my time in New Mexico and Colorado I would often hear about transfers of water from rural agricultural communities to municipal users (that said, most of the water in the western United States still goes to agriculture.) The ability of water markets to function like this in the western United States is based on the unbundling of water rights from land rights. This was meant to make water more portable so that users who did not own land right next to water could still obtain rights. This unbundling lowers the transaction costs of water markets since they do not have to contend with exchanges of land property at the same time; the general principle is that when we unbundle one right from others, the transaction costs in a market for this right will be lower.

When we talk about unbundling rights, we generally talk about separating a specific right (say extraction) from others. I believe that we can similarly talk about the individualization of collective rights as a form of unbundling, which similarly lowers transaction costs. In this case, the rights of an individual are being unbundled from the claims made by other members of a group. This similarly lowers transaction costs because an individual can then choose to sell their rights without consulting other community members or accounting for the costs that a sale would impose on them.

There are many examples of this dynamic. I have seen this in my own work in the New Mexico acequia farming communities of Taos, where the sale of water rights out of acequia communities has undermined the feasibility of these traditional systems by lowering the cost of exit, reflecting the theory of environmental reciprocity from Chapter 2. In response, many acequias have added formal bylaws that require community approval for an individual water sale to go through, increasing exit costs. These bylaws increase the transaction costs involved in water markets in New Mexico, but these costs also bring benefits in the form of a better recognition of the social costs of market exchange. As another example of a response to the threat of alienation to community interests, the 1990s agrarian reforms in Mexico, made it possible for ejido members to sell their parcels of agricultural land, but they could only do so to other ejido members unless they obtained community approval to sell it to a non-member.

The argument in this section is generalizable beyond the context of efficient markets. The desire to minimize transaction costs for increased efficiency is driven in part by the desire to scale up trade, as seen in the fact that long-distance markets are increasingly implicated in environmental degradation. When we scale up an activity we need to economize on our resources more than if we stay at a small scale. As we shall discuss in Chapter 6, this drive to scale up is an important feature of policy panaceas, and it can have similar consequences in that context, as we will explore.

Permanent versus temporary rights

Another dimension of exchange that relates to transaction costs is the permanence of rights transfers, with more permanent transfers usually involving much higher transaction costs because of the higher stakes involved. When we think about environmental markets, the most common scenario we probably imagine is one in which rights are permanently transferred; but this need not be the case. We already saw an example of temporary exchange in Chapter 3 through the gift economies that represent community building through indirect reciprocity (Hyde 2019).

A formal version of temporary exchange occurs through licences and leases that must be renewed periodically. These essentially grant usufruct use rights to resource users. An advantage of leasing arrangements is that they usually incur fewer transaction costs, and so are more easily implemented; they are also potentially more flexible, allowing resource users to adapt to changing circumstances in ways that reflect our discussion of contextual boundaries in Chapter 2. Under some regimes a fisher may, for example, lease rights to catch a particular species to make up for a decline in another livelihood stream.

There are other examples of the advantages of leases. A common refrain in the water rights literature is that leases could be used to provide the environment with water rights, for example as is done through Australia's water buyback programme (Wheeler et al. 2013). If the transaction costs of leasing water are lower than permanent transfers and they are more politically feasible, this may be an attractive option. A famous example of a concession being used to promote community rights comes from Guatemala, which has involved the "recognition and expansion of community rights in Petén where community forest concessions – 25-year concession contracts between the state and organized communities – have been granted in over 400,000 ha within the largest protected area of Mesoamerica, the Maya Biosphere Reserve" (Monterroso & Barry 2012: 137).

A disadvantage of temporary rights is that it can place the ownership of such rights in a less powerful position than the permanent owner. The communities who benefit from the state concession of forest concessions in Guatemala are ultimately dependent on the state continuing to grant them this benefit. Relatedly, based on the theory of environmental reciprocity from Chapter 2, we would predict temporary leases and concessions to diminish the motivations of the right-holder to steward the environment or the welfare of local people. This concern has played out in the use of corporate leases of oil and gas and short-term forest concessions (Jepson *et al.* 2001) that reflect the dynamic of roving banditry discussed in Chapter 1.

Corporate leases can also be used to alienate people from their land. A mechanism we have seen before is to de-collectivize rights. Earlier we discussed the leasing of public lands by corporations. In some cases, the leased environment is formally bestowed to local communities, such as in Papua New Guinea, where most of the country's land has been bestowed to Indigenous people. Corporations have used legal loopholes in this regime through what are known as special agricultural business leases to obtain de facto rights to forest land and proceed to clear this land against the will of Indigenous peoples. This often involves corporations manoeuvring to have community forest rights handed over to a single person, and then obtaining the signature of this one person to transfer lease rights to forest to a corporation (DiGirolamo 2021).

Permanent exchange also raises the spectre of dispossession of people from their lands and other resources. This has occurred for many families in the United States through the rules that govern property inheritance. Inheritance, like property itself, is a universal institution across cultures, arguably because it helps to resolve an unavoidable question: who owns someone's property when they die? In the absence of a specific principle for inheritance, it is difficult to effectively use land over time, as the default condition may be that the land is split among an owner's heirs. Over one or two generations, this can explode to an unmanageable number of owners. This requires a response, and unfortunately, in the United States, the law often does not help (Heller & Salzman 2021: 205). In the United States, if no will is written describing the inheritance procedures for a piece of land, that land is then considered "heir property". In the case of many property owners, US law requires unanimity in any decision taken about such partitioned heir property, and if someone is able to purchase a portion of this property, they can force a sale of this property and then buy it all themselves or have a partner do so. This process has led to the systematic alienation of black-owned land in the United States (Heller & Salzman 2021). Vaughan (2018: 104) describes how this system has similarly affected Native Hawaiian rights:

> Under Western private property law, kuleana lands are not collectively held by families, but owned in partial shares – which may be as small as 1/512 – by hundreds of distantly related individuals. Keeping lands requires organizing descendant owners, many of whom have never met one another or seen the land, and who live scattered throughout Hawai'i and the United States. With the addresses of home and land owners publicly available on the County of Kaua'i's real property website, realtors, most of whom have themselves moved to Hawai'i from elsewhere, routinely mail glossy brochures highlighting million-dollar sales of nearby properties and offering similarly lucrative results. Owners find it increasingly hard to resist selling, as both property values and tax burdens increase. Any single owner can sue to partition and force sale of the kuleana at public auction.

These examples show us that while we can make some broad statements about the degree of permanence of exchange, we should avoid relying too much on our stereotypes about what each category necessarily entails, and the details often depend on other aspects of exchange that we have discussed in this chapter. One thing that does consistently impact our evaluation of exchange is the identities of the actors involved: we feel one way about a lease by a predatory corporation and another about a lease by an individual fishery or local community.

Alienation and development: freehold-mortgage theory

In a previous section I have expressed some reasons to doubt the connection between alienation and stewardship incentives. But as I have emphasized before, stewardship is not necessarily the same thing as development. So what about the potential for alienation to promote development? One of the most important arguments in favour of alienation of resource systems comes from the agricultural sector. Here alienation is argued to enable a landowning farmer to use their land as collateral for a financial loan, which they need due to the high costs of farming and the low margins that farmers face for their goods, which is itself a function of their exchange entitlements and market dynamics. Shipton (2009: 8) describes this theory, which he calls the freehold-mortgage theory:

> The old theory and doctrine is this: (1) to raise agricultural productivity, farmers need more inputs and technology. (2) Farmers are too poor to save or to afford the inputs and new technology themselves. (3) They therefore need loans from better-endowed people until they can afford to finance their own needs. (4) Loans require collateral as security; this will ensure their repayment. (5) The best collateral is land, because it is immovable. (6) Land ought therefore to be negotiable (that is, transferable) for monetary or other consideration. (7) The way to make land transfers easier, and to keep track of them, is to issue title of land ownership (or else deeds of transactions), registered with the national government.

This theory has mostly been applied to inputs such as fertilizers and pesticides and the physical equipment needed to run an industrial-style farm, and less applied to more collective inputs such as irrigation infrastructure which is more likely to be supplied directly by external actors based on an assumption that farmers are less capable of acting collectively to do so themselves. As Shipton details, the theory has held a dominant place in agricultural economics and arguments about tenure reform. Shipton also describes the Western presumption that alienation is a "natural" or "evolutionary" culmination of property rights from more traditional arrangements, along with a transition from communal to individual property, with external actors interpreting the lack of commodification of cattle as a sign of underdevelopment, which itself implies a path of social evolution towards a desired goal (development).

Returning to the theory, it all sounds reasonable enough. But there are reasons to question each of these assumptions. First, we notice that we are assuming that the main problem to be solved is how to raise agricultural productivity and that input-intensive agriculture is the only way this can be done. But such capital-intensive agriculture brings with it high social and ecological costs. In the Dominican Republic, I have seen the negative consequences of the development that such alienation enables through the loans that Dominican rice farmers can take out. The Dominican rice sector is highly industrialized: rice monocultures are grown with the use of many chemical inputs and a lot of ecologically invasive machinery. The system, like most industrialized systems, is leaky, with fertilizer and pesticides seeping out and flowing downstream into mangrove and coral reef ecosystems. There are many important examples like these that represent a development versus stewardship trade-off. Following the 1980s agrarian reform in Nicaragua, for example, it was found that secure "property rights increase investment, increasing agricultural productivity and therefore the returns to deforestation" (Liscow 2013: 241).

Shipton tests the freehold-mortgage theory by studying the application of a land titling programme among the Luo People of western Kenya. Shipton (2009: 168) describes a cultural difference between how Luo farmers and financiers viewed loans and interest:

> Farmers are not just farmers, and farm loans to them are not just farm loans ... borrowers divert much, and probably most, of their ... credit to non-farming purposes like trade, housing, school fees, and consumption, and not least to the marriage payments and funeral contributions and travels that are so important in western Kenyan life.

Shipton also comments on the difficulties that farmers often had in understand the legalese they were presented with in the form of contracts and notices with respect to their loans, and how this contributed to farmers often not notifying government authorities of their land transactions, leading to a wide gap between the informal and formal distribution of land. Farmers and lenders also differed in how they viewed land. Among the Luo people, ancestors are commonly buried next to or close to houses, providing a sacred attachment between landowners and their land:

> The Luo case shows how different the meanings of land can be to farmers and financiers. To one it can be an occupation or a retirement plan, an expression of family and lineage (for a man), a challenge from a mother-in-law (for a woman), a link with the ancestors, and a place to sacrifice to spirits or divinity in a crisis – is short, a place in life. To the other, it is a collateral asset or a percentage: at the most immediate, a title deed pinned to a form with a signature or inky thumbprint, in a stack of faded folders.   (Shipton 2009: 180)

This very much reflects our discussion of intrinsic versus extrinsic value from Chapter 3. Finally, while alienation theoretically increases tenure security, Shipton (2009: 154) finds that:

> titling can ironically *reduce* it. It does so not only by introducing new temptations to gamble with mortgages, but also by vesting family rights and interests in individual hands in a way that renders them hard for other members to control. Not only kin of titleholders but also titleholders themselves are at new risk as it becomes easier for one member to hypothecate land others always considered held in trust.

We saw this issue earlier on when we talked about how unbundling of individual rights from collective rights lowers transaction costs of exchange. All this is not to say that alienation for collateral is not important. It is another example of leveraging an existing right to obtain additional rights and benefits, and for those who can avail themselves of these benefits, it can be critical, particularly in Western societies where other, intangible values do not conflict as much with formal exchange relationships. But as we have seen before with other models and theories, we cannot apply the theory as an assumption we make to any particular case.

Exchange value

We have been talking so far about the exchange of material rights: rights to resource units like fish or lumber, and rights to resource systems which provide streams of material benefits. But exchange can involve the trade of intangible goods as well. And we cannot understand the full impact of the formalization of markets in natural resources without understanding this fact. Formal exchange rights create a new object, an intangible right in the form of a contract, which itself can be subject to further trading, negotiation and manipulation. Modern resource markets often involve the trade of abstractions by people who often have no direct interest in the physical good underlying the abstraction; simply put, they are more interested in exchange value than use value. Their goals are primarily or purely financial: hedging their bets, diversifying their investment portfolios by adding a new asset class and thereby managing risk, and speculating based on expectations for future exchange values. The exchange value of a good is usually much more externally legible than use value as well, which is what leads to outcomes we call price bubbles, when exchange value is much higher than use value (it is also why policy analysts conducting cost–benefit analyses default to relying on market prices to measure costs and benefits).

An entertaining description of how this played out for oil markets during the Covid pandemic comes from a Planet Money Podcast episode from that period (Goldstein & Childs 2020). The motivation for the episode was the seemingly bizarre event that oil was trading for negative amounts. As Mary Childs states in the episode: "It's like there are two different kinds of oil – the actual black goo that comes out of the ground and a financial abstraction that people buy and sell to each other to hedge risk or to make bets."

An entire ecosystem of abstract goods can exist seemingly far above the physical reality, which is not inherently problematic, but definitely can be. When that becomes all we see, and we lose track of what is actually happening on the ground. One can easily imagine many office buildings (and maybe now living rooms) full of people moving around abstractions on their spreadsheets, far removed from the push and pull and real objects and people outside.

A good example of the role that formal exchange value plays in affecting the behaviour of property owners comes from the housing sector (Fischel 2015). In the 1970s, as inflation was increasing, housing was increasingly valued for its exchange value, as an investment, in addition to its use value as a home. During this time, zoning laws in the United States, which are the jurisdiction of local government, changed regimes from pro-growth to anti-growth (with exceptions being mostly in the south and in the city of Houston, Texas, in particular, which has no zoning laws).

Through his famous "homevoter hypothesis", Fischel argues that homeowners had a shared, group interest insofar as additional housing in their communities would decrease each of their property values. This is similar to the situation faced by Dominican dairy farmers who have a group interest in the price they receive for their milk. In many places the response of homeowners has been to change zoning laws to prevent such development. This is an example of successful collective action on their part to contribute to a local public good: housing prices. Notably, this also reflects the importance of exclusion, quite directly: the only way to promote this in-group public good is to exclude outsiders. And like before, how we feel about this exclusion likely depends on who is doing the exclusion and who is being excluded. Once again, we shouldn't lapse into a single supposedly representative image we have of this situation as wealthier owners keeping out poorer people. Many neighbourhoods of different socio-economic statuses exclude outsiders.

Conclusion

Some of the main ideas to take away from this chapter are the model of patron–client relationships and how these help us understand the dynamics of exchange entitlements. We have also seen the importance of the principles of efficiency and equity for the first time, and shown that there are multiple ways that we can interpret efficiency. With its focus on the minimization of transaction costs, efficiency excludes a more holistic understanding of the benefits and costs of exchange. We have also explored the relationship between alienation and development and stewardship, as well as the role that intangible goods can play in fundamentally changing how we interact with the environment.

If there is one conclusion to take from this chapter, it is that it should be hard to arrive at firm conclusions with respect to markets and exchange rights, because the world is complicated. This is particularly important to emphasize at this point because there is so much intergroup conflict about the role that markets play in society. One group conjures up the spectre of an all-consuming capitalist machine, and another other views markets as close to a modern-day deity of social organization. Angel or devil, which side to choose? The answer is that we shouldn't choose, for each is a little bit right. Markets represent our basic reciprocal instincts. And the overemphasis placed on efficiency through lowering transaction costs, particularly in formal markets, can drive out intrinsic values and remove us from each other and the world we depend on.

Moving forward, we turn to the topic of formalization in the final section of this book, and unpack the challenge of policy panaceas as formal solutions preferred by a group in part to set itself apart from other groups. Several of the most dominant policy panaceas we will consider are based on exchange rights and entitlements that we have discussed here.

PART III

Property regimes and policy panaceas

In this final part of the book, we will discuss two interrelated ideas: property regimes and policy panaceas. An environmental property regime refers to the type of actor claiming ownership over the environment. A policy panacea is a public policy that is promoted as a fix for a type of problem, regardless of case-based and political context. The connection between them comes from the fact that all policy panaceas with respect to environmental property rights are based on assumptions about property regimes.

We begin our discussion by unpacking the elements and enabling factors of policy panaceas in Chapter 6. From here, in Chapter 7 we move to one of the most important distinctions with respect to property regimes: individual rights versus common property. These are often thought of as being mutually exclusive, but as we will see in this chapter, they are not, and their relationship has multiple elements to it. Building on this, in Chapter 8 we discuss the meaning of public property and consider the role of the state in environmental governance. We also consider a relative newcomer to the property regime discourse: nature itself. Finally, we question the significance of property regimes as a broad way of classifying complex realities, and we introduce the idea of a hybrid property regime to help make sense of this complexity. We conclude Part III in Chapter 9 with a discussion of market policies as an example of a hybrid property regime, and maybe the most prominent example of environmental policy panaceas.

6

Policy panaceas

What is a policy panacea? One answer is that it is a solution that has been broadly applied, and panaceas are often talked about as being successful in this way. This is not the same thing as whether the policy is successful in producing the desired outcomes; it may or it may not be. The theory of panaceas I develop in this chapter is agnostic about this second type of success. Rather, the theory developed here is about the features of a policy that enable its spread: its evolutionary success as a panacea. For to spread, policies are often expressed in apolitical, highly legible terms and supported by top-down governance, and at the expense of more extensive cooperation across groups.

In this chapter we are doing two things at once. First, we are unpacking the dimensions that enable the panacea problem that I just mentioned. And in so doing, we discuss key issues of environmental policy analysis. Panaceas are about overgeneralizing, usually beyond the evidence, but how do we think about the trade-offs involved in making generalizations? In the first section of this chapter we tackle that question.

From there, we move on to discuss a set of enabling factors for the spread of a policy panacea, starting with a set of psychological biases and heuristics that we all have, and which lead us to favour the spread of a preferred solution, even in the face of contrary evidence. From here we discuss another social aspect of panaceas, and this comes from the fact that preference for any specific policy is closely related to one's social affiliations, to one's membership in a group. And here we tie this conversation back to our previous discussion of intergroup dynamics and the synergy between intergroup conflict and intragroup cooperation.

In the third section we discuss the role of politics. We have already talked about the role that apolitical framings can play in our discussion of the tragedy of the commons and collective action problems in Chapter 1. Panaceas are likewise often cast as apolitical, technical solutions; this helps them garner support by decision-makers who might feel threatened by the spectre of political controversy. Finally, we turn to the interrelated topics of scale, centralization and formality. Panaceas are about achieving outcomes at scale, and this requires more centralized governance programmes to carry out consistent interventions across different cases. The topic of centralization is also important for helping us understand the nature of property regimes, as this is one of defining differences between different types, at least based on our stereotypical ideas about them: we often think that "private" property means decentralization, and "public" means a centralized state is in charge. But we need to move beyond these simplistic associations, which we will do as we proceed through this section of the book. In this section of the chapter we will also draw a connection between centralization and the use of formal institutions, which are required to manage human relationships in large, top-down regimes where it is more difficult to maintain informal and flexible relationships.

Generalizations

Before diving into the factors that enable a policy panacea, we want to spend some time thinking about the good and the bad of generalizing. We all do this all of the time and we couldn't function in the world without it: generalizing is another way of saying learning from experience. But we can overgeneralize. And how are we supposed to know when we have done that? This section starts to answer that question.

Aggregation and levels of explanation

Panaceas are about making generalized prescriptions. In this first section, we explore the role of generalization and when it is or is not problematic. We start by discussing a trade-off between generality and specificity in our theoretical arguments and predictions. From here we observe that some very general statements can and should be made, including that environmental property rights are universal across all cultures; what varies is how these are implemented and how they relate to the cultures that employ them. We conclude with a discussion of the potential costs of over-generalizing.

To understand when generalizing might or might not be problematic, we turn to the well-known accuracy versus precision trade-off: the more precise (specific) we are, the less accurate we will be (Levin 2000: 26). This is true for any prediction: we can more easily predict changes in global temperature than we can for a particular location, because more aggregate predictions average out a lot of local variation, or noise. Thus, higher levels of aggregation associate with larger spatial and temporal extents. This is why, for example, we can make better predictions about average global temperatures than we can about the temperature in a particular place. This is also an important way to understand some of the adaptations of pastoralists discussed in Chapter 2: by moving around a landscape, they have a larger area of resources to use, and at this larger spatial scale there is less variation in resource availability than in smaller areas. There might be less water available in one smaller area, but this is often compensated for by the presence of water elsewhere.

We can also use this argument to better understand Ostrom's (1990) design principles for sustainable community-based resource management. In a paper I co-wrote with Ostrom and led by David Sloan Wilson (Wilson, Ostrom & Cox 2013), we argued that the reason Ostrom's principles were so accurate in explaining the success of communities in managing their resources was their level of aggregation. Ostrom did not say how her principles should be implemented and with which rules. Who, for example, should be responsible for maintaining social and environmental boundaries, which we discussed earlier? If Ostrom had tried to make predictions about the exact ways in which the principles were implemented, she would not have been nearly as accurate, since there is much more variation at this more specific level than there is in the presence or absence of the principles themselves. Being more general then has the advantage of allowing for more flexibility in implementation. The lesson from this discussion is that generalizations will be more accurate if they are made less precise, and if we are worried about overgeneralizing as a core part of the panacea problem, reducing our precision is one way to make sure that we are still making accurate statements.

We can also use this framework to understand the success of the self-determination theory pioneered by Ryan and Deci (2018), which we saw during our discussion of intrinsic motivation in Chapter 3. While the authors argue for the universality of the basic needs they identify, they allow for differences in understanding, and therefore implementations, to provide for these needs. Thus while we all value autonomy, we need to remember that autonomy is about fit between one's values and how one participates in the social environment. Change the social environment, and you change what is perceived to be autonomous. We return to this issue in Chapter 8 when we discuss participatory governance as a means to satisfy our basic need for autonomy.

The universality of rights

In keeping with the trade-off between accuracy and precision, we can make a very general statement about environmental rights: every social system has some concept of rights to the environment (Brown 1991). What varies are the rules and norms that express property rights. Amidst this variation, in any social system, there is some sense of some people being able to do some things with respect to the environment, and others not. There is no functional social system where access to and use of the environment is entirely random and chaotic, and the ways in which access and use are non-random reflect strategies taken and social functions played. It is a mistake to think that because norms in many cultures are radically different from the Western perspective, constraints on behaviour through property rights are not needed in such cultures. The Tlingit people discussed in Chapter 3, for example, have powerful narratives that establish stewardship norms, but this is not the same thing as saying that they have no conception of ownership. In Carothers *et al.* (2021: 20), co-author Steve Langdon describes the property rights arrangements among the Tlingit people:

> Tlingit society had/has exceptionally strong property concepts. Clans were corporate units in that they owned both tangible and intangible property … Salmon streams were under the control of stream chiefs (heen saati) who exercised governance by determining who had access, harvest timing, technology, and location of harvests. In general, other Tlingit respected clan claims to streams, but if they were violated, Tlingit would use violence to protect their claims.

On the other hand, it is important to avoid forcing the assumptions of the dominant perspective on marginalized knowledge systems and cultures. It is also fair to argue that the concept of "property" has been so imbued with a Western framework that claims of the universality of property can sound like a colonial imposition, forcing a dominant perspective onto local cultures. This is why terms like kuleana, as described by Vaughan (2018) and discussed in Chapter 3, are so important. On the other (other) hand, as I describe in this book, colonialist framings have been used to deny the universality of rights by arguing that certain types of rights don't "count" as true property claims. So, an argument that property is not universal could be used for opposite purposes.

Generality and meaning

Being general has clear advantages in that it helps to reveal broad patterns, as reflected in Ostrom's design principles. In practical terms, generality also enables more flexibility of implementation. Rose (2019) notes that many legal procedures have favoured muddier, less clear principles to allow more flexibility in the application of the law. So why not just always increase our generality? Because excessive generality becomes less meaningful, and we struggle to apply general statements to specific cases (Cox 2008). After all, if I am trying to improve the property rights arrangements in a particular time and place, how helpful is it to know that they are a cultural universal? It is a good starting point to know that I should look for some, but it doesn't help me much beyond that.

This lack of meaning problem applies squarely to the idea of tenure security, which is ubiquitous in theoretical and applied literatures or property, but which is also mostly an empty conceptual container that people assign to whatever aspects of an environmental right claim they think are most fundamental to its efficacy, with the most common attribute being that it is formally written down and enforced by a state actor. Claims about the importance of tenure security, then, unless they are unpacked with more specific arguments (e.g., see Albertus 2021) are more like initial framings rather than falsifiable theoretical claims. Similar comments can be made about concepts like "privatization" and other "izations" (Shipton 2009: 25).

I think a best-case scenario for highly general concepts is to serve as boundary objects, which can unite groups with different perspectives under a common, general cause. "Okay, we don't know what we mean by a concept like 'collective action problem' yet, but we know we need to think about how individual incentives produce outcomes for a group." Unpacking the meaning of a vaguely agreed-upon concept can itself serve as a means of bridging different perspectives of different groups. Although this does not automatically resolve all conflicts, as suggested by my previous discussion of the idea of "property" itself. Over time, however, more specificity is likely needed. Excessively vague language can be a source of loopholes when contingencies aren't covered, and can also create conflict over competing interpretations if there is no space to resolve these.

Ultimately, we need to balance the two extremes of generality and specificity. And the extent to which we should be concerned about overgeneralization depends on our level of analysis: I believe that extensive generalizing is much more problematic when it is accompanied by high degrees of specificity: "do exactly this and do exactly that, everywhere", rather than, "have you thought about this general issue that needs to be addressed?" Just because property rights are universal doesn't mean that we should expect their implementation to be homogenous: quite the contrary, as their universality in part represents the fact that they are a method for communities to adapt to the needs of local circumstances.

The psychology of policy preferences

To further explore the dynamics of policy panaceas, we have to consider the social and psychological nature of science. In this section we will cover several human biases that influence our own tendencies to adopt panacea thinking and maintain a preference for a particular policy solution, even in the face of contradictory or insufficient evidence.

Extrinsic motivation and crowding

In Chapter 3, we discussed the importance of intrinsic motivation as providing an incentive to better care for the environment and each other. It is tempting to ask if this could be scaled up so that such benefits can be shared more broadly. And to some extent we can, in part because of the transitivity of such motivation. If leaders of an organization show themselves to be intrinsically motivated and are supportive of others' basic needs of autonomy, efficacy and belonging, this can catch on and spread through an organization.

But there is also a limit here because of the highly specific nature of intrinsic motivation: it is by definition about a specific relationship between people or between people and their environment, as Vaughan describes in the case of Native Hawaiian people, who have different words to describe their affection for a specific place and a broader environmental appreciation. Intrinsic motivation is costly and therefore less efficient to formally produce than extrinsic motivation, and even in our own lives, we need to decide who and what we can intrinsically value, because it is a scarce resource. Policy panaceas thus tend to favour extrinsic motivation, because panaceas as much as anything are about scaling up a solution and applying it to many situations. In Chapter 8, we shall discuss an effort to formalize the intrinsic value of the environment through the "rights of nature" approach.

The previous discussion describes a process by which extrinsic motivation can crowd out intrinsic motivation when scaling up and efficiency become primary organizational goals. There is a broad literature on the relationship between these two types of motivation that has asked whether or not extrinsic motivations necessarily crowd out intrinsic motivations. In brief, the answer is no, not necessarily (Cerasoli, Nicklin & Ford 2014). It is best not to think about these two types of motivation as two ends of a scale, or as necessarily relating to each other in a zero-sum game, to use terminology we have used to describe social relationships. As we discussed in Chapter 3, intrinsic motivation can grow in a space initially motivated only by extrinsic motivation, and the two can then coexist. The two types of motivation can be either substitutes or complements. From the perspective of self-determination theory, whether or not an extrinsic incentive crowds out or crowds in intrinsic motivation depends on how it impacts people's basic needs (Bowles & Polania-Reyes 2012; Rode, Gómez-Baggethun & Krause 2015). An example would be if resource users could participate in deciding what extrinsic incentives they will face, this can satisfy their need for autonomy and lead to less crowding out and even some crowding in, which leads us to a discussion of the importance of political participation in Chapter 8.

Confirmation bias, false positives and representation

We can think of the establishment of a panacea as occurring in a few stages. First, a model is created, second, an initial round of evidence is collected, and third, the policy is applied to a larger population of cases. At the second and third stages, human psychology plays a large role in promoting a favoured policy. At the second stage of initially analysing a case where a policy is applied, confirmation bias influences how we interpret the evidence of a case and whether or not it supports the theories behind a particular policy. Confirmation bias leads us to believe what we believe; it causes us to view evidence that supports our beliefs as more salient, and to dismiss contradictory evidence, maybe by arguing that a case that contradicts the efficacy of our preferred policy does not represent the "true" version of this policy. If we already believe in a policy based on the model that we have created, then we are inclined to view all evidence through this lens. Our observations are "theory-laden".

False positive bias (List 2022) is another related bias that can occur in the initial interpretation of a case. In statistics, a false positive occurs when we infer that a pattern or relationship between variables exists (positive result) when it does not (but false). In our context, this relationship would be between a policy and an outcome, and the bias is to infer that this outcome is produced by the presence of the policy, rather than as a seemingly random occurrence. Humans are not good at judging what is truly random and often infer a pattern where there is none (Thaler & Sunstein 2009). In scientific practice there is a strong incentive to find "real" results that show some type of pattern and can therefore help tell a story (more on our bias towards stories in the next section). These two biases combined (false positive and confirmation) can be used to reinforce support for or criticism of a policy.

Finally, a panacea is expressed by the generalization from one case to many. This occurs through an assumption that an initial case is representative of a larger population. This assumption goes by the awkwardly long term "the representativeness heuristic". If a case that demonstrates success is in fact not representative of a larger set of cases to which a policy is to be applied, then we cannot necessarily use this case as a basis to predict the policy's future success. Moreover, if there is a bias towards paying more attention to successful cases, which can occur in part through survivorship bias, whereby we cannot see unsuccessful cases because they aren't around anymore, then we would expect such cases to not be representative of a larger population (Ellenberg 2014).

Group-based policy preferences

Different groups tend to align with different policy solutions. A great description of this is provided by Degnbol *et al.* (2006: 535) in their aptly named paper "Painting the floor with a hammer: technical fixes in fisheries management". In this paper they compare three solutions to fisheries depletion, each of which we discuss in this book, and argue that each tends to be favoured by a different group: individual transferable quotas (ITQs) otherwise known as catch shares are favoured by economists, marine protected areas or MPAs are more preferred by conservation biologists, and community-based natural resource management (CBNRM) has more support from anthropologists. Each of these policies is theoretically based in part on the discourse of property regimes, assigning ownership of the environment to some types of actors and not others.

This association between a policy preference and group affiliation is driven in part by conformity bias, a type of in-group bias, which leads individuals to bias their policy preferences based on the opinions of a majority in a group (Furth-Matzkin & Sunstein 2018). Beyond preferring a particular policy, members signal their adherence to the associated group by problematizing the approaches taken by other groups. In the book, *Order Without Law*, Ellickson (1991: 7) comments on the relationship between two groups of academics with similar substantive interests, but significantly different perspectives: "To exaggerate only a little, the law-and-economics scholars believe that the law-and-society group is deficient in both sophistication and rigor, and the law-and-society scholars believe that the law-and-economics theorists are not only out of touch with reality but also short on humanity."

This pattern extends beyond the study of law and rights; economists are stereotypically critical of the supposed lack of their version of analytical rigor of other social sciences. Cultural anthropology and sociology in turn are critical of the economist's lack of emphasis on inequality, treating it as a secondary concern that we can focus on once we take care of the overriding goal of efficiency. And so on, with each group thinking that, while others are conforming to arbitrary and unproductive group norms, its own members have seen the light and left Plato's cave. And in the meantime, in the above stereotypical descriptions, I am treating all of these groups as if they were homogenous, falling into the trap of out-group homogeneity bias, which is another type of in-group bias that downplays the diversity of individuals that are not a part of one's own group. This type of thinking is hard to escape.

Policy narratives

Within the literature on collective action, the important community-build role of narratives is often overlooked. Narratives are often told from a member of a community to the rest of the community about itself as a way of establishing collective identity; they also are used to make sense of events and argue for particular responses to problems (Fortmann 1995; Rose 2019). There is a close relationship between narratives and panaceas. Stories are often used to justify the use of a preferred intervention, and can be used to motivate overgeneralization. It has been found that anecdotal evidence is often more psychologically influential than statistical evidence, particularly when it is told with an appealing story (Eger *et al.* 2022).

I like the term "just-so story" for the types of stories that are meant to persuade more than they are meant to be tested. The term was popularized in evolutionary studies to describe stories proposing why a cultural or biological trait is adaptive, without much concern for alternative hypotheses that could also explain its persistence. And while I am problematizing the role of storytelling in the panacea process, we should remember there is nothing inherently good or bad about storytelling, just as there is nothing inherently good or bad about the formation of social groups and the associated exclusion of non-group members. We have already seen the importance of storytelling in the case of the salmon boy from Chapter 3.

Gottschall (2021: 107–9) argues that there is a universal grammar to storytelling, borrowing from the well-known universal grammar of language idea popularized by Noam Chomsky. Stories, according to Gottschall, tap into our negativity bias and moralistic bias. These go together: "Story's universal grammar conditions us to see the world in terms of proliferating problems and then to name, shame, and punish the villains who are responsible." Gottschall argues that through storytelling "love is generated, but so is hate. Community is forged, but enemies are identified. Empathy is created, but also callousness for those who haven't earned it." Here again is the dark synergy between in-group identity and out-group antagonism. Gottschall offers a cultural evolutionary argument for the persistence of some stories over others: those that fit with our tribal psychology.

From the point of view of collective action described in Part I, the promotion of a policy is a public good shared by those whose professional identity aligns them with it. This most obviously includes the experts who promote the panacea and directly benefit from its implementation, but can include other groups as well. These groups have a vested interest in the policy and play a critical role in promoting it. These groups are often led by charismatic leaders. The presence of such leaders strongly aligns with traditional collective action theory, going back to Mancur Olson's (1965) argument that leaders play an important role in leading the provision of public goods for their groups. Because a policy benefits those who promote it, organizational decision-making is often characterized at least as much by "solutions looking for problems" as it is "problems looking for solutions" (Cohen, March & Olsen 1972).

Narratives promoting a particular policy or approach will sometimes invoke a pseudo-evolutionary, "end of history" narrative, as if there is an inevitable social evolution towards the best, or most natural way of organizing society (committing the naturalistic fallacy). Similar to our discussion of Social Darwinism in Chapter 2, this represents an incorrect and inappropriate application of evolutionary ideas to society. This has been seen in the realm of environmental property rights via arguments for an inevitable "evolution" from open access to common property to private property through formal processes (Galaty 2016). In his discussion of the legal relationships between Native Americans and the US federal government, Duthu (2008: 173), provides an example of this that also reflects the pernicious out-grouping that Gottschall describes:

> Perpetuating the idea of Indians as a savage, primitive and dying race was a critical and necessary element in the grand theory of America's nation-building mythology. A fundamental tenet of that mythology was the idea that Western legal systems, philosophy, religion and social structures represented the height of civilization that was preordained to grow and dominate in the lands formerly occupied by infidels.

To me an important lesson is that when we find ourselves compelled by a story, we should ask if and how it feeds into our biases. We may say that a story is "good", but what we mean, at least in part, is that it fits well with our preference for problem resolution, in-group belonging, and concomitant out-group antagonism. This isn't to say that a popular story isn't "true", but it is to say that part of the reason it is popular is probably that it feeds into this psychology.

This point is particularly important to keep in mind as we proceed through the rest of this book. In Chapter 9, I shall be fairly critical of some aspects of market-based policies, which are the preferred solution by many economists. There I am running the risk of committing the same out-grouping behaviours I am describing, including treating everyone who calls themselves an economist as if they were identical. Non-economists need to avoid out-grouping all economists as the villains of panacea policymaking, and conversely, bestowing others (e.g., anthropologists) with the mantle of the heroes who bravely fight for us to better recognize complexity. Part of the reason why such a story might be tempting to us is explained by Gottschall's thesis, and this is not a good reason. Economists have by far the most influence of the social sciences on the formal practice of environmental property rights and policy discourses generally, and I do think a part of the reason for this has to do with one of the elements of policy panaceas: that their frameworks tend to avoid dealing with issue of power and inequality compared to the other social sciences. But if another group were to displace them, we can't be sure that this group would address the problems I am discussing any better. There are similar complaints to be made about the protected areas promoted by conservation biologists (Brockington, Duffy & Igoe 2008).

Unitary actors and technical framings

In Chapter 1 we discussed the issue of politically neutral framings of environmental problems by questioning the dominant narrative of the tragedy of the commons. Politically neutral, or technical, framings can also be used to promote the solutions to our problems, advancing policies as technical solutions. The assumption of political neutrality is one of the hallmarks of panacea thinking. My favourite definition of a technical solution comes from Hardin (1968: 1243) himself: "A technical solution may be defined as one that requires change only in the techniques of the natural sciences, demanding little or nothing in the way of change in human values or ideas of morality."

In the previous section, I argued that one of the reasons for the success of the discipline of economics in policy is due to its apolitical framing of ideas like efficiency (Berman 2022). Why would this framing be advantageous? The answer, according to Giridharadas (2018), is that win-win framings garner support from elite decision-makers. In his trenchant criticism of the ways in which the wealthy and powerful take it upon themselves to help the less wealthy and powerful, Giridharadas (2018) argues that "win-win" framings of solutions can be used to depoliticize our problems and promote coping-based solutions rather than fundamental solutions, because the fundamental solutions would require that some people (the powerful) lose something in real terms. According to Giridharadas, win-win framings, where we all lose or we all win, are safer spaces because they preclude observations that sometimes our problems are the cause and effect of having real winners and losers, and to solve these problems, we need to redress these inequalities. The reasons for the popularization of efficiency as a politically neutral policy goal as promoted by many economic policy experts are, ironically, political.

This win-win, apolitical thinking has influenced how we think about the solutions to environmental problems. A traditional, Western answer to the question of which property regime is best is that private property (meaning individual property) is best. Why is this? Part of the answer is that it is assumed that individuals are uniquely capable of acting in their own self-interest. And why should that matter? Going back to the theory of environmental reciprocity, this predicts that an actor will invest in the environment when their future interest is tied to the state of the environment. But this depends on the actor being able to act in their own best self-interest. If they can't, we cannot make this prediction.

Thus, the treatment of certain property regimes as panaceas is tied to the unitary actor assumption. By unitary I mean an actor who is absent of internal conflict with multiple identities, interests and motives, and who makes decisions in accordance with a single interest. This tricks us into thinking that collective actors can be thought of as individuals with single interests that we can tie to the state of the environment, without any messy internal politics getting in the way. In policy and political discussions, we talk loosely about what is happening in "Washington", or what "the government" should do, or isn't doing, and in so doing we trick ourselves into thinking that these are meaningful terms, as if large organizations can be stated as taking actions in ways that mirror what so-called individuals do. When we use a whole to refer to its parts we are using symbolic shorthand to describe a more complex reality, but often describing this reality poorly. In short, we are talking about collective actors as if they were unitary actors.

This simplification is often done through formalization, where each actor type becomes as much an administrative artefact as it does a real entity in the world. This formalization discounts the internal conflicts that occur in each actor, and therefore helps promote the associated regime as a technical fix that doesn't involve politics.

Centrality and formality

In this final section we talk about two closely related dimensions of governance: centralization and formality. The connection between these is straightforward: more centralized governance tends to be more formal. One way to think about the reason for this is through the principal–agent relationship that we introduced in Chapter 5. The most common example of this is between a boss and an employee. The information asymmetry between the principal and an agent is exacerbated in a more highly centralized system, where one boss oversees many employees. The most common solution for this is to develop formal rules to ensure the accountability of the agent. Panaceas tend to be promoted by top-down, formalized governance processes, although ironically, as we shall see in Chapter 8, decentralized governance can become a panacea itself. In this section we discuss centrality and formality and their relationship to the panacea problem.

Bottom-up and top-down

Centrality plays a strong role in the theory of panaceas because of the common desire to scale-up the implementation of a preferred policy, which requires some measure of centralized governance to ensure consistency of implementation. A governance system is more centralized when the distribution of authority over people and the environment is more unequally distributed, which occurs in social systems through taller organizational hierarchies. As discussed by Easterly (2008: 95–6), the top-down view looks at context more as a blank slate to impose its own models on, whereas a bottom-up governance approach is more path dependent, taking into account how things are currently working. This also has implications for the role of expertise, with top-down expertise being more interventionist and less incrementalist.

Despite these stark differences, these categories are not mutually exclusive, as we will discuss in the next two chapters. Top-down and bottom-up governance have been combined under the rubric of co-management, which we will discuss in more depth in Chapter 8. We also need to be careful not to assume that certain regimes are bottom-up or top-down. Common property, for example, indicates that a resource is owned by a community, but often the control rights in these settings are held by powerful local actors or by external actors. Conversely, when we think about states or corporations or NGOs as owners of the environment, we shouldn't be misled by the largest and most salient examples to think that all such actors are highly centralized.

Formality and legibility

There is a strong connection between centralization and formality. In short: the more top-down a governance regime is, the more likely it is that a larger number of people need to coordinate their behaviours and that this is done so through formal institutions: rules that are codified by written language. To see why this is, we need to unpack what we mean by formal institutions, and a related term, legibility. Formality implies the presence of a third party (usually a governmental actor) who can make sense of agreements between two or more parties (Leach, Mearns & Scoones 1999: 238). A formal institution is legible to an external party who can then interpret it and help to enforce it. By legible I mean both visible and comprehensible (O'Donnell 2018): something is visually perceivable and can be interpreted by an actor through some analytical framework. When we talk about legibility, we can only do so by talking about "legibility to" a particular type of actor or organization. Formal legibility, then, means that an agreement between two actors is legible to a third actor, who can then understand this agreement and enforce it.

Is it good to be formally legible? Yes and no. In apartheid-era South Africa, individuals were given identity cards which identified them by race (as defined by the apartheid government) with oppressive limitations on the rights of those who weren't classified as white. Being illegible to the state can often be a sign of power (Scott 2009). It is surprisingly difficult, for example, to find out which wealthy landowners own much of the land in England (Shrubsole 2019). On the other side, formalizing rights of citizenship in many countries is seen as a way to empower those individuals who can finally be "seen" by their government.

The issue of legibility also extends beyond the issue of legibility of local systems to external actors. In this context of local versus external, legibility is a two-way street, as Scott (1998: 35–6) recognizes in his discussion of property law as an "impenetrable thicket for ordinary citizens … and decipherable only for those who have sufficient training and a grasp of state statutes". Scott concludes that the supposed simplicity of formality "is lost on those who cannot break the code, just as the relative clarity of customary tenure is lost on those who live outside the village". Formal rules and laws have become increasingly complex in many societies, and are often illegible to all but the most expert actors with the "local knowledge" of such formalities, which then serve as a barrier to those who don't have the resources to navigate with them. Stoll *et al.* (2019: 7), for example, analyse the extent to which fishers in the US state of Maine are able to diversify their livelihoods by obtaining aquaculture licences, and find that they largely are not. The authors conclude that one of the barriers that transitioning fishers are likely to face is the increasing bureaucratic costs of obtaining licences.

Formality and politics

Formality works better at scale than does informality and is more consistent in its expression. That is its great advantage, as it can help to clarify common understandings of a set of rules for a group of actors. Formal rules can then be taken and applied elsewhere seemingly automatically, if we are only thinking about the fidelity of the formal rules themselves and not how their implementation fits with local context. Often formal consistency satisfies important norms of equality (treat everyone the same) that we would not want to do without.

The most popular term for the formal consistency we just described is the "rule of law", which also implies the presence of an independent judiciary to ensure that such consistency is maintained. The "rule of law" is related to a group of movements that have attempted to take the "politics" out of decision-making, with the implications that politics includes efforts of some to benefit themselves or their in-groups at the expense of a broader public. This is the impetus behind the "progressive era" from the 1900s to the 1920s in the United States, which emphasized professionalization of governmental officials and greater transparency of decision-making.

Formal institutions are often framed as being apolitical, but this is not the case. Easterly (2008: 97), for example, describes Shipton's (1988) analysis of a land titling programme among the Luo people of western Kenya. Among the key points that Easterly summarizes are the ways that the programme created new uncertainties and disrupted power relationships among local resource users, and enabled opportunistic behaviour for land owners to game the system. Formal land registration policies also create space for public certifiers to act strategically. In a study of land registration in Ethiopia, Chinigò (2015: 182–3) found that local officials leveraged their powers to allocate land and extension services for personal and political gain.

Often, formal land registration policies may act against common property in favour of private individual property and serve to dispossess local owners of their land, as occurred to Native Americans under the US allotment acts, and to Mayan landowners in Mexico, partly as a result of disempowered Mayan landowners who faced barriers to engaging with formal processes (Torres-Mazuera 2022). We shall discuss governmental aversions to common property in depth in Chapter 8.

Formal legibility and simplification

One concern with legibility is that it is an asymmetric relationship between an observer and what they are making sense of. The observer is imposing a framework of understanding on this system to make sense of it from their perspective (Rose 2019). We see this concern play out in Scott's (1998) aptly named book, *Seeing Like a State*, in which he argues that state bureaucracies have difficulty "reading" local, informal social institutions and complex ecologies. Formal legibility, or the legibility of a local system to an external actor like a government agency, is enabled by certain objects, and a primary example that Scott uses is the cadastral map, which outlines land rights in a community in a highly simplified and formalized way. Through this object, a complex land tenure reality is "made legible" to an external actor.

What is the purpose of this analytical simplification? In short, it increases efficiency by lowering transaction costs, and such efficiency is required when a policy solution is being scaled up to apply to many cases. We saw this argument in Chapter 5 when we discussed the impacts of efficient, long-distance markets. Simplification enables the state to engage with complex local realities without incurring too many costs. If we think of the state as a principal and local implementing actors as agents in a principal–agent relationship as mentioned earlier, then simplifying target systems and outcomes of interest is a good way for the principal to hold local partners accountable by increasing accountability through formally legible metrics. Simplification can also clarify patterns that are not easily recognized from the ground. Rose (2019: 9) points out that in some circumstances maps of a territory can reveal patterns that cannot be discerned from the ground, with a famous example being John Snow's map of cholera outbreaks in London showing that they correlated with proximity to a pump for drinking water.

The need for legibility has implications for the types of rules that a policy panacea will use, reflecting our discussion from Chapter 4. Policy panaceas tend to favour more measurable factors such as quantitative rules over qualitative rules. They also tend to favour direct allocations of rights and endowments, as these are less complex than indirect processes which, as we discussed in the section on access in Chapter 4, are more subtle and less formally legible.

But as the saying goes, "the map is not the territory". Formal depictions should not be confused for the informal reality on the ground. A term that encapsulates the departure of the de facto from the de jure is the "paper park", or a park that exists only on paper (formally), but not in reality (informally). It is always easier to draw up a park on a map than it is to enforce the rules and norms associated with this park.

What are the downsides of this analytical simplification? One of Scott's main concerns is that this simplification is imposed on the target system it was initially claiming to describe (say with the replacement of common property with individual property). This resonates with Easterly's argument that top-down governance tends more to replace existing systems than adapt to them. Scott also argues that, because the more complex and invisible reality that is then undercut is essential to the functioning of the overall system, the system itself begins to deteriorate and become less resilient (Holling & Meffe 1996). Thus, programmes that optimize for the most measurable variables may not be able to sustain themselves in the long run, or ultimately promote the changes that they seek. In his critique of what he calls metric fixation, Muller (2018: 156) argues that there is a negative relationship between measurability and transformative potential: that the more we focus on what can be measured, the less likely we are to affect lasting change.

An important critique of top-down, formalized governance is that it in fact misses the most fundamental drivers of behaviour: intrinsic motivations based on social norms and values. This resonates with the framing offered by Meadows (1999), who offers a hierarchy of leverage points for changing complex systems, from the most proximate to the most underlying. She places "rules" as the fourth category, less fundamental than (3) the distribution of power over such rules, (2) the goals of the system, and (1) the paradigm that gives rise to the system.

Gamification

Earlier in this chapter we talked about the dynamics of extrinsic motivation and motivational crowding, and most of the literature on crowding has focused on the incentives of the recipients of the incentives. But what about the incentives of policy makers and implementers? Another concern with the analytical simplification described in the previous section is that it can crowd out intrinsic motivations. This reflects our discussion in Chapter 3, where we used the example of a loss of intrinsic motivation on the part of health-care professionals, who had started to see their patients as flat lists of symptoms to be treated rather than as whole people. How this transformation can unfold in the context of a policy design and implementation is described by what Nguyen (2020) refers to as gamification, or the application of values and principles from a game context to real life. Nguyen argues that the primary function of games is to provide participants with agency. In the language of self-determination theory, games provide us with a sense of efficacy, one of our basic needs. They do this in large part by simplifying our decision space, giving us clear signals about what success looks like, and not making players wait too long for at least incremental rewards. Most games are also highly simplified in terms of the criteria for success: there is almost always a point system or a set of win criteria.

Nguyen argues that games offer a respite from a world that is otherwise deeply motivationally challenging, without incremental rewards that show us how we are progressing along a linear path. They offer us the chance to pick up a new identity and provide identifiable criteria for success and socially visible accomplishment. The panacea designer then is like a game designer, who shows how implementers can gain points by following the constraints of the game.

A major problem with games when they are applied to "real life", as Nguyen describes, is that they change our motivations. The main concept that Nguyen uses to describe this is value capture. This is the process by which our multiple values are replaced with the highly simplified criteria for success as measured by a game. We become preoccupied with winning based on simple criteria, and the one goal that matters becomes intrinsically important to us, with everything else becoming instrumental. The modern gamification of life is ubiquitous, and Nguyen (2020: 201) provides several examples that hit home to me:

> You might start to use a fitness tracker like FitBit, which measures the number of steps you take per day, for the sake of your health but, over time, come to chase only high step counts. Or you might go into academia for the love of wisdom and truth, but come out of graduate school valuing only publication in high-status journals and measurable research impact factors. Or you might get onto Twitter for the sake of communication and connection, but come to value high numbers of likes and retweets.

I like this quotation in part because it helps to demonstrate that the issues we are discussing in this chapter are widespread. When I was growing up, my brothers and I would sometimes play Dungeons and Dragons, a tabletop role-playing game where you get to imagine that you are someone else with extravagant powers living in a world where thoughts of danger bring excitement without the genuine risk. I would gaze at my "character sheet", a piece of paper that documented all the important aspects of my alternate identity that seemed so much more interesting than myself. I have thought about how similar this behaviour is to the way that academics look upon our "Google Scholar" pages which publicly document our publications and citations. Are we not also looking at an alternate version of ourselves with a mix of pride and insecurity?

In his podcast Plain English, Derek Thompson suggests a theory that "the incentive structure of modern science encourages too much research that doesn't serve any purpose except to get published. In other words, science has a bullshit paper problem" (Thompson 2023). I have written that academia faces its own type of collective action problem via the arms race of publishing (Cox & Schoon 2020), where more and more papers must be written because of the deflation of the value of papers, which occurs because more and more papers are written and so on, reflecting the common issue of oversupply not unlike the collective action problems faced by say dairy farmers who produce too much milk. And this is based partly on the simplistic framing that scientific knowledge is a public good, and therefore cannot be overproduced (since this framing argues that we are only worried about under-provision of public goods). In Thompson's conversation with Professor Robert Funk, they frame this as the "paradox of choice", which is a critique applied to the capitalistic proliferation of products available to consumers. Also relevant here is Goodhart's law (which also goes by Campbell's law) that states that once a measurable variable has become a performance metric, it motivates strategic behaviour that undercuts its own validity. And Thompson's theory illustrates a critical point, that what is supposed to be an instrumental good, the implementation of a policy or the publication of a paper, becomes seen as an inherent good. The inputs become the outputs and scaling up is seen as good for its own sake.

This can also occur when the proliferation of a certain policy becomes seen as progress, which is also encouraged because in this case this input is much more easily measured than the outputs it might enable. And so we have protected areas placed in highly mountainous areas where they are not serving any purpose other than to add to the metric of "formally protected area" (in language we will use in Chapter 9, they don't provide any additionality). Arguably, some parts of the 30 by 30 initiative (conserve 30 per cent of the world by 2030) suffer from an opposite version of the same problem by disregarding the presence of humans throughout much of earth's surface when arguing for massively upscaling formal area-based protection. The cost–benefit calculations promoting this goal have been argued to embody the terra nullius assumption that disregards current property ownership, and that has been used on other settler colonial contexts (Kashwan *et al.* 2021).

Conclusion

The term panacea has a negative connotation because it is generally used to criticize prescriptive overreach. But several caveats present themselves. First, there is no part of the panacea problem that predicts that a policy solution will necessarily fail. Assuming this would be going too far, arguing against one policy potentially in favour of some alternative solution that is in danger of being treated like a panacea. A policy panacea may be associated with a positive outcome, although even in this case, we need to understand why to also avoid giving it undue credit. As we shall discuss in Chapter 9, some policies are given more credit than they deserve, as sometimes what makes them work is complementing them with other policies, or with more idiosyncratic factors like the personalities in the room. The problem with panacea thinking is that it can foreclose the option to think about the diversity of options available to us, and how elements of this diversity might work together.

A second caveat is that the aspects of the panacea problem we have discussed cannot be entirely avoided, or maybe it is better to say that we wouldn't want to entirely avoid them given the benefits that some measure of formalization and centralization can have. I have framed this discussion as a "problem" because of the audience that I have imagined for this book being people who are interested in implementing policies and inherently interested in formal generalizations, and I think anyone who calls themselves a policy expert needs to be sensitive to the trade-offs and potential pitfalls of policy development and implementation.

Finally, some of the criticisms levied at panacea thinking can be applied to these same criticisms. Just like the different groups identified with different policy solutions, we can think of a group that prides itself on critiquing what others are doing, bemoaning the complexities that others miss in their analytical simplifications. I think this is itself a trap that we can fall into, one tinged with its own type of pride and social identity and potential overreach. It is easier to tear down than to build up. Or as the saying goes, when you have a hammer the whole world looks like a nail, and critique itself can feel like an empowering hammer.

With all of this in mind, we now proceed to consider specific types of environmental property regimes, starting with the relationship between individual and collective property.

7

Individual and common property

In the previous chapter, we explored the idea of a policy panacea. In this chapter we build on this discussion by unpacking the idea of a property regime, which broadly points to who owns the environment. Because the panaceas that we discuss in this book make assumptions about the actors involved, unpacking the concept of property regimes help us understand policy panaceas.

In this chapter and the next chapter, we will address three interrelated questions. First, what do we mean when we talk about a particular property regime, such as individual or public or common property? Second, what are the relationships between these types of property? And third, is there evidence that one or another type of property performs better than the others?

To begin to answer these questions, this chapter focuses on the difference between individual and common property. And to do this, we need to clarify what we mean by each of these property regimes. Common property is an example of collective property, and means ownership by a community. Collective property can also mean ownership by a non-profit organization, by a corporation, or by a state. Individual property means property by individuals, and is often referred to with the term "private property". But private property really means ownership by any actor other than the state, and so includes other collective property regimes. There is thus a spectrum of ownership from the most individual to the most collective, and to me the transition to the collective level occurs when we move beyond the household unit, even though households are technically made up of multiple individuals.

Let's return to the hypothetical scenario of the Dominican fishery where I have worked. In Chapters 4 and 5, we explored the different rules that the fishers could use to create a system of property rights. But unasked in those chapters was, should the fishers adopt a more individual or common property regime? A tension exists between individual and common property that reflects the divergence between individual and group interests discussed in Chapter 1. Should rights be granted to individuals for their benefit or to the group for its collective benefit? Or can the two types of ownership work together? In this chapter we will unpack what we mean by each type of property, consider the relationships between them, and explore arguments in favour of each one.

Common and individual property

In this first section, we begin by exploring the nature of common property, which as we will see, includes individual property. From here we explore the common situation of common and individual property existing side-by-side, and relate this to arguments about the relative merits of form of property under certain environmental conditions.

Nested institutions

Individual and common property are not mutually exclusive, as is commonly assumed. Rather, the conceptual boundaries between rights regimes are fuzzy. To understand this, we need to unpack what we mean by common property. What does it mean to say that a community "owns" say, a plot of land? This is potentially confusing because individuals within the community use land or some other resource that the community "owns". Common property is a situation in which a community grants usufruct rights to its members over parts of that property (Bromley 1992; Cronon 2011: 65)

A usufruct right, as introduced in Chapter 2, is a right to use or otherwise benefit from a property that belongs to someone else for specific purposes and under certain conditions. Usually, usufruct rights are imagined to be granted to an individual actor by another individual actor (e.g., I can walk through someone's property). But applying this to community ownership is straightforward. If, for example, a community owns a fishery, members of that fishing community are granted fishing rights, which generally means that they can physically access the fishery to extract certain types of fish for a certain period of time and/or with certain gear.

We can better understand this situation through what Ellickson (1993: 1334) refers to as external general-purpose boundaries and internal special-purpose boundaries. General purpose boundaries are more exclusionary, while special purpose boundaries are specific to a certain set of rights and a subset of a larger resource. As Ellickson says, owning property generally involves both external and internal rights. In the context of common property, there is a general-purpose boundary around a resource that a community owns, and within this boundary, members of the community are granted special purpose individual rights. And this ties back to our discussion of rigid versus contextual boundaries from Chapter 2: special purpose boundaries tend to be more contextual, and general boundaries tend to be more rigid.

Usufruct or special purpose individual property rights are nested inside common property regimes. And this relationship can be reversed: common property regimes can grant usufruct-type rights to communities on individually owned land, as it does, for example, in the New Mexico acequias, who have what are referred to as easements, or rights of access, to individual parcels in order to maintain irrigation ditches that travel along and through such parcels.

This nesting scales up as well. Reflecting the distinction between intra- and intergroup cooperation, we need to also distinguish between common property that exists within a group, which is often what we imagine with the term, and common property that occurs among several groups. Ellickson calls this "horde" property. I saw an example of the difference between intragroup property and intergroup property in my work on the New Mexico acequias. Each could be described as common property, but the details were different. Within acequias, farmers had rights expressed in units of time, and took turns conveying the water onto their fields. Mayordomos historically patrolled the canals, and organized ditch cleanings, with each landowner required to contribute. Between acequias, agreements known as repartimientos were used. These often relied on proportional physical divisions of the water to different communities and were implemented by representatives of each of the communities, who would meet in times of drought in order to reassure each other that they would share the water in times of scarcity.

Comparing individual acequias with inter-acequia agreements here resonates with Ellickson's comparison of individual and common property. Ellickson argues that for what he calls "small events", individual property is better, but for larger, rarer events, more coordination is required. Ellickson (1993: 1329) also describes the advantage of individual property over common property: "a shift from group to individual ownership of land substitutes the relatively cheap systems of self-control and boundary monitoring for the relatively costly system of pervasive intragroup monitoring". But one could say the same thing about a shift from inter-community property to community property. This comparison to me highlights how helpful the multilevel perspective promoted by Wilson (2016) and discussed in Chapter 2 is: we stop thinking about "individuals" as being only single people and think about them more from the perspective of a level in a social hierarchy. This is particularly helpful to remember in the context of collective action. For just as we can have collective action problems among individual people in a group, we can have a higher-level collective action problem among individual groups within a larger group, and much of the same logic remains.

Competitors or complements?

Insisting on clear boundaries between concepts is arguably a Western perspective, and this may also reflect a difference between European and some Indigenous land rights systems, as documented by Lockhart (1992) and cited by Sauls, Galeana and Lawry (2022). Lockhart, who studied the Nahua people of Central America, argued that there were clearer distinctions between private and public property in European systems than in the Indigenous communities he studied. He described the institutional nesting of the Nahua, from the *altepetl* (city-state) to *calpulli* (neighbourhood) to the household and individual. There is a gradient from one property regime to the next within this system, with ongoing tensions at the boundaries between each regime, with each wanting to capture more property for itself. Two conclusions we can draw from this are that the boundaries between property regimes are fuzzy, and that there are political tensions between individual and common property and other types of collective ownership based over who gets to own what.

Despite these tensions, individual and common property can complement each other based on the relative adaptiveness of each to context. In a classic study of the commons and property, Netting (1976: 144) presents several attributes that are conducive to common property (with the implication being that the opposite values are more amenable to individual property). I have used these attributes as the basis for my own list of factors that favour the use of common property: (1) resource availability is low and unpredictable; (2) there are public goods present that if provided would help all members, and these are characterized by economies of scale; and (3) risks are present that require coordination to mitigate.

In many situations, the first item is a driver of each of the second two, and we can start by exploring an example that illustrates how the first item leads to the second. In the acequia irrigation systems that I studied in Taos, New Mexico, the irrigation infrastructure and the water it conveys were held as common property. And this pattern is extremely common around the world, which poses several questions. First, why is water held as common property? The first part of the answer is that this is a dry area with little production value and unpredictable water availability. The practice of agriculture therefore requires building an irrigation system, and there are significant economies of scale with such infrastructure, since one headgate and canal off of a river can serve multiple sub-canals and fields; it is thus a public good. Building the irrigation system requires that individuals work together to produce the needed canals and headgates off local rivers (the collective action problem). The common property water regime follows from this as a means for ensuring that the benefits of irrigation are shared reasonably among those who paid the costs for the infrastructure with time, labour or in some cases, money. Common property is made available based on capital inputs, which was discussed as an allocational principle in Part II.

Another instance of the public good argument can be found in common interest communities, better known as homeowner associations (HOAs) in the United States (Lehavi 2008). These combine privately owned residences with commonly owned public spaces such as hallways and lawns, which make more sense to be held in common because of their economies of scale: it is less efficient to create an individual hallway to each person's apartment in a building rather than share hallways, or to create a separate common green space for each resident. HOAs can also include "limited common" spaces such as patios which don't include economies of scale, but the use of which is perceived to impact other homeowners. The possibility of such negative externalities or spillover effects is a primary concern with decentralized governance, and while I don't view it as necessarily an argument against individual property in this case, as I think it is correctly used to constrain the rights associated with individual property.

Common property as an adaptation to scarcity and risk

An additional component of the acequia system, as well as the Swiss communities that inspired Netting's work, is that irrigated lands near rivers are always held individually, and drier, non-irrigated lands used for pasture are held in common, with individual and common property held side-by-side, similarly to the previous HOA example. And why does it make sense to have pastures owned in common? The answer is the same argument we saw for contextual boundaries, which as we have now discussed, common property generally entails. Common property therefore provides a flexible mechanism to ensure access to a resource under conditions of scarcity and unpredictability. At the same time, it is important to note that flexibility is not necessarily thwarted by individual property, if, for example, individuals can exchange temporary use rights with each other to adapt to fluctuations in scarcity and need as we discussed in Chapter 5.

In the acequia governance system and others like it, access to water or pasture as common property is largely based on the ownership of individually held agricultural plots that associate a farmer with a larger group through a version of the proximity principle, which bases ownership of one resource on the ownership of a nearby resource. This is an extremely common relationship between individual and common property, although access to the commons is not always limited to landowners; in some cases it may be extended, for example, to others whose labour is important to landowners as an expression of reciprocity (Zückert 2014). Thus, in many systems, land is owned individually and communally, side-by-side. In some instances, the same land can cycle between individual and communal ownership if, for example, cows are allowed onto farm fields to graze on stubble once crops have been harvested, thereby also suppling agricultural fields with nutrients via their manure (Zückert 2014).

As the acequia example illustrates, one of the most prominent functions of common property is to adapt to scarcity. A similar scenario plays out in many pastoralist systems. Niamir-Fuller (1999: 105), whose work we discussed in Chapter 2 with respect to contextual boundaries, describes the patterns that many African pastoralists must adapt to: low rainfall leading to low and unpredictable productivity across a landscape:

> The drier the ecosystem is, the greater is the incentive to manage the natural resource communally. In arid lands, uncertainty is high, and the risks of production and survival are higher. The risk burden is too much for an individual to bear; therefore, common-property regimes are devised to share the risk and spread the burden. The productivity of arid and semi-arid lands is both marginal and variable, and therefore these areas have a benefit–cost ratio that discourages investment in exclusionary, private, mechanisms.

Agrawal (1998) discusses the relationship between pastoralism and the choice between collective versus individual property, noting that the Raikas of India travel in groups, thereby engaging in common property. The reasons that Agrawal proposes for this largely have to do with risk mitigation and economies of scale. In terms of economies of scale, the herders can work together in groups to provide security for their flocks more efficiently, and they can conduct the business of herding more efficiently as well (while one herder may be able to manage and protect 100 animals, two can manage 300). Agrawal also mentions that herders have more agency in local markets when they act collectively, which in the United States is referred to as collective bargaining.

There are other examples from other resource sectors. In the fisheries sector, (Holland 2018) describes the potential advantages of collective fishing rights within the context of fisheries governance and catch shares policies, which we shall discuss in further depth in Chapter 9. One of Holland's arguments is that pooling fishing rights could reduce individual risk if fishers can make transfers between each other to balance their "portfolios", which mirrors the insurance function described in the pastoral sector. More specifically, Holland (2018) explains how "risk pools" can help individual fishers adapt to risk associated with the limited quota for "choke species". These are species with low catch limits, such that if a fisher catches them even incidentally as bycatch, they may be forced to stop fishing. A response to reduce this risk in some places has been for fishers to pool their fishing rights of bycatch species into a pool, reflecting the risk-sharing function of common property described earlier.

In conclusion, there are reasons when individual versus collective rights might be preferred. While I took a rather asymmetric approach to this discussion, the underlying argument provides just as strong support for the use of individual rights under situations of high resource availability, low risk, and few interdependencies resulting from the presence of public goods.

Excludability

Readers who are familiar with traditional arguments about common versus individual property may have expected excludability to be on the list of factors above. The traditional argument is that excludability favours private (usually assumed to be individual) property. And there is an intuition behind this: I have argued that common property includes flexible, contextual boundaries, and exclusion sounds more rigid: if I put up a fence, which is the single most prominent type of physical exclusion, this represents a loss of flexibility. The invention of barbed wire and its availability at scale has been associated with the enclosure of pasture commons in the western United States.

This said, I think the argument that excludability promotes individual property is overly simplistic. To understand why, we need to remember that excludability, as I discussed in Chapter 2, is a relational concept: while it is supposedly describing a natural resource's inherent characteristics, it is also describing the social and technological context of this resource. Excludability is also assuming a particular scale: excludable by whom? The argument that excludability promotes individual property assumes that we are talking about excludability by individuals: it is assuming an individual's perspective. But if we are talking about excludability by a community, then the same logic holds: if a community can exclude outsiders from using a resource, then this helps promote common property. Or, if a state can also use barbed wire and put a fence all around a protected area, then this enables state property. The issue of excludability then does not point towards a particular property regime; it is simply a statement about the "ownability" of a resource.

Individuals and communities

So far, we have discussed common and individual property without much of a discussion of the nature of the actors claiming ownership. And a key component of this discussion is the extent to which such actors are thought to be able to act in their own self-interest, in other words as unitary actors. Arguments for individual rights are often referred to simply with arguments for property rights in general, and individuals have a special place in the pantheon of property regimes because of their supposedly unique degree of self-interest. Arguments for individual property rely on an assumption that individuals know what is best for their single self, and the theory of environmental reciprocity that we introduced in Chapter 2 implies this. For what this theory argues is that an actor will invest in the environment if the state of this environment impacts their future interest. But if there is not a clear sense of this interest, then the mechanism for this theory falls apart. So, how self-interested are we individually, or collectively? In the rest of this chapter I present reasons to question the unitary nature of both communities and individuals.

Before proceeding, we should also acknowledge that our ability to act self-interestedly (at the individual or collective level) is itself a function of property rights. This follows straightforwardly our discussion in Chapter 2 of the role of boundaries around groups in promoting collective action. And property rights are a kind of boundary. This endogeneity of interest to property regime was demonstrated empirically in a recent article by Kaur, Chang and Andersson (2023). Based on an observational analysis of forest user groups and a behavioural experiment, the authors argue that receiving de jure collective rights promotes cohesion and collective action within groups. One conclusion from this is that, with respect to property regimes and the importance of self-interest, any property regime can be at least somewhat self-fulfilling, promoting self-interest at its level of ownership.

Gendered interests and divergent adaptation

I want to further unpack the non-unitary character of communities by discussing an important dimension that has so far been underemphasized in this book: the different interests of men and women. Women's interests and preferences often diverge from men's, both within households and within their larger communities. Part of this is biological: women bear larger biological costs of reproduction than do men regardless of culture, and surveys have shown that across cultures men tend to prefer larger family sizes than do women

(Duflo & Banerjee 2011). And it doesn't stop there. Women systematically do more childcare, more unpaid and invisible work that doesn't show up on economic indicators biased towards formal exchange value, and have fewer economic resources and therefore less bargaining power within the household (Perez 2019). Duflo and Banerjee (2011: 116) report on a study in Peru (Field 2004) that found that if women were granted greater property rights, fertility declined, with one explanation being that "with her name on a property title, the woman acquired more bargaining power in the family and was therefore able to weigh more heavily on the decision of family size".

Historically, household-level data has been used to measure asset and wealth levels (Kilic, Moylan & Koolwal 2021), but this commits the ecological fallacy of assuming that we can use an aggregate statistic for a group to infer the attributes of its members, and we usually cannot in the case of households. A study by Kieran *et al.* (2017) in Bangladesh, Tajikistan, Timor-Leste and Vietnam, for example, has shown that gender gaps in land rights persist even as household wealth increases.

Women also have different preferences than men within households because of their cultural roles. This is powerfully seen in the history of improved cook stoves, which is a common example of the inability of a new technology to gain traction despite it offering some obvious social and environmental benefits. In most cultures women do more of the cooking than do men, and so have different perspectives on what is needed for the activity and what the effects of it are. In the case of traditional cook stoves, this means that women experience the harmful effects of indoor smoke more than the average man. But women also tend to have less access to economic resources of their own and are less often the decision-makers regarding household finances. This leads to a finding in India that when women are empowered as decision-makers, the household they are a part of is more likely to purchase clean-burning technologies (Gould & Urpelainen 2020).

The bovine mystique and gendered rights

In this section I want to explore the two main assumptions about communities as rights-holders. First that they are adaptive, and second, that they are unitary. One of the main arguments in favour of allocating rights to communities is the idea that local communities adapt their institutions to local circumstances based on the argument for common property just discussed as well as concepts like "local ecological knowledge" (Berkes 2018) and "customary tenure" arrangements (Sauls, Galeana & Lawry 2022). The great advantage of the adaptationist perspective that supports such arguments is that it opens our eyes to the functional possibilities around us, which otherwise we might discard as "irrational". From this perspective, any cultural trait is fair game to be interpreted as an adaptation to local circumstances.

The primary trap we can fall into in identifying adaptations is to be a naive adaptationist: to infer that if something exists and has for some time, that it must have gone through some evolutionarily selective process and therefore be adaptive. But as I have discussed on multiple occasions, such evolutionary thinking about institutional evolution as an optimizing process can be a trap that hides the significance of political conflict and inequality. This presumption that a given trait is adaptive ignores other possible reasons for the persistence of a trait. Evolutionary biologists have long been aware of this problematic inference (Gould & Lewontin 1979). Within the social sciences there exists a somewhat similar debate over functionalism, or the assumption that institutions arise for some collective benefit, as opposed to through social conflict (Knight 1992).

The story that Ferguson (1994) tells about a development project in the mountain kingdom of Lesotho illustrates these points well, and shows us just how non-unitary communities and the households within them can be. Ferguson describes several outsider interpretations of a tradition among Basotho livestock owners in rural Lesotho known as the "bovine mystique". This tradition places cattle in a special category of property that cannot be simply bought or sold the way that other goods in the Basotho society can. Rather, cattle are seen more as an investment to plan for the future and less as a commodity. Ferguson (1994) describes one hypothetical explanation posed by outsiders of the bovine mystique being that Lesotho is still an "underdeveloped country", meaning that it simply has not proceeded far enough down the developmental path to a more market-oriented economy for Basotho people to think about trading cows as commodities, reflecting the pseudo-evolutionary discourse that we have seen before, and which we reflected on in the previous chapter as a part of the panacea problem.

Another interpretation of this behaviour was based on what has been referred to elsewhere as the "safety-first" principle (Scott 1977). This being the argument that "when individuals face a choice between economic strategies, they will select the strategy that gives them the lowest probability of falling below some 'subsistence threshold' or economic minimum, regardless of the expected yields generated by alternative strategies" (Henrich & McElreath 2002: 173). And to call this a "just-so story" is unfair, insofar as the term is popularly used to describe hypotheses that haven't been put to the test. Henrich and McElreath, for example, conducted an experiment with several distinct cultural groups and found only limited support for the safety-first hypothesis, although they acknowledge that their results do not bear as directly on the principle as they could have. Nevertheless, Ferguson's discussion implies that some external actors were making a "safety first" assumption about the behaviour of local actors.

This is also a case where local communities seem to be resisting the pull of commodification (of their cattle), and the market integration that elsewhere has found to be detrimental to community-oriented natural resource use and management.

To understand Ferguson's alternative interpretation, we have to start with the idea of what he calls a "category interest", or a type of person identified by their combination of interests. This concept emphasizes the fact that one's interests and the way one experiences the world result from a combination of our characteristics (e.g., gender, sex, age, ethnicity, job, nationality), rather than just one characteristic at a time. One prominent category interest in Ferguson's story is the young male migrant worker. Ferguson describes how the majority of wealth in rural Lesotho is garnered by young men who go to South Africa to work in the mines. During this time, they accrue livestock with the money from their wages. Basotho women are not permitted to do the same.

The unusual position of cattle as a kind of property extends beyond the fact that they are not straightforwardly commodified. In addition, there is a norm that assigns them to be the property of Basotho men within a household, rather than of women. Other types of property are more contestable. It is therefore advantageous for a man to keep wealth in livestock, since it empowers him within his household (while disempowering women). Because of this, the special place that cattle have is in fact constantly contested between Basotho men, most of whom spend most of their working lives in the mines of South Africa, and Basotho women. To men, cattle are an investment, a retirement fund for them to draw upon once they are back in Lesotho and retired from the mines. To women, this takes away from the needs of their household in the near future. So, the bovine mystique does represent an adaptation – by men to the gender norms that allocate livestock as a male property. It is an adaptation within the household that enables men to save money – often for themselves – into the future. But this falls far short of the collective or holistic scenario that is evoked by functionalism or adaptationism. It is instead what Snorek, Renaud and Kloos (2014) refer to as divergent adaptation: an adaptation by one group that imposes costs on and creates vulnerabilities for other groups. This is also similar to the concept of a negative externality that we first saw in Chapter 1.

A final part of the story that Ferguson tells relates to elder men. Their position is different from young men, in that they have retired from mine work, and no longer have access to the same level of remuneration as they used to. Older men, Ferguson argues, also have a vested interest in the bovine mystique, as they are able to benefit from it through marriage payments known as "bridewealth" through which a young man getting married generally has to pay his in-laws. Custom holds that this is often paid in cattle. A similar pattern emerges: if a husband comes into some wealth of some other variety, this is not owed to his in-laws. But if it is cattle, then they will have some claim to it.

While Ferguson acknowledges that the story he tells is somewhat tentative, it does sound more realistic than the simple safety-first explanation because of its complexity and the presence of multiple competing interests. Social systems involve constant tension and synergy between cooperation and competition. Working within the communities of our own lives, I think this is how we understand things to be. And we shouldn't be too tempted by the supposed dichotomy of adaptation versus interests, as there are clearly elements of both here: young men are adapting to their own situations to maximize their own interest, and there are elements of the bovine mystique that could be interpreted to be in the interest of the larger community in the form of the patron–client relationships that livestock owners have with others. And yet the women who Ferguson describes as disempowered by this situation presumably do not see these aspects of their culture as adaptive. One of Ferguson's most important points is that the situation is fluid and constantly being recreated by its participants: you don't just adapt and then you're done, since interests and conflict don't go away. As a final point, we should always ask ourselves when talking about an adaptation, adaptation for whom? Ferguson's story is a story of adaptation, by the men who are adapting to a combination of circumstances including a gender-based norm that grants them priority rights over livestock.

The ultimate unitary actor?

From the previous section we should question the unitary nature of communities and consider the implications this has for common property. Does this then turn us to individual property as the best option? For many of us, being unitary is a part of our sense of self: that we are one thing, not many (Gazzaniga 2012). To have several selves is sometimes pathologized, and we face pressures to present one face to the world. As Henrich describes, in Western societies, we are particularly invested in the primacy of the unitary individual and inclined to attribute agency and identity to this level before others (such as the communities we engage with). Building on the unitary actor assumption, the discipline of economics often assumes that individuals are "rationally self-interested". Notice that they are "self" interested, not "selves" interested; an assumption of unitary identity is baked in here.

The behavioural economics literature has identified a litany of exceptions to these assumptions, labelling these as biases (Thaler & Sunstein 2009). This is arguably an outcome of the field insisting on sticking with a standard model, forcing future findings to adapt to the dominance of this idea. As Collins (2015: np) argues, "behavioural economics has some similarities to the state of astronomy in 1500 – it is still at the collection of deviation stage. There aren't 165 human biases. There are 165 deviations from the wrong model." Labelling a behaviour as a (supposedly universal) bias is fine in one way, because it reflects the fact that none of us have uniquely privileged access to objectivity. At the same time, it disregards the fact that there are adaptive reasons for our many so-called irrational behaviours. Collins (2015) advocates for what he refers to as an "evolutionary rationality" that understands that we have multiple adaptations to specific challenges, and our success in addressing our current challenges will depend on how well they match these previous challenges. This is the standard interpretation associated with the field of evolutionary psychology.

Multiple schools of psychology and neuroscience and their leading figures, including William James and Carl Jung, have argued for the multiplicity of the self (Gazzaniga 2012; Van der Kolk 2015). Similarly, the subdiscipline of evolutionary psychology has argued that the mind is made up of adapted modules that have each evolved to fulfil their own function: the self is run by committee, not by an executive (Kurzban 2012). And there is no part of the brain that knows everything that the other parts know. Even within a single brain, there is such a thing as "local knowledge".

One prominent example of these different modules comes from the field of behavioural economics, where it is commonly argued that human beings have two dominant methods for processing information and making decisions, commonly labelled as our more automatic (fast) versus deliberative (slow) systems (Kahneman 2011). Our automatic systems rely on heuristics and are rife with biases that can steer us towards poor decisions for ourselves and others. The most well-known policy-relevant outcome of this work is the "nudge" movement, led by Richard Thaler and others (Thaler & Sunstein 2009). This movement recognizes that our heuristics often lead us to make decisions that, upon reflection, we would consider to be against our best "interest". From this perspective the goal of policymakers is to nudge our automatic systems towards more prosocial behaviours.

In reading this literature, the picture of the mind and the self that appears is more of a federation of agents, each of which is jockeying with the others for attention and to emerge to consciousness, direct attention and behaviour. An important governance implication of this is that we ought to consider how our institutions engage with our different modules, just as we should consider how policies impact the power relationships among different individuals in a household, community, firm or agency.

We have seen an example of this in Chapter 3, where we described how some indigenous institutions build on our psychologies of kinship and reciprocity. Each of these can be thought of as its own behavioural module, with a set of rules for governing perception and behaviour. Recognition of such institutions and the adaptive role they can play is implicitly dependent on this modular theory of the mind.

Conclusion

Individual and common property have a complicated relationship. Common property includes individual usufruct property through special-purpose boundaries, and in many instances common and individual property are found side-by-side. Despite this, much of the discourse surrounding these arrangements focuses on which is preferrable overall. In response, we should be leery of assumptions regarding the nature of individuality, particularly based on Western cultural arguments that dismiss the role that society plays, and we should be sceptical of the romanticization of common ownership based on a narrative that in Western cultures we have been led astray, away from our communal roots, even if this may to some extent be true. Common ownership means having to deal with other people and their personalities and their problems and sometimes their unwillingness to contribute, all of which we might ignore when we are only theorizing about common property and not actively participating in it ourselves. Just as common property can empower communities, individual property can empower individuals, which matters for the same reasons. Individual property also facilitates market exchange, since it is easier for one individual to agree to a transaction than it is for dozens, although as we discussed in Chapter 5, this is a double-edged sword with both benefits and potential costs.

Having considered individual and common property and their relationships, we now add a third actor: the state.

8

States and hybrid regimes

In the previous chapter, I introduced three questions. First, what do we mean when we talk about a particular property regime, such as individual or public or common property? Second, what are the relationships between these types of property? And third, is there evidence that one or another type of property performs better than the others? In this chapter we continue to address these questions by adding more complexity to our discussion by considering the nature and behaviour of state actors with regard to the environment and the other forms of property we have examined.

We begin this chapter by examining the third question about the superiority of any given property regime. Most studies that have looked at this question have compared individual, common, and public property. We review this literature, and conclude that the emphasis on broad categories of ownership has been overblown relative to their importance in explaining outcomes. One reason for this pertains to our first question about the nature of property regimes: broad categories of ownership are not always very meaningful because they are very vague terms, which we problematized in our discussion of generality in Chapter 6. There is a lot of variation within each property regime category relative to the variation between categories, which does not reflect a successful classification scheme. For example, in some cases small-scale corporate property has a lot more in common with common property than with large-scale international corporations. As we saw in Chapters 4 and 5, much of this analytical cloudiness comes from how bundles of rights are distributed across actors. In the second section of the chapter we discuss how the distribution of bundles of rights complicates the meaning of property regimes.

While much attention has been paid to whether or not one property regime is better than the others, our discussion will point us back to the other two questions: what do we mean when we talk about a specific property regime, and how do regimes relate to each other? We spend the remainder of the chapter answering these two questions in more depth, with a primary focus on the relationships that have existed between states and public property and communities and common property. We conclude with a discussion of a new legal movement to bestow nature itself with environmental rights and discuss the assumptions of this perspective and how feasible it may be as a new approach to environmental governance.

Empirical evidence comparing property regimes

What empirical evidence is there that one property regime may perform better than others? One research programme that has dedicated substantial time and effort in answering this question is the International Forestry Resources and Institutions (IFRI) research programme. The IFRI began at the Ostrom Workshop at Indiana University, and has involved a network of 12 collaborating research centres across 11 countries. This programme has studied forest governance mostly in the Global South across 241 unique sites and 350 forests in 17 countries over time. Ostrom and Cole (2012: 51–2) provide a summary of IFRI findings with respect to property rights and governance:

> IFRI research shows that forests under different property regimes (government, private, or communal) sometimes meet enhanced social goals, such as biodiversity protection, carbon storage, or improved livelihoods. At other times, any of these general property systems may fail to meet such goals. Thus, it is not the general system of property rights used for forest governance that is crucial in predicting whether forest conditions are sustainable. Rather, it is how a particular governance arrangement fits the local ecology, how the specific rules of a governance regime are developed and adapted over time, and whether users consider the system to be legitimate and equitable ... Property rights are indeed important in affecting resource conditions, but the general names assigned to government, private, or community property regimes do not discriminate among the types of rules used in practice.

In short, much of the IFRI work has found that the most important factors are not the property regimes themselves, but the accompanying governance processes that exist to enforce institutions. And what about work that has compared regimes across sectors? Ojanen *et al.* (2017) conducted a systematic review of 80 studies that compared the regimes of government, individual, common and some mixed property regimes for forests, fisheries and rangelands. The cases described by the studies came from Latin America, Africa and Asia in roughly equal numbers. The authors failed to find that any single property regime regularly performed better than others when it came to improving the state of the environment, although each regime performed better than no regime, or open access. Interestingly, they found that those cases examining fisheries governance mostly compared a regime to an open-access condition rather than to an alternative regime, which is more likely to favourably evaluate the regime being analysed. The authors also note that most studies do not extensively explore how parts of the property rights bundle are allocated to which actors, and tend to define property concepts inconsistently. This variation and lack of detail makes it more difficult to uncover broad trends.

One way to interpret these results is to think back to our discussion of common versus individual property in the previous chapter. There, the main argument wasn't that either regime is better than the other per se, but that it depended on local conditions. If this is true, then we are unlikely to find broad trends that don't account for such conditionality. These findings also point us to our next topics, which start with the problem of vagueness that characterizes how we talk about these different property regimes, and that some of this vagueness comes from the diversity with which bundles of rights can be distributed across actors in a given case.

Diversity of regimes

In Chapter 6, I criticized excessively vague arguments and concepts such as tenure security for their lack of meaning. The problem of excessive vagueness also impacts discourses about property regimes (Ellickson 1993: 1322). By public, after all, we mean government property, not a literal public, whose interests are presumed to be represented by a state actor. And if private is everything that is not public property, that could be a lot of different things, including for example individual property and common property as we discussed in Chapter 7. Because of this gap in meaning, we tend to fill it with our own assumptions and images of what each property regime signifies. In this way, we underestimate the diversity of actors referred to by one type of property regime.

The bundles of rights concept that we unpacked in Chapters 4 and 5 help us understand heterogeneity across instances of a property regime. Different actors can have different rights bundles with respect to a natural resource: some could have rights to access a field but not develop it, others could develop it but not sell it, etc. In their classic discussion of property rights, Alchian and Demsetz (1973: 18–19) point this out:

> There is some ambiguity in the notion of state or private ownership of a resource, because the bundle of property rights associated with a resource is divisible. There can and does exist much confusion about whether a resource or "property" is state or privately owned. Some rights to some uses of the resource may be state owned and others privately owned. While it is true that the degree of private control is increased when additional rights of use become privately owned, it is somewhat arbitrary to pass judgment on when the conversion to private control can be said to change the ownership of the bundle of rights from public to private.

Saying that a regime is private tells us nothing about a whole suite of questions that we addressed in Chapters 4 and 5. How are rights distributed, and based on which principles? Which rights are allocated or withheld? The question of how rights bundles are allocated can be asked both within groups and between groups. Between groups, we might have a community of resource users having use rights but a government having control rights. Within groups, we can likewise have heterogeneity of rights endowments leading to differences in interest and in power, thus violating the unitary actor assumption introduced in Chapter 6.

Let's start by asking how this argument affects our view of common property. An idealized view of common property would bestow control rights to the community rather than the individuals, and I think to many people this partly defines what we mean by common property: that the community is in charge of collectively deciding how individuals use their shared resource. Based on this example, we can think of adopting a principle that we label a property regime based on the actor that has control rights, since these grant substantial power. But there are several ways to complicate this picture.

First, communities often have formal and informal hierarchies and local elites, and systematic gender-based and other inequalities. Sometimes, when we talk about "common" property, we are really talking about property owned by local leader, often a chief was the case in precolonial Hawaii as Vaughan (2018) mentions. Niamir-Fuller (1999), for example, describes the role of chiefs and subchiefs as having substantial control rights within pastoral property regimes in Africa. The presence of local leaders and authoritative individuals is an important complication on our understanding of communities and common property. Historically and still in modern times, in many so-called common property systems a powerful individual such as a local chief or lord of the manor has control over common property "owned" by a village.

An example of a state holding control rights comes from the case of the ejidos of Mexico, which are a longstanding, supposedly common property regime supported by the Mexican state. Here the state claims formal ownership over ejido common lands, granting ejido communities usufruct rights to formally government-owned land. In referring to this as a common property regime, we are not privileging a state's claim to formal control. Rather, we think that the most influential part of the property regime is who is actually using the resource, because it is this actor who influences the character of resource management. So we have conflicting principles for how to label a property regime.

A similar logic could apply to public property that is leased out or granted to private actors via resource concessions, often to powerful corporate actors who can act quite differently from states. In his article, "Seeing like an oil company", Ferguson (2005) argues that oil companies are distinct from states through their mobility: they are able to move from place to place, extracting resources as they go without benefitting local society. Ferguson's primary example is of an oil company in Angola, but the image is generalizable, for example to the banana empires in twentieth-century Latin America (Koeppel 2008) or forest concessions in Indonesia (Jepson *et al.* 2001).

And at the same time, we need to be wary of having this image of corporations trigger our representativeness heuristic. The reality of a corporation can range from multinational corporations all the way down to small collectives that don't look all that different from community-based governance and have aspects of common property. In the western United States, for example, irrigation and water companies have long been used as formalized vehicles for collective action among irrigators (Ostrom 2011). The concept of the corporation can also include larger, more integrated firms, or firms that only own and manage one factor of production as we discussed in Chapter 4 through the example of the transition to forest management via TIMOs and REITs.

So we have numerous complications, and we haven't touched on use entitlements or exchange rights and entitlements. As an example of this we can return to the ejidos of Mexico. Bray (2020) examined a group of ejidos who manage forest lands, known as community forest enterprises, or CFEs. This is a market-oriented community ownership model that blends common and corporate property. Bray describes the indigenous Zapotec community of San Pedro de Alto near Oaxaca, which has worked for some time with the Forest Company of Oaxaca. This company had harvested timber for the community, while the community held use and exchange entitlements. How should we think about this as a hybrid property regime that might seem to be primarily community-oriented? The community has since transitioned to obtain full rights over its forest lands.

This discussion indicates a need to systematically recognize what could be called mixed (Lehavi 2008) or hybrid property regimes (Lemos & Agrawal 2006). Using the classification scheme proposed by Lemos and Agrawal (2006), we could label the case of the San Pedro de Alto forest governance regime a private–social partnership, and the combination of state and corporate property via the resource concession example a public–private partnership.

In addition to the examples covered in this section, we have already seen an example of a hybrid regime in our discussion of individual and common property in Chapter 7. There, we observed several examples of how individual and common property are mixed within the same case. One example involved a group of farmers, each individually owning agricultural land and jointly owning a nearby pasture. Another example comes in the form of community land trusts (Lehavi 2008), which are non-profit organizations that buy up tracts of land, and then lease out homes on this land to individual homeowners, with the primary aim of making tenancy more affordable. As a final example of a hybrid regime, market-based policies, which we will discuss in Chapter 9, are often thought of as bestowing rights primarily to private actors, individually or corporately. But these often reserve control rights to determine use rights for governmental agencies.

States, communities and the commons

We have argued that it is difficult to systematically associate a particular property regime with a particular outcome, and this is due in large part to the diversity of cases that each regime describes and the relationships between regimes. To build on these observations, in this section we further unpack the nature of common property and public property, the relationship between them, and the actors involved: communities and the state. This relationship has exhibited conflicting tendencies on the part of state actors towards communities, historically with dismissiveness, and more recently with formal recognition, which, as we will discuss, can bring with it new promise as well as its own problems.

State challenges to the commons

Common property is complex. This is not to say that individual property cannot become complex through extensive formalization, for example, but collective ownership has posed a challenge to external actors. In this section we look at why common property has been dismissed and antagonized.

Common property as illegible

Common property is poorly legible to external actors, reflecting the same issue that we discussed with contextual boundaries in Chapter 2, which common property entails. In Scott's (1998) account, this resulted from the fact that common property often involves many different uses of a property by different sets of people, with these arrangements shifting informally over time. Such complexity can create an "impenetrable muddle" (Mabey 1980: 166) from the perspective of outsiders. An additional source of formal illegibility of common property may also come from the fact that communities tend to use qualitative rules rather than quantitative rules, as we discussed in Chapter 4.

Common property has been additionally illegible to the individualistic Western mindset that tends not to recognize group ownership as authentic. In colonial New England, for example, white settlers dismissed Native American land rights because they weren't legible to the Western mindset that views property claims as consisting of individually developed plots of land (Cronon 2011). This disregard culminated in what are known as the US allotment policies in the nineteenth century, which systematically privatized commonly held native property, often leading to the outright dispossession of native lands. This disregard for local property traditions has been used in many settler colonial contexts from Australia to New Zealand to South Africa, and is referred to as the terra nullius, or "empty or vacant land theory" (Verkuyten & Martinovic 2017: 1026). This represents a wilful ignorance of local traditions on the part of expansionist cultures.

Common versus open access property

Another reason for the dismissal of common property is based on the collective action problems that groups must resolve in order to manage a shared resource as we discussed in Chapter 1. It has been assumed that groups cannot resolve such problems, leading to an open access regime, with no limitations on use. "Common land" can sound like it means that it is open to anyone. And in academic and popular discourses, common or communal property is often used to refer to what is really an open access situation with few rights to exclude, with a popular corollary argument being that common property is then inherently "unstable", to be inevitably replaced with private property (Alchian & Demsetz 1973). Dunn (2000) appropriately labels much of this discourse as "armchair reasoning".

The most famous counterargument to this assumption took place in Ostrom's book *Governing the Commons*, in which she argued that communities of resource users such as fishers or groundwater users could work together to avoid the tragedy of the commons, and that this was more likely if one or more of a set of institutional design principles are present. Ostrom was not arguing for the superiority of common property, but was saying that we shouldn't disregard it as an important solution to local problems. A further argument against this framing is made by Rose (2019), who observes that any property regime is inherently a collective venture. This follows from the fact that even individual property is a claim made against a social group by an individual, and that the enforcement of such claims is itself a social process. Individual property is not thought of as being equivalent to anarchy, and so an argument against the viability of common property, if it is based on doubts about our ability to act collectively, is an argument against the viability of any property regime.

Common property as unproductive

It has long been argued that common property is less productive than other forms of property, in part because of its conflation with open access and the presumption that only with individual property will owners be incentivized to invest in their property by physically developing it, thereby increasing its productivity. Much of this argument then is about the best use of land, and arguments for the increased economic efficiency of land use have been used to justify many enclosure movements, including the famous enclosures of common lands in England. Enclosures for the sake of agricultural conversion have continued to the modern day, with large-scale land acquisitions in poor countries being argued to constitute "commons grabs" due to their disproportionate targeting of common lands to convert to individual and corporate property (Dell'Angelo et al. 2017, 2021).

There are several points to make with respect to the criticism of common property as less productive. First, this theory may be reversing the causal arrow: differences in productive potential of the environment are leading to the adoption of specific property regimes, not the other way around. And there are several ways in which this can play out. First, as we discussed in Chapter 7, common property is potentially an adaptation to less productive environments. And second, as reflected in the commons grabs movement just mentioned, there is a historical trend of individual or corporate property displacing common and public property from the most desirable land through politics and coercion (Bromley 1991).

A second line of thinking allows that common property may be less productive than individual or corporate property, but notes that one person's productivity is another's conservation. And this remark belies a third response: that when we talk about productivity, we need to ask, productivity for whom? The type of productivity that is implicitly used in this argument is one that is externally legible and measured in formalized exchanges of goods, and much of the conversion of common property to some other form of private property has included the commodification of the commons as well, meaning that natural resource products are traded in formal markets. So the productivity that is valued by this argument is one that is easily measurable by external actors, but this does not mean that this is the only kind of productivity we could think of. Productivity is a form of efficiency, and so just as we asked in Chapter 5, we need to ask, productivity for whom?

Government support of communities

Following in part on the success of works like Ostrom's (1990), in the 1990s a wave of decentralization enthusiasm swept the conservation and development sectors. The problem to be solved was the onerous, traditional top-down governance with its bureaucracy, its metric fixation, and disregard for local institutions and local knowledge. It was also a response to the soulless market and the negative impact it had on social capital. In the commons community[1] there exists scepticism with respect to anything that sounds too top-down and technocratic, and a corresponding sympathy for local, community-based solutions.

The rhetoric in favour of community-based natural resource management contains multiple narratives, several of which relate to the instrumental value of decentralization of resource management to communities. First, there is the argument that local communities are better able to better adapt to their local ecological context (Berkes 2018), and to develop strong norms of stewardship through the psychologies of kinship and reciprocity as discussed in Chapter 3. The other narratives regard what I call political participation, or your ability to influence the rules that affect you. This is in fact one of Ostrom's design principles for effective community-based resource management: that a community is able to impact the rules that govern how it uses its shared resources. Using the language from Chapter 4, this amounts to the same actor having both use and control rights with respect to a resource.

Political participation has several important benefits, each related to our basic needs as identified by self-determination theory: autonomy, efficacy and belonging (Ryan & Deci 2018). These needs are important both inherently,

1. As formally represented by the International Association for the Study of the Commons.

because they partly constitute our well-being, and instrumentally through the behaviours they motivate. Participation in a rule-making exercise increases the extent to which the resulting rules are internalized and complied with, because doing so then meets our basic need of autonomy. Participating in designing use rules allows a community to empower itself and make these rules reflect its interests, also potentially increasing its sense of efficacy, or belief that its actions can achieve the outcomes it hopes to achieve. Self and collective efficacy are critical motivators for action. Finally, participation has the potential to increase a sense of belonging if one's values are affirmed during the process.

In Chapter 4, we discussed the importance of self-enforcement on collective action through the work of DeCaro, Janssen and Lee (2015), who found that the ability to vote on rules and self-enforce them increased collective action in a set of experiments in which participants are put in situations to model the tragedy of the commons scenario. This work is relevant here, as the authors also examined the relationship between participation, collective action and basic needs. They showed that participation by voting on the rules to be used increased participant's sense of autonomy and efficacy, but did not impact belonging. Overall they found that voting was important to legitimize the sanctions that followed, and that the combination of voting and self-enforcement helped participants internalize the rules governing resource use and increased rule acceptance. These findings were largely replicated in a follow-up study (DeCaro, Janssen & Lee 2021).

At the group level, we often see the need for autonomy expressed through the concept of sovereignty. As Duthu (2008: 164) observes in his discussion of tribal sovereignty, sovereignty is itself a relational concept: it describes a relationship between a group and other groups. However, I don't think the same thinking about autonomy necessarily applies at the level of group sovereignty: while individuals require socially supportive environments to thrive and develop a sense of self within a group, groups do not have this same need with respect to other groups. Nevertheless, I believe the principles of participation and autonomy support claims to the importance of group sovereignty.

Co-management and protected areas

In this section we describe an approach to community participation through co-management. Earlier in this chapter, we talked about the importance of examining hybrid property regimes, or regimes that combine multiple types of actors. A shift from top-down to more bottom-up governance has often taken place under the rubric of co-management as a hybrid property regime shared by communities and the state. In this section we explore the meaning of this as a hybrid property regime involving both common and governmental ownership.

The concept of co-management has increasingly been implemented within the design and implementation of protected areas (PAs), which define a certain area and then constrain resource use within this area. Protected areas are particularly popular among conservation biologists and in the field of conservation as a policy tool. One prominent critique of PAs has been that they represent an approach known as fortress conservation and that they are motivated by a set of assumptions associated with Western science. Like all policies, PAs are supported by several narratives. One dominant narrative has motivated the implementation of PAs as a response to environmental degradation caused by too many people who are mismanaging local resources, and the idea that these people are perceived to be an "alien" (non-Indigenous) presence, poorly adapted to local circumstances in ways that enable them to effectively steward their resources. The lens through which this environmental degradation is presumably documented is Western-oriented scientific practice (Brockington 2002). This narrative is also associated with an idea about what nature should look like, potentially without human interference, and it concludes with the prediction that drastic intervention is needed in order to rescue the environment from human interference by excluding people from the environment. Such exclusion in fact has meant that there is less mixing of property regime types, reflecting an argument that Western systems impose boundaries between property regimes onto the world, whereas in non-Western cultures the boundaries are fuzzier (Lockhart 1992).

This is one model for protected area governance. But it is not the only one. In South Africa there are many private protected areas as well (De Vos *et al.* 2019). And this model also excludes a long history of area-based stewardship, such as sacred groves that are prominent in Africa and India (Brockington, Duffy & Igoe 2008). The US model for protected areas, which has been exported to other parts of the world, grants limited (primarily access) rights to recreational users. Finally, an interesting counter-example to the exclusionist PA model is presented by Freitas (2021), who describes how in two adjacent protected areas on either side of the border between Brazil and Argentina, people were actively encouraged to move into the parks to further establish each nation's claim to the border area that contained a beautiful site known as the Iguazu Falls (although this policy was later reversed and each country tried to evict its park's inhabitants).

It is tempting to see fortress conservation as a thing of the past. But critiques of a new policy initiative known as 30 × 30 have represented some of the same concerns expressed about fortress conservation. 30 × 30 is a conservation initiative to conserve 30 per cent of the earth's total land area by the year 2030. One prominent line of critique of this initiative has been that its discourse disregards the people who live on land that is targeted for conservation as well as other locally important details. The most famous example of this was a paper that argued that afforestation could help the climate change problem through natural carbon capture (Bastin *et al.* 2019). In their response, Veldman *et al.* (2019) argue that the original authors made some key errors that are also reminiscent of the panacea problem from Chapter 6. One error was that the original authors argued that afforestation could take place in grasslands and savannas because these areas have a climate that could support forest growth, inferring that a lack of trees in these areas represented degradation and an opportunity for restoration. But by only looking at climate, Bastin *et al.* (2019) ignored the fact that these ecosystems have persisted not just because of climate, but because of natural, and more recently anthropogenic, fire regimes. So the original analysis was naïve about the evolutionary history of these ecosystems and the role that humans now play in them.

More generally, the literature on protected areas has tended to underemphasize social outcomes, privileging biophysical goals instead (Ban *et al.* 2017). There has also been a greater emphasis on more legible inputs as a measure of progress, such as the amount of land formally conserved, rather than impacts on the ground. As I mentioned in the beginning of this book, this can lead to a proliferation of paper parks, or protected areas that only exist on paper, and which aren't actually doing much conserving.

A part of the response to fortress conservation, which has also made its way into the 30 × 30 initiative, has been to encourage collaborations between governments and communities under the rubric of co-management. This has the potential to combine the best of both worlds: all the benefits of community governance described earlier in this section and the support of an external government that can fill in the gaps with technical and scientific expertise. But employing the idea of co-management has the same issues of potential vagueness that the property regime concept does. Carlsson and Berkes (2005: 65) describe each of these, pointing out that we cannot assume that co-management entails a win-win arrangement between "a unitary state and a homogeneous community".

We certainly can't assume that the combination of a set of communities and a state government share a single interest that is not subject to political manoeuvring. Cundill *et al.* (2013) describe a case of co-management in post-apartheid South Africa, in which black South Africans who had been forcibly removed from their lands by the apartheid regime were offered the opportunity to reclaim these through a formal land claims process. Many of these claims were made against land in formal protected areas, in which case a special provision was offered for the land to be co-managed by the state and reclaiming communities. While formal language about valuing both conservation and community livelihoods was presented in key documents describing these arrangements, the reality for the cases that the authors analyse was that the state prioritized its own view of conservation that came at the expense of community participation and livelihoods. Cundill *et al.* (2013: 176) also echo some of the criticisms of the unitary community assumption. In this process the "community" is an artefact of the claims process, forming groups of people who "were largely united by their dispossession and marginalisation, and the expected benefits associated with land restitution. Unsurprisingly, the post-settlement period in this case has been characterised by social fragmentation and intra- and inter-community conflict."

Moreover, there are different images that we might think of under the rubric of co-management. To me, the dominant image is one of nested governance, with communities exercising use rights while the state maintains most control rights, and this is one of the scenarios that Carlsson and Berkes (2005) discuss. But there are other models. The nesting could go in the other direction, or there could be no nesting at all, and it could be a joint collaboration between communities and the state. Or there could be other actors (e.g., NGOs, corporations) involved, complicating the idea of a hybrid property regime.

Brockington, Duffy and Igoe (2008) describe how the governance of protected areas often results from a network of state, NGO and corporate actors. The role of NGOs in supporting or playing quasi-state roles is not surprising; NGOs are often considered to be a third sector (between public and private) that fulfils governmental roles in the absence of a fully functional state. In their description of protected area governance and conservation in Madagascar, Brockington *et al.* (2008: 168) describe the complex relationships that governed a network of formally state-run protected areas:

> Donors and environmental NGOs have been involved in directly running state-owned national parks in Madagascar. For example, Association Nationale pour la Gestion des Aires Protégées (ANGAP), the national agency responsible for managing protected areas in Madagascar, is run and funded by a group of international NGOs and donors in conjunction with Malagasy state agencies. ANGAP is essentially a private organization that runs a public utility, and has received funding from CI [Conservation International], the World Bank, WWF [World Wildlife Federation], USAID [United States Agency for International Development], the German development agency, and the French and British governments. The board of directors is drawn from government ministries, such as the Ministry of Tourism and the Ministry of the Environment, but donors including the World Bank and WWF also have seats on the board.

Brockington *et al.* (2008: 4) provide another example from Madagascar that represents a confluence of state, corporate and NGO actors, with users being granted some entitlement rights through ecotourism:

> Consider the development of the ilmenite (titanium dioxide) mine in the Fort Dauphin area of Madagascar by Qit Minerals Madagascar (80 per cent owned by Rio Tinto and 20 per cent owned by the Government of Madagascar) ... The company has set aside zones in the mining project for conservation, which will form part of the national system of protected areas in Madagascar. It also set up an ecotourism project, which has been running since 2000, to allow local communities to benefit from the conservation initiatives established by Rio Tinto.

What type of property regime is this? This discussion complicates how we think about co-management as a supposedly hybrid property regime as well as what we think a protected area is.

Communities and participation as policy instruments

The rise in appreciation for communities that could potentially manage their own affairs has been seen in numerous conservation and development projects, particularly since the 1980s and 1990s (Agrawal & Gibson 1999). The World Bank, along with many other organizations, maintains an active community-based governance programme, which it calls community-driven development (CDD), the original sourcebook for which Ostrom co-authored. CDD requires community involvement in the selection and implementation of development projects that affect them. A specific example of this movement is reflected in community-based forest projects in India, the Philippines and elsewhere. Similarly, in the fisheries sector, co-management approaches have been popular in the literature for some time, and territorial user rights fisheries, or TURFs, often represent the formalization of community-based fisheries management. Within the conservation space, a recent development has been the introduction of "other effective area-based conservation measures", or OECMs.

In valuing and formalizing communities, we can end up treating them as panaceas. The ideal of "the community" can come to be seen as an administrative tool, or a governance modality, rather than a process that reflects the facts on the ground (Cleaver 1999). Ironically, programmes that formally empower local communities also simplify and abstract their understanding of these communities for administrative purposes.

There are several aspects of the panacea problem to unpack here. To start, using a just-so story to promote an idealized version of a complex reality as a policy solution. An important criticism of the community-as-policy approach has questioned the assumption that local communities are necessarily conservationist, because they "had been relatively isolated in the past (and therefore used their resources sustainably)" (Agrawal & Gibson 1999: 632). The importance of isolation here reflects the theory of environmental reciprocity from Chapter 2, in that it represents high costs of exit for resource users due to a lack of resource alternatives. Idealized narratives about local communities may assume that they have a unitary interest, and moreover that they engage in win-win interactions with the environment, which itself is discussed as a single, unitary interest, an assumption that we will question later in this chapter.

Agrawal and Gibson (1999: 630) describe how the most often bureaucratically assumed aspects of communities are "as a small spatial unit, as a homogenous social structure, and as shared norms". These are interrelated: the first component is seen to promote social cohesion among a limited and therefore fairly homogenous set of actors with common values and beliefs. Most arguments that critique communities as administrative artefacts focus on how this is done to single communities. But in some cases, whole groups can be artificially grouped into a larger administrative category, as was done in the 1855 Yakama treaty between the United States government and a group of Native American tribes, which "displayed remarkable ignorance or disregard of tribal political structures in that it lumped fourteen distinct tribes into 'one nation' under the name 'Yakama'" (Duthu 2008: xxii).

Despite these convenient assumptions, communities are non-unitary in multiple ways. As we saw in Chapter 3, they often break into sub-groups based on networks of kinship and reciprocity. And as we saw earlier in this chapter, rights can be distributed unevenly within a community, for example when a local chief holds most of the control rights over a resource. And as we saw in the previous chapter, there are also significant inequalities between men and women in many communities. Underlying inequalities can impact the influence of a supposedly equitable rights-based policy. Sikor and Lund (2009: 5), for example, describe the inequality in the devolution of forest use rights to individual households of the Dak Lak province in the highlands of Vietnam. Despite a relatively egalitarian formal allocation, underlying variation in resources held by different houses served as an indirect allocation mechanism. Households with more resources such as machinery and labour were able to benefit more from their formal rights.

Power asymmetries within a community can also lead to an outcome known as elite capture, whereby local elites are able to funnel the benefits of a new programme to themselves (Persha & Andersson 2014). Through what he calls the "paradox of participation", Lund (2015: 4) describes how elite capture can result from the process of professionalization and upskilling that many projects involve, giving some local actors resources that they can then leverage to disproportionately benefit from such projects.

Just calling something "participatory" or checking attendance records at a meeting is unlikely to suffice. Individuals might not feel that their voices are really being heard, and they might not feel like they belong in a public forum, even if they are legally entitled to be there. People formally granted access to a participatory forum might face obstacles to attending, if, for example, they have other obligations (work, childcare) during this forum. Because of this, participation must be actively inclusive through outreach and other strategies (Newig *et al.* 2018), again reflecting the importance of positive liberty as freedom based on a supportive environment.

One of the main arguments in favour of political participation is that it leads to the internalization of the resulting rules by satisfying the basic need of autonomy. However we need to recognize, as we did in Chapter 6, that there are multiple, culturally specific ways in which such needs can be satisfied. If participation is to achieve better compliance by satisfying our basic needs, and there are multiple ways to satisfy needs based on context, then we need to think about what DeCaro and Stokes (2013) call participatory fit, or the extent to which participatory processes satisfy our basic needs, with the authors highlighting the importance of autonomy and procedural equity. DeCaro and Stokes (2013: 14), describe how experimental work conducted by Vollan (2008) among farming communities in Namibia and South Africa demonstrates the importance of participatory fit:

> residents of Karas, Namibia, where there is a long history of successful self-governance and strong norms of trust and reciprocity, successfully managed a shared resource when they voted on rules and could not use economic sanctions to enforce them. In contrast, residents of Namaqualand, South Africa, where self-organization is limited and norms of trust and reciprocity are relatively weak, only benefited from voting when the rules were also backed by economic sanctions. Vollan attributed these results to cultural differences in subjective definitions of self-determination, hypothesizing that Namaqualand residents were best empowered by rules backed with economic enforcement, whereas this undermined definitions of self-determination among Karas citizens.

At this point it is worth asking, are there other broad principles that can guide the implementation of community-based participation? Based on their analysis of participation-based policies in India and Mexico, Fleischman and Solorzano (2018: 164) answer this question: "three elements are jointly necessary for a stable participatory programme: A supply of institutions that enable and provide benefits from participation, a demand from citizens to participate, and a citizenry with the capability to participate". To me much of this boils down to the concept of coproduction as discussed by Ostrom (1996), who argues that when it comes to the delivery of services (as opposed to goods production) such as education, the best outcomes are produced by a collaboration between the supposed service providers and receivers.

The importance of the components described by Fleischman and Solorzano is reflected in cases of so-called collectivization where they are largely absent. The worst scenario for formalized community-based governance are the examples of "forced collectivization", through which "regimes can force beneficiaries into collective farms or cooperatives with elements of communal land ownership and then provide members with ill-defined or highly incomplete property rights. Examples include Cuba, the Soviet Union, Peru, and much of Eastern Europe after WWII" (Albertus 2021: 90). Another example of this is the movement towards compulsory villagization that occurred in Tanzania that Scott (1998) describes. Such cases represent an often-horrific exercise of power by extremely top-down, dictatorial governance regimes, and can involve large-scale dispossession of local land holdings.

Formalizing kuleana

We have seen in this chapter that there are reasons to be sceptical of the enthusiasm to decentralize use and control rights to local communities. But this doesn't mean that every co-management effort must go awry. I have seen a case of government supported local collective action in the San Luis Valley of Colorado, where a series of state-supported roundtables helped create an arena for dialogue about declining aquifer levels, and state-produced data on declining aquifer levels over time increased the salience of the problem to local farmers (Cody *et al.* 2015; Smith *et al.* 2017). These measures helped to enable the implementation of a self-imposed groundwater use tax among a set of farmers in the valley.

To further explore both the challenges and potential of formally recognized community governance, we return to Hawaii and the case described by Mehana Vaughan (2018), which we last discussed in depth in Chapter 3. Historically, the state of Hawaii has undermined the customary practices that Vaughan describes, but there have been efforts by several Hawaiian communities to work within this formalized system to have it better recognize their rights and historical practices.

Vaughan describes how one community, Hāʻena, has worked with the government of Hawaii to formalize their traditional environmental institutions. In 1994, they began a movement to designate community-based subsistence fishing areas (CBSFAs) that would reflect traditional Hawaiian resource norms. After much delay, the community of Hāʻena worked to support the passage of Act 241, which required the Department of Land and Natural Resources (DLNR) and its subsidiary, the Department of Aquatic Resources (DAR) to work with the community of Hāʻena to develop new rules based on local traditions.

The experience of the Hāʻena community reflects some standard tensions between informal and more formal processes. Several of these related to the inherent limitations of bureaucratization and professionalization. One challenge was that government personnel were not naturally equipped to work with local communities based on their training more as fisheries biologists than community liaisons. Vaughan (2018: 152) also describes how the professional tunnel vision that results from bureaucratic specialization created barriers to more holistic management. One agency would be in charge of freshwater, another of forests, and another of aquatic resources, creating coordination challenges. This is a standard challenge of formalization and professionalization: as a group focuses more on a specific aspect of a system, it becomes intellectually and administratively blind to other aspects. Government can become a parallel processing system with no central processing unit, to use a computational metaphor.

This depiction also should make us question language about "the government". We often talk quite loosely about "the government" or "the state" or in the United States, "Washington" or "the administration" as if they are unitary entities. But like the other social actors we have discussed, they are not. In Chapter 2 we discussed the challenge of intergroup and intragroup cooperation and conflict. Similarly, we should view larger organizations as consisting of multiple groups that dynamically form and dissolve coalitions over time. "The government" is made of multiple groups with often conflicting goals and values.

Vaughan (2018: 153) also argues that administrative management was slow to adapt to changing circumstances in comparison to local management which could change local rules based on real-time observations. This represents a common trade-off between formal and informal governance, or between consistency and flexibility.

Several challenges related to the heterogeneity of the Hāʻena community. As we have established in this chapter, communities are not unitary, and intra-community conflict was an important issue for Hāʻena to address. The state, however, did not reflect this heterogeneity either within the community or between the community and the rest of the state. It administratively homogenized members of the community, not recognizing traditional rules that allowed, for example, community elders to access certain seaweed beds. And it refused to prioritize rights of the community to its fishing grounds by excluding outsiders from fishing there. While there were limitations put on who could access the community's fishing grounds, this was enabled in part by local community members agreeing to abide by these restrictions themselves, scarifying some of their rights in order to prevent overfishing by outsiders. And the spirit of kuleana, or combining rights with responsibilities, was not strongly reflected in these rules.

Nevertheless, through the persistence of community leaders as well as governmental staff, the community of Hā'ena did achieve increased formal recognition of local practices. And much of this success came from multiple actors working together over time, developing skills that they hadn't initially possessed, and bridging different worldviews in part with extensive face-to-face communication. The NGO KUA acted as an effective boundary actor between communities and the government. And the community worked with the formal system rather than against it. This initial success has since inspired communities to better formalize their own traditions.

This example shows us how we might try to understand many similar cases: it shows that co-management is ultimately a process of muddling through that requires the efforts of multiple actors to be present and push their own boundaries over time. The formalization of customary Hawaiian practices has not entirely a success or a failure, and it gives us reason to believe that it can be built upon in the future.

Nature as a property regime

We have so far been talking about the decentralization of rights from states to communities. Another type of "decentralization" is increasingly taking place in the form of the "rights of nature" movement (as opposed to rights to nature). This rights movement can be seen in part as a formalization of psychologies of reciprocity and kinship with nature discussed in Chapter 3. The story told to motivate the rights of nature approach is that we must value nature intrinsically in order to adequately engage with it; that our dominant, instrumental motivations are insufficient for motivating environmental stewardship. By formally valuing nature per se, we can move towards a more holistic relationship with it (Stone 2010; O'Donnell 2018). In this section we discuss nature as an environmental rights-holder in the same way that we have for other property regimes. In the previous section we discussed the challenge of formalizing customary Hawaiian resource practices in the context of a Westernized bureaucracy and cultural milieu. We will see that challenge repeated here.

In this section we explore the idea of nature as a rights-holder itself. We start by asking whether nature can be thought of as a unitary actor, the same way we have for other types of actors. This question is important for the same reason it was before: unitary actors do not have internal conflicts to account for when we prescribe or implement a property regime. We proceed from here with several case studies of the rights of nature approach, namely the Endangered Species Act (ESA) in the United States, and the movement to grant rights to rivers that has occurred in several countries.

Unitary nature

Boyd (2017) describes a case that illustrates the tensions involved in granting rights to nature within Western societies. In the midst of the fracking boom in Pennsylvania, Grant Township passed a community bill of rights to prevent the disposal of toxic wastewater into their watershed, the Little Mahoning. This document contains language that claimed the township's watershed status as a legal rights-holder. This language was used in court to declare and defend the rights of the watershed in a suit brought by Pennsylvania General Energy (PGE), which wanted to develop a wastewater injection site there. The company's response dismissed this language, calling the watershed an "artificial construct". Boyd notes that the company itself, as a rights-holder, is likewise an artificial construct, no more real than nature itself. Still, the notion that nature has agency and legal standing is historically mostly anathema to the Western legal discourse.

Even if we don't necessarily take seriously the vociferous complaints that have been logged against the rights for nature movement, there are some important questions that the approach must answer. First, does nature have a single interest, or are there win-lose relationships in nature in which case we have to decide whose interests we favor at the expense of others? Second, which human actors will represent nature and her interests?

Turning to the first question, there is legal precedent for this line of thinking: laws that have formalized a rights for nature approach have consistently invoked a whole nature interest rhetoric with terms like "indivisible", "interdependent" and "complementary" (Harden-Davies *et al.* 2020). So we need to ask ourselves whether or not, and to what extent, we can be thinking of "nature", or parts of nature, as a unitary actor. If we can, then those parts that are more unitary can be thought of as having a single interest, and therefore are more promising holders of rights. If not, then the allocation question becomes more complicated if we have to pick winners and losers.

Some lines of research have shown that cooperative relationships are more common in nature than an evolutionary lens based on "survival of the fittest" might assume, as we discussed in Chapter 2 where we saw that cooperation within a group can help it outcompete other groups. A particularly arresting example comes from Suzanne Simard's (2021) work. Simard documented the ways in which trees within a forest shared carbon through a fungal network within the soil. Simard shows several patterns of cooperation among the trees that she studied, two of which are particularly interesting. First, she describes how "mother trees", highly connected in the fungal network, share resources with their younger kin. Simard (2021) also describes cooperation across species, most notably Douglas fir and birch trees exchanging carbon during different seasons of the year in what she describes as a "quid pro quo" arrangement, otherwise known as reciprocity. Ideas of the unity of nature have been quite grand: there is a history of advocating for a unitary nature view among scientists, for example in the Gaia hypothesis about a global environmental interest, to the "balance of nature" idea, which implies that there is a single state that is best for a whole ecosystem.

Simard's story is intoxicating, and a part of me strongly wants to embrace it, which maybe reflects my own desire to intrinsically identify with nature as we discussed in Chapter 3. Simard's findings have jumped into the cultural mainstream through terms like the "wood wide web". But there is also reason to be cautious, as these findings have produced an enthusiasm that many now think stretches beyond what the evidence can support, as discussed in a recent *New York Times* article (Popkin 2022). Additionally, it is fair to say that the balance of nature and Gaia ideas have been discredited by the scientific communities that have engaged with them. And overall, the scientific consensus is that, just like in social systems, while patches of cooperation can exist and sometimes reach surprising scales, there are always winners and losers in a complex ecosystem, and individual interest often conflicts with collective interest. In general, we should not assume that an entire ecosystem has a single unitary interest, just as we cannot for humanity. Some species, populations, and individuals are going to benefit at the expense of others. Just as humans do, species in nature will tend to form groups of cooperating individuals, pushing out free-riders when they can.

Another complication is that humans have tended to pick sides in nature, and the sides we pick are often based on who is most like us. As Boyd (2017) describes, arguments about whether or not animals should be granted rights have often hinged in part on how much they seem like us: do they have thoughts, or are they "mere" instinct? Do they suffer? Do they have social emotions and cultural learning? This perspective places humanity at the centre of a moral space and allocates rights to other parties based on their proximity to our defining features.

A final complication of the personification of nature is that it could equally be used to assign responsibility to nature as it is to assign rights. And what could it mean to hold nature responsible? Lahsen and Ribot (2022) provide one answer to this question, arguing that attributing only to "climate" the suffering that is caused by climate-related disasters can be used to obfuscate the role that human decisions, inequalities and vulnerabilities play. So the rights of nature approach is not a panacea, as it brings with it its own difficult, political decisions. In the next two sections we explore several examples of this approach that demonstrate its challenges and opportunities.

The Endangered Species Act as a rights of nature approach

An example of the inherently political nature of the rights of nature approach can be found in the US Endangered Species Act (ESA), which is not always mentioned in the burgeoning rights of nature literature, but which is arguably the longest-standing law granting rights to nature. The ESA requires the US Fish and Wildlife Services (FWS) to identify endangered species and recommend that they be "listed" as endangered by the secretary of the Department of the Interior. The ESA grants legal standing to nature by allowing any person to claim that they have been injured in connection to a threatened species, and then bring a suit on behalf of a listed species.

The ESA is one of the world's most powerful environmental laws because of the strength of the rights it bestows onto species. It has been used to change the course of entire ecosystems through lawsuits in support of the spotted owl in the northwestern United States, or the snail darter in Tennessee which threatened to derail the construction of a major dam. The ESA favours a holistic approach to environmental management because of the common argument that the preservation of a species requires that its habit be preserved. By some accounts it is a major success story and arguably one of the most powerful environmental laws in the world.

On the other hand, it has left a trail of intense political conflict and increased distrust between landowners and the government in many places. Duthu (2008: 95), for example, describes how the Apache tribe in Arizona responded to the ESA out of concern that "federal officials would unilaterally declare large portions of the tribe's reservation critical habitat for threatened or endangered species" by "barring any federal or state agency official from entering its lands to conduct studies related to natural resource management". Duthu quotes a tribal chairman, Ronnie Lupe, who criticizes the ESA as an effort to impose conservation on tribal lands to make up for environmental degradation outside of such lands; this critique has been brought up again in criticisms over carbon offset policies that we shall discuss in Chapter 9.

In the most well-known example, the northern spotted owl in the forests of Oregon and Washington was listed under the act in 1990. After many years of conflict between logging and environmental activists, a new adversary has emerged: the barred owl, which is now actively encroaching on the spotted owl and displacing it. This is putting conservationists in a strange place, as some of them have advocated for actively limiting this other owl's advances, sometimes with lethal means. Which of the two closely related owl species, if that matters, should receive protection and rights? It seems that many are applying the priority principle in granting the spotted owl precedence in its claims over forest habitat.

Rights for and of a river

Many states in the western United States have adopted programmes that enable NGOs and state agencies to purchase rights for the environment as instream flows rights, or rights for rivers themselves (O'Donnell 2018). These aren't commonly thought of as a part of the rights of nature approach, in part because of their operating within a resource market context, (see "shared resource markets" in Chapter 9) but they do lean in this direction. These programmes are also partly motivated by the ESA and the need to keep water in streams to avoid endangering species that depend on them for habitat.

This case is particularly interesting because of how it relates to the role of transaction costs as described in Chapter 5. There, we argued that minimizing transaction costs increases the efficiency of trade by ignoring the side-effects of trades, and we used water markets in New Mexico as an example. Water markets in the western United States have high transaction costs due to what is known as a "no injury rule", which states that any rights transfer must not create negative externalities or costs for those not involved in the trade. And as Smith (2019: 191) describes, transfers to instream flows have unusually high transaction costs because of the difficulty in determining just how much water is going where when it being used by the environment instead of a human. In her discussion of these programmes, O'Donnell (2018) emphasizes the political balancing act that water rights purchasers have had to make in working with local communities and farmers to purchase water. The transfer of water to environmental use has needed to be framed as something non-threatening and potentially beneficial to agricultural interests in the areas where water rights purchasers work. Here we see high transaction costs as potentially thwarting the promotion of environmental conservation.

Moreover, the hierarchy between senior and junior water-rights-holders that the prior appropriation regime creates means that new users, including the environment, are placed at the bottom of the priority ladder, only receiving water when everyone senior to them has their fill. If there is a drought, these instream rights will not be prioritized. This represents another example of path dependence, whereby new institutional innovations must cope with the existing property regimes in place: see Abrams (2019) for a more thorough discussion of the challenges that the instream flow initiative has faced in navigating the prior appropriation model. Despite these challenges, Smith (2019) argues that instream flow transfers may have had positive indirect environmental effects due to increase monitoring and enforcement of water use rules in areas that involve such transfers.

Other approaches to river rights reflect more intrinsic values. One of the most famous examples of the rights of nature approach has taken place in New Zealand, which in 2014 and 2017 respectively recognized a forest in a national park and the Whanganui river as having legal personhood. An important element of this case is the extent to which the case was motivated by traditional Māori cosmology that reflects the Indigenous perspective described in Chapter 3. As Boyd (2017: 140) remarks, the statute formalizing the river's identity as Te Awa Tupua, a personified entity, states that: "Te Awa Tupua is a singular entity comprised of many elements and communities, working collaboratively for the common purpose of the health and well-being of Te Awa Tupua."

This act moves us further towards an intrinsic valuation of nature as embodied in law, but it itself is not perfect in this regard. It is the result of a political compromise between the Whanganui Iwi tribe and the New Zealand government, and created two guardians of the river, one from each side. And political challenges regarding how the river will be managed holistically remain: the act does not actually grant Te Awa Tupua its own riverbed, because of an existing natural resource law.

As always, the devil is in the details. Will this approach be used to formalize the cultural traditions of people that hold the environment to be a sacred partner, or might it be used to support more NIMBY-type behaviour, with more powerful actors declaring that we must protect the rights of nature at the expense of those who most closely depend on it, creating a new version of fortress conservation?

Conclusion

We have spent the last two chapters unpacking just how complicated it is to definitely say who owns the environment, and this builds on our conversation in Chapters 4 and 5 about the complexity of defining what it means to own the environment. I have attempted to show that these dimensions of ownership are closely related to each other: because ownership is not unitary but has multiple components, different actors can have different portions of a bundle of rights, complicating the meaning of any property regime.

The cases examined in this chapter present a tug of war between the complexity of reality and the models that we want to impose on this reality to make sense of it. In applying such models, we may be simplifying for the sake of external legibility to ourselves. If we want to have a meaningful discussion about the relative merits of property regimes and the relationships between them, we need more complex typologies of hybrid property regimes. But even then, I'm not sure that the reality will easily yield to meaningful comparative analysis. This conclusion is based on my own experience leading the very academic-sounding social-ecological systems meta-analysis database (SESMAD) project (Cox 2014). In this project we attempted to code the aspects of large and complex governance systems with multiple actors and institutional arrangements governing different parts of equally complicated and extensive ecosystems. In this project we experienced a hard trade-off between the complexity of coding individual cases and our ability to compare such systems. The more we recognized the multiple regimes within each system, the more difficult it was to aggregate these fine-grained descriptions to characterizations that could be compared across cases.

A part of me still thinks that a quantitative comparison of large and complex social-ecological systems such as the protected areas of Madagascar (as described by Brockington *et al.* 2008) is the holy grail of environmental governance research. But another part of me recognizes that facilitating such comparisons would require a massive amount of collective action within the relevant research communities. The IFRI project that I described earlier represents one particularly successful effort to meet these challenges, and there are others that we could learn from (Cox *et al.* 2021). Such efforts must also contend with the potential biases in favour of one policy type or another that different research groups may have.

In the next chapter we move on to our final topic of the book: market policies. This chapter will build most directly on our discussions from Chapter 5 on exchange rights, Chapter 6 on panaceas, and from this chapter on hybrid property regimes.

9

Market policies

This chapter pulls together content from several previous chapters to discuss arguably the most popular type of property-based policies: markets. We have already discussed markets through our examination of exchange rights in Chapter 5. There we associated exchange with reciprocity, establishing trade as a culturally ubiquitous phenomenon. As such we need to distinguish "markets", which include informal exchange and are found everywhere but are less legible to state actors, with market-based policies, which are public policies that include the allocation of exchange rights and are our subject for this chapter. In Chapter 5 we also considered the goals of equity and efficiency that are a strong part of the dominant market discourse. Efficiency is a primary theoretical motivation for most market-based policies, and so we build further on that discussion here.

In Chapter 6, we introduced the idea of a policy panacea, which we will reflect on a fair amount in this chapter, since the market-based policies we will discuss in this chapter have often received the panacea treatment from their promoters. In Chapter 8 we introduced the idea of a hybrid property regime involving multiple types of actors, each with its own set of rights. In this chapter we unpack market policies as their own kind of hybrid property regime, commonly involving a state actor (or in some cases an NGO) with control rights and resource users with use and exchange rights.

We will explore three types of market-based environmental policies, based on O'Donnell's (2018) classification:[1] (1) public goods markets (e.g., PES policies, conservation easements, certifications); (2) tradeable environmental allowances: shared resource markets (e.g., catch shares); and (3) tradeable environmental allowances: regulatory markets (e.g., cap-and-trade).

---

1. My thanks to Erin O'Donnell for helping me think through these categories.

A public goods market involves an external actor paying a local actor for the provision of a public good, based on a formalized evaluation or certification scheme. A prominent example of what O'Donnell (2018) refers to as a public goods market are payment for ecosystem services policies. In this case, money is being exchanged for environmental benefits – such as avoided deforestation – that are framed as public goods, and entitlements are granted to landowners.

A public goods market is about incentivizing the provision of social and environmental benefits, or positive externalities that are shared by people other than those who provide them. Tradeable environmental allowances (TEA), on the other hand, seek to decrease the provision of social and environmental costs, or negative externalities in the form of pollution or resource degradation. If it is natural resource degradation that we are addressing, then we call it a shared resource market, and if it is pollution, we call it a regulatory market. The most popular example of a shared resource market is catch shares in the fisheries sector, and the most popular regulatory market programmes are carbon markets designed to curtail the emission of greenhouse gases. In this chapter I will primarily focus on these two specific examples, but as we will see, in the carbon policy space there is now a strong connection between regulatory markets and public goods markets. TEAs involve two quantitative output rules: a cap on the overall amount of pollution or resource extraction allowed, and tradeable rights in shares of the overall cap (e.g., pollution permits or fishing quotas). In the fisheries sector, the cap is referred to as the total allowable catch, or TAC.

Each of these policies have received the panacea treatment from their promoters: both have been promoted in apolitical terms, with a strong emphasis on the allocational and efficiency benefits each provides. Specifically, it is argued that these schemes allow for the allocation of rights through markets in TEAs to the most cost-effective actors. Here we need to remember that there are many possible definitions of efficiency. At least in some contexts, a carbon market policy is less efficient than a carbon tax because of the transaction costs that a functional market in emissions rights entails, and these costs are exacerbated when we add a forest-based offset programme to the mix (van Kooten, Shaikh & Suchánek 2002) as we will discuss later on in this chapter.

It is also important to remember that TEAs involve two stages of allocation: an initial distribution of shares of a cap and ongoing redistributions of these rights via market exchanges. Equity concerns have been expressed regarding each stage of allocation, and it is during the second stage of rights trading where efficiency arguments are most commonly made.

Public goods markets

A public goods market involves a "buyer" who pays a public good "seller". This can be thought of as another example of the principal–agent relationship, with the buyer being the principal and the seller being the agent. We can think of different types of public goods markets based on the rights they bestow on the seller. In some cases, they grant the seller use entitlements: the right to benefit financially from how they use their resources, which is how payment for ecosystem services policies work. Other examples include the conservation easements that many environmental NGOs direct as a primary part of their conservation portfolios. Here, landowners give up development rights on their land, often in exchange for tax benefits as use entitlements.

Paying for ecosystem services

We conclude our discussion of public goods markets with a discussion of payment for ecosystem services, or PES policies, in which one actor, often but not always a government, pays a private actor to provide an ecosystem service, such as clean water or forest conservation. PES policies depend on local resource users having formally legible land rights so that governmental actors can connect conservation outcomes achieved on land to the behaviour of landowners. This connection is needed to ensure that payments are rewarding the right behaviours and outputs, which in the case of rewarding outputs or outcomes, also assumes a strong connection between the behaviours of resource users and conservation outcomes. The theory of environmental reciprocity from Chapter 2, with its emphasis on exclusion as a motivator for environmental investment, is relevant here. If an outsider can cut down a forest, this reduces the incentive a forest landowner would have to conserve this forest, as they would not receive the payment that is tied to conservation outcomes that are now undercut. One of the main challenges that PES policies have is that local users frequently do not have secure rights, let alone rights that are sufficiently formalized to be legible to outside actors.

The application of PES schemes has at times involved several aspects of policy panaceas as discussed in Chapter 6. One common concern raised with them is that they may crowd out intrinsic incentives to produce public environmental goods, although in line with our conclusions from Chapter 6, this likely depends on the how an intervention relates to our basic needs as described by self-determination theory. Akers and Yasué (2019) report on the results of a systematic review of PES schemes based on SDT. This study found that more autonomy-supportive PES schemes were more participatory and crowded out less and crowded in more. Surprisingly, they did not find that such schemes tended to be more ecologically successful, although this may be a result of a measurability bias in how this variable was coded (holistic outcomes are not emphasized in the paper).

One popular example of the biases that we discussed in Chapter 6 has been found in the popularization of a PES scheme out of Costa Rica, which has been argued as a model or template for other countries (Rodriguez 2016). Using the Costa Rican case as a template for future interventions is an example of the representativeness heuristic that we discussed earlier. However, the case of Costa Rica is unique in some important ways. As Fletcher and Breitling (2012) argue, the Costa Rican case deviates substantially from the idealized vision of a PES scheme and involved factors that are not easily generalized, such as a large population of pro-conservation expatriates who were inclined to productively respond to the programme as payees. The authors also question the extent to which the Costa Rican PES case is a "true" (as opposed to false) positive, based in part on the fact that deforestation had been dropping already by the time the programme was implemented.

One interesting example of a PES scheme's development and implementation that demonstrates the panacea process from Chapter 6 is described by Milne (2022), based in large part on her experiences in implementing the programme in Cambodia. This programme is known as the Conservation Agreements Model, or CAM, and it was developed by the large environmental NGO Conservation International. Milne describes how supporters of the CAM sought to displace a previous model known as integrated conservation and development projects, or ICDPs. In Milne's words, a "dichotomy" was created between this old policy and the new one, reinforcing the boundaries between the groups who favoured each approach. And it wasn't just the old approach that was criticized, but its adherents, likely reflecting our ongoing discussion of in-group versus out-group conflict.

An interesting aspect of the programme is that the agreements were made with whole communities, granting collective property in the form of collective use entitlements. This has the potential advantage of lowering transaction costs compared to dealing with individuals, but it also meant the programme had to deal with some of the challenges we have discussed before. Several of these revolve around the nature of the community. Milne and Adams (2012) argue that during the implementation of the CAM programme in Cambodia there was an assumption that land clearing was a collective action problem with all community members contributing equally. They also point out that the "communes" that were engaged with were not naturally occurring communities, undercutting some of the logic of community participation as we discussed in Chapter 7. And I think most fundamentally, much of Milne's discussion centres around the analytical simplifications of people and place that the programme promoted, and how national and regional politics disrupted the implementation of the programme in Cambodia. While the conservation agreements were framed as "community choice", Milne describes how she observed that these agreements seemed to be mostly determined by private meetings between individuals, as well as "Cambodian tendencies to bypass community participation to favor elite interests" (Milne 2022: 147).

And while the programme included a multi-criteria matrix to help with evaluation of the programme, Milne describes how the implementation of the programme led to several analytical simplifications, including the prioritization of particular, simplified measures such as "number of hectares of forest protected per annum" over other criteria, even if these were formally part of the conservation agreements. Arguably, filling out such a matrix starts to "gamify" the implementation of the programme, in the sense discussed in Chapter 6. This has the important benefit of providing efficacy to staff who implement the programme but can again crowd out the benefits of intrinsic values that can sustain staff and help the programme maintain a more holistic perspective on the issues it is addressing. Reflecting this dynamic, Milne (2022: 83) describes how

> Ultimately, the conservation agreements' logic and language influenced how CI staff conceptualized their work. Their problem-solving and analysis of human-environment relations in the field soon become frame mainly in economic terms ... thus the presence of the agreements encouraged staff to see the field according to the CSP matrix of economic costs and incentives.

These problems notwithstanding, I think we need to be careful in how much we conclude from this discussion about the nature of PES schemes in general or the CAM version more specifically, particularly in comparison with other policies. The programmes were implemented within the context of a set of five protected areas that suffered from many of the same problems of political influence polluting the process. And indeed, Milne describes how over time the CAM programme was "subsumed" into the protected area regime, through which the Cambodian government was able to extend its problematic influence over the programme. The CAM programme could have served as an opportunity for community participation in the context of an otherwise top-down protected area regime, although as Milne and Adams (2012: 146) argue, the CAM programme itself turned this more into "community participation by contract". I emphasize all of this here because a dismissal of the PES approach based on this case could be simply another turn of the panacea wheel in favour of some other policy consigned to deal with the same problems.

Certifying sustainably harvested rice

A more indirect example of a public goods market that is based on exchange entitlements and involves many buyers is environmental certification programmes. I have seen an example of this in my work with farmers in the Dominican Republic. Here, a local partner of mine, AgroFrontera, is working with a set of rice farmers to improve their farming practices, mostly by decreasing the amounts of fertilizers, pesticides and water that they use. The system faces a challenge in transition to these practices, in part because of the influence that local agrochemical companies have on farming practices as powerful market intermediaries (Cox, Payton & Pimentel 2019). Farmers take out loans from these companies at high interest rates in order to purchase chemical inputs and receive technical advice from these same actors about how, and how much, to use such inputs. This reflects the challenges of patron–client relationships discussed in Chapter 5, and AgroFrontera is effectively trying to insert itself as a kind of beneficent market intermediary into the system by offering farmers better rates and more environmentally sound advice.

AgroFrontera is working to help around 100 rice farmers become collectively certified as sustainable rice growers. The costs of doing so include coping with a lot of uncertainty, learning new techniques, and facing the fear of producing less. The benefit is the higher price that would be paid for sustainably produced rice, and AgroFrontera is working with a Dominican rice company to help market the new product. This can be thought of as a public good market in the sense that consumers are paying for the public good of sustainably produced rice. Because a share of the premium goes to the farmers, this is also an exchange entitlement programme, although it can also be thought of as an indirect use entitlement, since this premium is ultimately about how the environment is used. Finally, the collective nature of the certification creates a collective action problem among the farmers who are involved. Each may want to free-ride on the efforts of others to transition to the new techniques while still benefiting from the market premium that is shared by the whole group.

Allocating rights

All market-based policies create a new set of rights for resource users, and one of the questions policymakers face is, how to allocate such rights. Before moving on to our discussion of TEAs I want to explore this problem. One prominent answer by public goods markets has been to use auctions. Auctions have been used for example in the Conservation Reserve Program in the United States, in which farmers bid on conservation contracts that then require them to take land out of production, which is seen as a cost-effective way to reveal their preferences and to promote conservation. These are known as reverse auctions because it is the seller (of conservation) who is bidding.

The standard justification for using reverse auctions in the context of PES schemes is offered by Ferraro (2008), who argues that such auctions are a way of addressing the information asymmetry between ecosystem service providers and a paying agency. Using a social model we have seen before we can think of these policies as creating a principal–agent relationship between a payer and service provider. Because potential service providers aren't sure that they will secure a contract, they have an incentive to not under-bid, and thereby more accurately represent their opportunity costs of conservation. If someone asks for more money, it is assumed that their opportunity costs of conservation are higher, and the paying agency can be assured that more conservation will occur with a payment than without. The difference between outcomes observed with and without a policy is known as additionality, which we will discuss in more depth in the context of carbon offsets. Ensuring additionality is why auctions are seen to be cost-effective, although the extent to which this is true depends on other details spelled out by Ferraro (2008).

Without reverse auctions in a PES scheme, a separate method needs to be used to estimate the correct amount to compensate service providers. One popular alternative is a direct estimation of opportunity costs of conservation, which is a hard thing to try to characterize, based as it is on counterfactual scenarios of what opportunities would have been available in the absence of a policy. In the CAM programme in Cambodia, this was done by calculating the opportunity costs of conservation as measured by forgone rice yields, which Milne (2022: 82) argues overly simplified the opportunity costs involved by excluding forest use benefits such as obtain "vegetables, forest products, customary user rights, and the Indigenous way of life".

Turning to TEA policies, as I mentioned earlier, these involve a cap on total emissions or extraction, and then distribute rights to emit or extract based on this cap. TEA allocations have a problem that public goods markets do not because of the nature of the issue being addressed. TEAs seek to decrease certain activities, not increase them, and so excessive allocations of rights is one of the primary challenges these programmes face, in part because of political pressures by regulated actors to allocate more emission rights. Carbon markets in California and the European Union, for example, have historically suffered from over-allocation of emissions licences (Cullenward & Victor 2020).

Auctions are used by several carbon markets to initially allocate emission rights. As Lynham (2014) describes, auctions are not used much by catch share policies, with the most common principle for freely allocating fishing rights policies being historic use levels. In both cases here, the main advantage of freely giving away rights is that it gains political support from regulated actors. And as we discussed in Chapter 4, historic use is one of the most prominent principles for allocating resources.

But formally implementing this principle does bring with it several challenges. Cullenward and Victor (2020) argue for the preferability of auctions over the alternative of freely granting carbon emission rights, which is the alternative that most emitters prefer for obvious reasons. The authors argue that freely allocating rights to emitting "incumbents" can lead to situations where emitters have no incentive to curtail emissions and amounts to a giveaway of the environmental commons. Furthermore, in the context of environmental overuse, freely allocating rights faces the potential problem of rewarding those who most contributed to the problem that a market policy is trying to address. Second, we need to decide what timeframe to use to start counting use, and third, there is the possibility that if resource users see an allocation coming, they will be incentivized to increase their emissions or extractions to increase future use rights. Auctions are not a panacea either, as they may reinforce existing inequalities in resources themselves. For this reason some have proposed to use equity-based principles for the allocation of fishing rights, although these have also been contentious (Lynham 2014).

The initial allocation is a required step based on the setting of the cap, but neither the cap nor this allocation make a market policy. In the case of TEAs, it is the fact that the allocated rights are then tradeable. This is the "trade" part of "cap-and-trade". We now turn to a discussion of the two types of TEAs: shared resource markets and regulatory markets.

Shared resource markets: the case of catch shares

A catch share is considered a "share" because fishers receive "shares" of a total allowable catch. It is thus a regime primarily based on output rules rather than input rules, to refer back to our discussion in Chapter 4. Shares are also sometimes referred to as individual trading quotas (ITQs), individual fishing quotas (IFQs), or individual vessel quotas, based on the unit and basis for ownership. It can be confusing to try to ascertain the exact theoretical motivation for catch shares. Sometimes they are framed as being a way to prevent the tragedy of the commons of open access; more often they are argued to prevent the "race to fish" or the "fishing derbies" that in many places had been caused by rules that limited the length of a fishing season, causing fishers to get in as much fishing as possible in a short amount of time (popularized in the television show *The Deadliest Catch*). The core economic argument for catch shares, however, is that they increase the efficiency of catching fish, with the accompanying implication that such efficiency is also associated with ecological sustainability since declines in fish stocks will make it harder to fish and thus lower what is known as catch per unit effort (CPUE).

The promotion of catch shares

Catch shares, along with marine protected areas, are arguably the most popular fishing policy globally. They have achieved status as a policy panacea based on many of the criteria developed in section one. In their discussion of catch shares, Holm and Nielsen (2007: 175) cite Francis Christy, the originator of the catch share idea, as stating that "The transition to property rights regimes in fisheries is occurring with a speed which, I think, is not fully appreciated. The process is inexorable" (Christy 1996: 288).

We can notice some common themes that we have observed before with panaceas. First there is a conflation of the idea of property rights generally with a very specific version of a rights-based intervention, which I usually interpret in part as an attempt to leverage the valid logic of property rights to promote one's own preferred flavour of rights-based governance. Second, we have the claim that this is part of an unavoidable evolution towards "the best" way of doing things. This is particularly striking given that most catch shares have been a response to dire conditions in the fisheries where they are implemented, not representing the next step in a series of inevitable improvements. Catch shares are mostly implemented opportunistically in response to crises, as many policies are (Webster 2015).

Heller and Salzman (2021: 252), similarly praise catch share policy (using the term individual fishing quotas or IFQs) stating that "to date, catch shares have been adopted in forty countries and already account for about one-fifth of the global catch. It's no surprise the strategy has been called 'the greatest unknown policy success of our time'." Harkening back to our discussion of how to interpret policy success for panaceas, this statement conflates the idea of success as an outcome versus the spread of an idea.

Allocations, incentives and outcomes

TEAs share a common narrative that the alienation of use rights promotes cost-effectiveness. In the case of environmental pollution, cap-and-trade schemes are seen as a way to minimize the costs of pollution abatement (lowering emissions) by allowing less efficient actors to buy credits from more efficiently abating actors, as most famously touted in the 1990 Clean Air Act amendments that effectively addressed the acid rain problem in the United States. Cap-and-trade is thus argued to be a cost-effective way to combat pollution. In catch share policy, it is argued that the tradability of fishing rights will likewise lead to more efficient fishing, based on the presumption that willingness to pay for fishing quota positively correlates with fishing efficiency. The theory of catch shares revolves around efficiency as an outcome, but this leaves out several other important outcomes that we should consider.

Holland *et al.* (2017) for example, explore the impacts that catch shares have on catch and livelihood diversification. This an important relationship to explore because of the theory that such diversity can promote resilience, and that in many contexts a drive for increased efficiency, and the maximization for a particular output, can make an actor or system less resilient. Holland *et al.* (2017) explore the impacts of catch shares on diversification across 13 fisheries, finding that they do systematically reduce diversification of catch. Possible reasons for this include the consolidation inherent in the tradability of fishing quota, fishers having comparative advantages in catching certain species, and use of the quota market to specialize fishing activities. As the authors state, a primary reason for concern with reduced catch diversity is a loss of livelihood resilience. They do not, however, find that catch shares have had a similarly negative impact on inter-annual income variation. There is an important literature on resilience of fisheries and its relationship to efficiency and productivity, with my favourite example being the description of the fragility of the highly productive Maine lobster fishery provided by Steneck *et al.* (2011).

Stewardship outcomes are also important, and in fact are often emphasized more in popular discourses than efficiency, as Carothers and Chambers (2012: 42) observe in their critique of catch share policy:

> Strikingly, current proponents of fisheries privatization do not often cite rent maximization as a primary goal. The Environmental Defense Fund (2012), for example, states that catch shares can "bring back fish populations, save commercial fishing jobs, ensure fishing communities prosper and thrive, preserve our fishing heritage, and attract new participants." Conservation of fish stocks is first among these benefits and is increasingly used as a rationale for fisheries privatization in both academic and popular media and discourse.

To me, multiple overlapping narratives that amount to saying that a policy can do just about everything is a telltale sign of panacea thinking. So, can we expect catch shares to promote stewardship? Building on our discussion of exchange rights in Chapter 5, we should say that there is no necessary answer to this question, as it depends in part on what markets value. To more fully answer this in the context of market policy, we need to unpack a key difference between the two types of TEA policies. In the case of regulatory markets and emissions, we are allocating rights towards those who can more cost-effectively do something we want them to do more: abate emissions. So we are trying to help them do it more cheaply. In the case of natural resources, we are supposedly allocating rights towards those who can most cost-effectively do something we want them to do less of (at least from a stewardship perspective): catch fish. The primary underlying driver of overfishing is over-capitalization, not inefficient fishing. A failure to address the politically thorny root causes of overfishing has been a primary critique of catch share policy (Carothers & Chambers 2012: 45).

There cannot, therefore, be a single stewardship-based TEA theory of alienation and stewardship, because of this critical difference: making emission abatement cheaper intuitively can encourage more abatement. But how does making fishing more cost-effective by allocating it to more efficient fishers promote less fishing or more stewardship? Is there is a plausible scenario in which alienation could promote stewardship in the catch share context? The TAC of a catch share needs to accurately reflect the state of a fishery resource such that overfishing will lead to it declining, and if fishing quotas are proportional to the TAC, these will decline as well. In this case, more fishing would lead to a decline in the use value of rights, and exchange value if the quota market is working well. But why is exchange value needed to incentivize stewardship here? If the use value of my rights is declining, why isn't this enough to incentivize me to steward the resource, insofar as I see a connection between my actions and changes in the use value of my fishing rights? One possible answer to this question, which reflects the theory of environmental reciprocity, is that if I am not planning on continuing to fish in an area for much longer, and so I am not invested in the long-term use value of a resource. The exchange value in this case may motivate me to conserve a resource until I sell it.

To further address this and related topics, we can consider how catch shares allocate rights, which they do in two stages: initially with the beginning of the policy, and then through the alienation of rights. A common criticism of catch share policies has been that most often they initially allocate fishing quotas to those who own fishing boats at the beginning of the programme (arguably because it is easier to measure boat ownership than a more slippery concept of long-term investment in the fishery via labour inputs). This has created a patron–client relationship between boat owners and their crews, who are often disenfranchised by the new policy, and must lease quota if they are to fish for themselves. A potential benefit of this is the added flexibility that leasing arrangements can provide, which is also seen in other sectors, where for example, the leasing of water in irrigation systems can help farmers meet unforeseen needs. At the same time, the patron–client arrangement, as we have discussed, can lead to decreased incentives to steward and subsequent environmental degradation, although this may be counterbalanced by fishers' existing place attachment and intrinsic stewardship incentives (see Van Putten *et al.* 2014: 40).

Moving to trade-based allocations, it is not clear that we are in fact rewarding more efficient fishers via catch shares (Høst 2015). As Webster (2015: 310) observes: "access to capital is a larger determinant of dominance in basic ITQ systems, which means that large corporations can push smaller fishers out of the market for ITQs even if there are not substantial efficiency differences between the two". Much of what determines willingness to pay is the availability of capital, which rewards larger organizations, and has led to concerns about consolidation. Many catch shares had been integrated into the "financialization" movement, which represents "particular kind of economic rationalization that emphasizes returns to financial capital over all other values", a strategy that has impacted other sectors such as forestry (Gunnoe, Bailey & Ameyaw 2018: 800). In such situations rights increasingly reside in an investor class which views such rights as a means to monetary compensation over a fairly short time horizon. And this type of owner is likely not attached to the fishery in any psychological sense as discussed in Chapter 3: they view the environment in instrumentalist terms: as an asset class that they can use to diversify their portfolios. Because of their distance from the environment, they are unlikely to develop strong feelings of psychological ownership (Wang, Fielding & Dean 2022: 267). At the same time, it is important to not homogenize such actors, as there are examples of such remote corporate actors working to promote stewardship, such as Austral Fisheries in Australia (van Putten *et al.* 2014).

Additionally, just as exclusion is not an all-or-nothing concept, there can be alienation with limitations imposed onto it. The most common way this is done in catch shares is through what are known as aggregation or consolidation limits, which impose a limit on how much of a quota can be bought up by an individual owner. Limits can also be placed on who is allowed to buy quota. In the Alaskan halibut fishery, for example, there are classes of quota that can only be sold to community members, rather than to outside parties, exhibiting a version of the proximity principle described earlier. This is an important policy, since one of the main concerns with catch shares is the alienation of rights from local communities that they can cause.

Finally, some of these issues do not apply only to policies labelled as catch share programmes. Basurto *et al.* (2012: 605) describe the national fishing permitting programme in Mexico as having some of the same problems, despite not having issues related to alienation:

> The permit system in Mexico as implemented in the study area dispro-portionately empowers permit holders – who generally are not fish-ers – while disempowering and marginalizing the fishers in such way that neither group has incentives to coordinate and effectively limit outsider access to their fisheries. Permit holders act as middlemen in control of the entire fishing process and behave as roving bandits … They have low dependency on a specific set of local resources and have the economic power to "hire" fishers to fish where they are told. Permit holders and independent buyers are often the reason why large numbers of outsider boats arrive to fish generating conflict among local fishermen. Permit holders find no incentives to encourage local fishers to limit fishing and these fishers find themselves in a constant race to harvest local – and other communities' – resources farther away, before others do the same.

Basurto *et al.* (2012) also note that there is no limit on the number of permits that an individual or organization can hold. But since fishing rights are not tradeable in Mexico, this policy does not bring with it the some of the concerns about consolidation as occur under catch share programmes.

What is a catch share?

Some of these issues challenge our understanding of what a catch share most essentially is. Catch shares, like property regimes, are not unitary, but have multiple parts that may work well together or may conflict, and there is much heterogeneity across instances of catch share programmes. Catch shares are an example of a hybrid property regime that reserves control rights for state actors (Holm & Nielsen 2007). In the United States, for example, which has several catch share programmes, the TAC is set by regional fisheries management councils, and local users often have few management rights. At the same time, some catch shares are arguably more like the co-management arrangements that we discussed in Chapter 8. In New Zealand, for example, which has one of the oldest and most famous catch share programmes established in 1986, the catch share programme has since 1999 provided for the rights of a set of com-mercial stakeholder organizations, or CSOs. This approximates a version of the co-management model that we discussed in Chapter 8, with CSOs now often conducting monitoring of fisheries and fishing activities (Yandle 2008, cited in

Holland 2018). Still, as Yandle (2008: 134) mentions, this model is quite different from the image of a set of communities working together with a supportive government. Rather, the co-management regime has united communities more as an administrative artefact (with the indigenous Māori communities being an important exception). So, like our discussion of co-management from Chapter 8, there are multiple ways in which rights can be distributed under a catch share policy, and multiple ways of understanding what the "community" part of this model means.

Beyond the question of labelling the property regime of a catch share, we need to ask about the contributions that different aspects of a catch share make to which outcomes. Teasing out the impacts that marketization has on the fisheries themselves is difficult, because alienation is part of a larger package of policies and their implementation. How do we know if simply setting a TAC and divvying up rights, without making these rights tradeable, would have led to a worse result? Even a TAC in the absence of individual quotas could feasibly incentivize some conservation, it would just do so inefficiently, which individual quotas can address by stopping the race to fish. In her analysis of catch share programmes, van der Voo (2016: 107) reaches the conclusion that the "science that showed that catch shares ended overfishing failed to acknowledge that the features of the programmes – hard caps on catch, defined by quality science – were the chief achievers of those goals, rather than the privatization itself".

A catch share is often referred to as a market-based or incentive-based instrument, and in analyses of the effects of catch shares, we often see statements such as "market-based management ends the race to fish" (Birkenbach, Kaczan & Smith 2017: 223), giving rhetorical credit to the "market" part of catch share policy. But without the TAC limit, which in other contexts would likely be referred to as a "command and control" rule, no one would argue that a catch share would work, at least if it wasn't somehow accompanied by some other way to limit extraction as discussed in Chapter 4 (e.g., based on input controls). I am not saying that I think that a TAC with associated quota allocations will necessarily work on its own, as it does not necessarily prevent quota busting (not following the limitations of the TAC and associated fishing limits) and high-grading, or discarding poor quality fish so that they do contribute to one's quota (Acheson, Apollonio & Wilson 2015). But if not sufficient, a TAC does seem necessary to promote the outcomes that catch shares aim to achieve.

Another issue is that catch shares have often involved complementary policies. Some of these relate to concerns that catch shares may poorly reflect ecological complexity and move us away from holistic, ecosystem management. Acheson, Apollonio and Wilson (2015) provide a good example of how a catch share might ignore ecological complexity through the concept of a meta-population. The authors observe that fishing populations are commonly spatially distributed into sub-populations, and argue that if a catch share doesn't take this into account, it could allow fishers to serially deplete sub-populations within a larger population. This would intuitively call for quotas to be specific to sub-populations rather than species. And indeed, Emery *et al.* (2012), cited by van Putten *et al.* (2014), found that many catch share systems have added or maintained complementary input controls such as gear restrictions and limitations on vessel size in order to move closer to the approach of holistic ecosystem management. We can also harken back to our discussion of the potential advantages of common property from Chapter 7. There we referenced work by Dan Holland (2018), who pointed out that an important adaptation to catch shares by some groups of fishermen has been to form quota pools. These facilitate the exchange of rights within a pool, which helps fishers ensure that they maintain the ability to fish even in the face of fluctuating resource conditions and the case of reaching their quota for a choke species as described earlier.

To conclude, just as we have seen in our discussion of property regimes, there are fuzzy boundaries between broad institutional categories, and we insist on these being rigid in part because rigid boundaries are more legible to external parties: it is empowering to an external actor if they can label a case as belonging to just one category or another, because this enables comparisons among a group of cases categorized this way, and supports a preferred policy if it compares favourably. But when should we label a case as catch share policy with additional input controls, and when does it become a case of input controls with an additional catch share policy?

Regulatory markets: the case of carbon markets

The theory that justifies cap-and-trade policy is quite similar to the theory of catch shares, with the notable difference in the role that alienation plays as I mentioned above. The basic theory argues that the cap and associated emissions quotas provide a financial incentive to curtail emissions, and that the alienation of emission rights allows pollution abatement to be done cost-effectively from the perspective of the regulated entities. If company X finds it more expensive than company Y to reduce emissions, X can buy emissions permits from Y, and we are therefore channelling pollution abatement to the places where it can be done at the least cost.

Many of the observations we made about catch shares apply to carbon markets. For one, there is the concern about the spatial distribution of the resource in question. A well-known issue in cap-and-trade policy is the possibility for hot zones, whereby you can end up concentrating abatement, and therefore pollution, in one location and crossing thresholds for health and safety. Another similarity is the status of these two policies as policy panaceas. As Cullenward and Victor (2020) describe, cap-and-trade has been the darling of climate policy wonks for some time, with their enthusiasm outpacing the evidence that cap-and-trade addresses the climate problem better than other approaches.

Cullenward and Victor (2020) comment at length about the divergence between the theory of cap-and-trade and the complicated, political reality that must be faced during implementation. In part this lack of evidence comes from the fact that where cap-and-trade policies are implemented, they are being integrated with existing policies such as renewable portfolio standards, for which a new policy may be taking credit, creating what we referred to in Chapter 6 as a false positive (a false conclusion about the success of a policy that is then used to argue for further applications of the policy). And this results in part from what I referred to in the introduction as the missing variable problem: if we leave out variables such as other policies that positively affect outcomes from an analysis, it can look like a policy is successful because it is taking credit for these other policies. Cullenward and Victor argue that the California carbon market programme, which is one of the most prominent and arguably well-functioning in the world, has acted as a false positive in this way.

The other part of this story is that the politics of implementation disrupted the idealized schemes that had been written down on paper about how such schemes should work. In the case of California's carbon market, regulated actors have consistently lobbied for a less stringent cap and lower carbon prices. This reflects a pattern that is also seen in many catch share programmes (Webster 2015), which has led to the TAC being set too high in that sector as well. This situation is sometimes referred to as regulatory capture, and it should dampen our enthusiasm for the political participation discussed in Chapter 8.

The concern here is less with carbon markets or regulatory markets per se, which can be successful. It is well known that much of the enthusiasm for carbon markets comes from the highly successful cap-and-trade programme created by the Clean Air Act Amendments of 1990 in the United States to address the problem of acid rain. The issue here is more with their treatment as panaceas, which includes the exclusion of other policy options. This exclusion presumes that different options are mutually exclusive. But like catch shares, the boundaries between carbon markets and other policies can become fuzzy, depending on what complementary practices are put into place. It is possible to create a hybrid policy, for example, by adding a price floor (or ceiling) to a carbon market, which can make the policy behave more like a carbon tax, which is the alternative with which carbon markets are most commonly compared. In their comparison of these two policies Goulder and Schein (2013: 28) conclude that "when comparably designed, a carbon tax, cap-and-trade system, and hybrid policy yield very similar incentives to reduce emissions". The idea of a hybrid policy is similar to a hybrid property regime, and it should similarly influence our thinking about environmental property and policy.

Forests and carbon offsets: back to PES

Speaking of complementary policies, an increasingly popular policy that is often added to carbon markets is known as carbon offsets, but in practice these two policies have become closely connected, often under the rubric of an initiative known as Reducing Emissions from Deforestation and Forest Degradation, or REDD. Carbon offsets are essentially a PES policy and therefore a public good market: someone pays someone else to provide for a public good. In the context of a carbon market the actor who pays receives carbon credits and the public good is carbon sequestration measured in tons of carbon dioxide equivalent. Each of these policies benefits the other one. The carbon market provides the answer to the question of who is paying for the ecosystem services, and offsets act as a pressure release valve for regulated entities, who can acquire them as a means to exceed their emission limits as defined by a carbon market. So instead of emitting less, regulated entities can pay someone to change their behaviour to sequester carbon somewhere else, with the idea that emissions in one place are balanced out by sequestration in another place. Like other policies we have discussed, the carbon offset space is very complex from a property regime perspective, with large NGOs often stepping in as certifiers where one might expect a governmental actor to be leading the way. This is particularly true with voluntary carbon markets.

The main advantage of carbon offsets is the same as the role of exchange that we have seen before: they offer additional flexibility to regulated actors and lower the costs of compliance. They also shift the benefits of climate policy towards extra-governmental actors (e.g., NGOs and academics) who have led the charge in setting up and running carbon offset certifying processes, particularly in the voluntary market space (Cullenward & Victor 2020). A challenge introduced here is that those doing the certifying are sometimes paid by those who want to be certified, which is a conflict of interest and can lead to regulatory capture.

Offsets create a strong connection between carbon policy and forest management because of how popular forest-based offset projects are. Forest projects account for roughly 80 per cent of offset projects in the California cap-and-trade scheme. Some of the issues that offsets face are specific to the forestry context and others are not. We have seen some of the challenges such programmes face in our discussion of the CAM programme in Cambodia. Here, external actors struggled to make a complex social and ecological landscape legible so that it could be managed from afar. Additionally, three issues are critical for any PES scheme to address: additionality, permanence and leakage. Additionality receives the most attention among these, and it represents the concern that a carbon offset project may not represent any additional carbon storage over and above what would have happened in its absence. This is the fundamental challenge of all observational science; that it cannot establish a counterfactual to clearly establish causality, the way an experiment can.

There is evidence that many carbon offsets do not represent additional storage (Cullenward & Victor 2020). Badgley *et al.* (2022) analyse the California cap-and-trade offset programme and find that the protocol it uses has led to a systematic overestimation in the amount of carbon being stored. This has resulted from the California Air Resources Board, which runs the programme, using regional averages of carbon storage as a baseline against which offset programmes are judged, representing the analytical (in this case ecological) simplification that we discussed in Chapter 6. As Badgley *et al.* describe, this commits the ecological fallacy of assuming that a population average represents the averages found in subgroups, and this enabled the strategic implementation of offset projects in forests that naturally store more carbon than the regional average to gain more offset credits under the programme's accounting protocol. As a final note, this lack of recognition of sub-groups is shared with some catch share policies which, as I noted in the previous section, could lead to serial depletion of sub-populations within a catch share regime.

Leakage is a standard governance issue as well, and it reflects the possibility that increased carbon sequestration in one place (say by avoided deforestation) could lead to decreased sequestration (increased deforestation) elsewhere. This complicates the carbon accounting problem, and the methods by which it is accounted for by California's programme have been controversial (Badgley *et al.* 2022). Finally, a project has permanence if the benefits it produces can last, particularly beyond the horizon of the project itself. This issue strongly relates to our previous conversations about motivational crowding: if a PES policy crowds out intrinsic motivations to conserve, whatever benefits it produces may not last once payments cease, although we should remember that such crowding will not necessarily happen if the autonomy of recipients is supported by the policy.

Shifting the burden

In Chapter 1, we talked about the problem of shifting the burden, or coping with the symptoms of a problem as a way to avoid dealing with its underlying drivers. A final concern that we should have with carbon offsets is that they enable the continuance of business as usual. It does so by allowing us to avoid decreasing greenhouse gas emission and all of the larger-scale economic transitions this would involve. The advantage of coping with symptoms rather than dealing with the underlying drivers is that it is less expensive and therefore more politically feasible. It therefore isn't surprising that a burgeoning voluntary carbon credit market is sweeping through the world's most developed economies. But dangling the promise of technologizing or incentivizing our way out of the climate crisis can create a moral hazard, whereby people take on more risk when they are insured against its negative consequences.

On an individual level, a mental accounting may occur whereby if I purchase a carbon offset for a flight that I take, this makes me feel like I have satisfied any obligation I might have to help with the climate crisis, and this allows me to go on with my life, guilt-free. This would be fine if we could be assured that offsets worked, but they often likely do not. At the organizational level, the challenge is that, as Cullenward and Victor (2020) describe, there is no incentive for regulated bodies to ensure that carbon offset projects are delivering on their promise. Quite the opposite: regulated firms should seek to maximize the number of offsets for the lowest price. It is much more tempting to simply add carbon offsets as a new item on a corporate balance sheet than it is to fundamentally change a firm's activities to move towards decarbonization. Critics have argued that offset projects amount to asking less wealthy countries and people to continue to bear the burden of climate change that is disproportionately caused by wealthier countries and people, who are using them as a means to exculpate themselves from any collective sense of guilt they may have.

Finally, much of how carbon offsets work depends on who the governing bodies are, and who works within these with which incentives and information. Much of the activity here is done outside the auspices of a centralized government actor. Once again, we cannot assume that "the government" should just come in and solve these problems. This is particularly the case in the new voluntary carbon offset programmes that are currently receiving a lot of attention and interest from private industry.

These criticisms are important, but we also have to recognize that not all carbon offset policies are the same. We have seen throughout this book that the world is more diverse than is implied by the abstract adjectives and nouns that we throw at it. Greenleaf (2020), for example, describes a different take on carbon offset PES policy in the state of Acre in Brazil. Here, payments for ecosystem services are not distributed only to those with full land tenure, including the right to exclude. Instead, the designers and implements of the programme attempted to skirt the difficulties of complex, illegible and unequal land endowments by compensating local users for their "green labour" (or compensating based on inputs instead of outputs or outcomes. This represents a departure from the orthodoxy of PES thinking, although most broadly it is still based on the rights of beneficiaries to access and use the land. And the programme introduces its own inequalities based on who is able and willing to perform the activities that the programme rewards.

More broadly, not all of the issues that forest-based carbon offsets face should be applied to offsets generally, or to tradeable permits similar to off-set programmes even more generally. The issues of additionality, leakage and permanence would look quite different if carbon capture technologies were scalable and a company could pay to have carbon physically removed from the atmosphere. In that case we wouldn't have to deal with a complex social and ecological system to ensure that the carbon accounting works out. Or in the energy space, we have renewable energy credits, or RECs, which are an attribute of electricity as having been produced by renewable technology. A REC is similar to an offset in that it is essentially a certificate for a certain quantity, in this case referring to units of energy, that is produced to comply with a policy-imposed limit, in this case a renewable portfolio standard (Harvey, Orvis & Rissman 2018). Both are based on accounting frameworks and promise to increase flexibility of policy compliance. RECs can also be unbundled and transacted separately from the energy they represent, enabling a situation similar to an emissions cap-and-trade scheme. But the concerns that we have about carbon markets and offsets do not straightforwardly apply to RECs and renewable portfolio standards.

Conclusion

Markets may be the most popular policy panacea in the world today. Sometimes there is confusion about the theoretical motivation for these and the empirical evidence behind the enthusiasm. In this context I do think we need to be clear about the theoretical arguments and evidence available to support a preferred policy. For example, there is no theoretical reason to suppose that the increased efficiency enabled by catch shares should lead to increased stewardship; if I were to bet, I would bet on the opposite relationship.

At the same time, this chapter has made arguments about market policies that mirror the broader themes of this book, and arguments about property regimes in particular. Market policies are best thought of as hybrid property regimes, with some rights to emit or extract allocated to one group of actors, and control rights allocated to government actors or sometimes an NGO. And like the property regimes we have discussed, market policies are not unitary. Rather they contain multiple sub-components that can work independently or together to enable or inhibit programme success. Because of these sub-parts, market policies are also more diverse than is often understood, and because of this, we should not lapse into an us versus them with respect to markets and the environment, assuming that we need to be either pro or anti. This conclusion is reinforced by our observation in Chapter 5 that reciprocal exchange is a cultural universal, and informal markets are employed beneficially by communities around the world.

Finally, this discussion reinforces a point made in Chapter 8: we need to think about the process of implementation as much as we pay attention to the broad category that a case or policy is put into. The concepts of additionality, leakage and permanence point to broad design and implementation challenges, as do Ostrom's design principles. We need broad categories to have a discourse that compares many different cases, but we should always be aware that in doing so we are artificially simplifying a complex reality for the sake of making reality legible to us.

10

Conclusion

The goal of this book is to synthesize multiple perspectives and evidence on environmental property rights, and thereby improve understanding and decision-making. I begin this final chapter by reflecting on the methods used to conduct this synthesis. After this, I outline two ways in which we can use this synthesis to make better environmental policy decisions. First, I discuss a process of institutional diagnosis (Ostrom *et al.* 2007a; Young 2002). This is a process of ascertaining the relevant features of a problem to explore their implications for the design of responses. In the second section below, I describe how this book can be used to diagnose environmental problems by drawing questions from each chapter that we should ask about a problem and its possible solutions. Second, I discuss how expertise depends on the qualities of the expert. Here I am drawing on work by Matson, Clark and Andersson (2016), who describe qualities of effective sustainability leaders. The third and final section in this chapter explores the qualities of the experts who would be making the prescriptions based on these diagnoses.

Methods

Much of the motivation for this book is my perception of the synthesis bottleneck in the study of environmental property rights that results from the siloed nature of research. The goal here was to pull together multiple disciplines to tell a more comprehensive story about the meaning and role of environmental ownership. It is worth reflecting here on the methods that I used and the implications these have for how we should interpret this work. Poteete, Janssen and Ostrom (2010) reflect on the various methods that are used by scholars in the study of environmental commons governance. The types of studies that they consider are found through the pages of this book: individual and comparative case studies, experiments, large-n analyses and synthetic meta-analyses. And the method for the book as a whole is reflected in what Poteete *et al.* (2010) call a qualitative "narrative synthesis", with their prime example of this being the well-known work on natural resource management by Baland and Platteau (1996). This is a relatively uncommon type of synthesis, with most approaches being primarily or exclusively quantitative. So why take a qualitative approach? First, qualitative, narrative synthesis is particularly appropriate when a diversity of study types with different research designs because these are hard to consistently characterize for quantitative comparison (Poteete *et al.* 2010). Second, qualitative methods often have an advantage over quantitative methods when it comes to unpacking social-ecological complexity (Schlüter *et al.* 2021). In this study I view complexity as being represented by the interdisciplinary connections we have made and by the conditionality of our conclusions: we have mostly avoided making definitive conclusions, and opted instead for "on the one hand, and on the other hand (and then on the other hand)" thinking, meaning that we are always looking for both patterns as well as exceptions. Exploring this complexity here was well supported by a qualitative approach and the flexibility it provides in folding around the evidence. In making these comments I do not mean to reinforce the qualitative versus quantitative divide, since this has served as yet another example of unproductive intergroup conflict and mutual dismissiveness, and it is worth noting that I have drawn on a mix of qualitative and quantitative studies in this synthesis.

Despite these arguments, from a traditional comparative social science perspective, there are some important limitations of this work to acknowledge. Here it is helpful to distinguish between the cases versus the studies that I have synthesized, and we can discuss the decisions and biases that influenced my selection of each. Cases and studies are not necessarily the same, since a published study may describe a single case, or several, or many, or not discuss any cases at all. That said, a fair amount of my evidence comes in the form of case studies. My goal in selecting these was primarily to find cases that did a particularly good job of representing certain issues or concepts, which is not the same thing as being representative of a larger population. While this is recognized as a valid logic for case study selection, there are two concerns that arise. One is that I am looking at cases through a particular lens as representing a set of ideas: I am using them instrumentally rather than holistically. There is a danger here that in applying this lens I will artificially simplify their points in order to fit my need of slotting them into my narrative synthesis. This is a weakness of all synthetic work, even when it is done qualitatively. We should therefore take the cases I discuss to be illustrative of the topics they highlight, and not necessarily generalizable in all their aspects. Not every case of indigenous governance will look exactly like Vaughan's (2018) discussion of the Native Hawaiian practices, and not every PES policy, or CAM programme implemented by Conservation International more specifically, will look like the example that Milne (2022) describes in Cambodia. Indeed, a major theme of this book is to avoid this type of overgeneralization. My goal for each of these cases was less to make an argument about indigenous practices generally or about PES schemes generally, and more to illustrate the underlying concepts at stake, and help us understand their connections to the study of environmental property rights.

We can also think about the nature of the studies that I examined. Here, in addition to looking for studies with illustrative cases, I was biased towards studies that are considered foundational within a particular field. A downside of this is that it reinforces the cumulative advantage of papers (and their authors) with many citations as they become even more popular, helping fulfil the very criteria that are the basis for the selection (this is also known as the "Matthew effect"). The reason for selecting foundational papers, particularly when exploring a new field of knowledge, is that foundational papers can better represent a large portion of a field, often quite directly by examining a broad evidence base. This is similar to a social scientist conducting an interview with an expert about a particular case: to learn about the larger case, you want to talk to someone who is unrepresentative with respect to the level of their knowledge about this case.

The most obvious limitation of this discussion for my own methods is the potential lack of reliability of the results: if someone else were to conduct this research, they would come up with at least somewhat different results, and I would say that if I were to do it again, the book would look rather different. On one hand, I see this as a limitation of the approach, and one that will only become more difficult to surmount as the amount of evidence and scholarship to synthesize continues to grow. It is also tempting to view this as a result of the qualitative rather than quantitative result that was taken, and to an extent I agree, but there is nothing automatically reliable about quantitative measurement and analysis: it takes work to make sure that data are collected consistently, and quantitative analyses can often appear like a black box to readers and reviewers.

On the other hand, I believe that the nature of an exercise like this means that we need to be more flexible in terms of the standard evaluative criteria. This is an exploratory analysis, hopefully making new connections between a range of ideas and evidence. My primary goal here was to maximize the number of meaningful connections between and among concepts and evidence, and this was therefore a creative process, and one not fully amenable to the standard of reliability. Finally, while acknowledging the weaknesses just described, to some extent I think these are weaknesses within the confines of a particular scientific paradigm. When we are moving between paradigms, it is harder to hold fast to a particular set of rules, as Kuhn (2012) so famously argued.

Institutional diagnosis

In the previous section I mentioned the importance of conditional thinking, and I think the ability to always be aware of both broad trends and exceptions is an important marker of expertise, which I want to develop further in this section. I will go through each chapter and highlight questions that have the strongest implications for how we might address an environmental problem with the language and tools of property rights.

Part I: Collective action and groups

Chapter 1 shows us that we should ask about the role of collective action and the role collective action problems play. Does the source of a problem follow the traditional framing of the tragedy of the commons, or does cooperation in fact play a role in causing the problem, or both? In either case, we should also ask if there are other causes of the problem, such as the presence of social asymmetries between actors that enable some to cause more harm without suffering the consequences. Are some actors "upstream" of others, such as in an irrigation system, or through the hierarchical arrangement of rights? We need to also ask if other models are appropriate, such as roving banditry and serial resource depletion, as these play just as important a role in contributing to environmental degradation. An example we used in Chapter 1 was the serial depletion of forest lands by banana companies in Latin America (Koeppel 2008).

The concepts in Chapter 2 lead us to ask about the role of boundaries, both around a resource and around its users. The theory of environmental reciprocity, which argues that boundaries in the form of high costs of exit and entry motivate investment in the environment (defined as either stewardship or development), may be relevant here. We also need to ask about the presence of rigid versus contextual boundaries and the roles these may be playing. Based on our observations about the role of contextual boundaries in pastoral systems, we may find or prescribe contextual boundaries in situations of high resource scarcity and low human impact, and also expect to see this accompanied by high user mobility as an adaptive package, keeping an eye out for the potential for such mobility to enable serial resource depletion. This scenario represents an additional departure from the tragedy of the commons model as the motivational framing of environmental property rights, and should make us question the standard definition of common-pool resources as being subtractable, as this depends on how they are used.

This chapter also introduced some important concepts to keep in mind moving forward. First is the proximity principle, whereby rights are allocated to one resource based on ownership of a nearby one, which represents our first foray into the question of rights allocation. Like all allocational principles, we should evaluate proximity as a basis for rights at least in part based on which actors are making ownership claims about which resources. Finally, we learned in this chapter that usufruct rights are ubiquitous, and we should be sensitive to the presence of these even if they are not as obvious to external actors.

Based on Chapter 3, we need to ask about the role of intrinsic value and the psychologies of kinship and reciprocity, which can play an important role in promoting environmental stewardship and a more holistic approach to environmental use. These have played a less prominent role in the dominant property policy discourse, arguably because they are hard to prescribe: such psychologies must be developed over time with respect to a particular place. But still, they speak to the importance of attachment, and we should ask about factors that are disrupting the ability of communities to maintain attachment to place. We should leave this chapter with a greater sensitivity to the potential adaptive functions of local institutions such as sacred groves, rather than disregarding them as "irrational" religious artefacts.

Part II: Bundles of rights

Part II of the book deals with the idea of bundles of rights. If we think that rights play an important role in addressing environmental problems, we have to be clear on what we mean by environmental ownership. In Chapter 4 we unpack the notion of what it means to use the environment, and we begin a fuller conversation about how rights should be allocated. An important part of this discussion was the broadening of the concept of access to help us understand that rights are allocated in very indirect ways that we need to be on the lookout for, and understand that such indirect allocations are often based on complex social arrangements and inequalities that we may not be able to easily influence.

Chapter 4 also tells us that we ask questions about what types of use rights are most appropriate, distinguishing between rules that regulate how the environment is to be used (e.g., gear restrictions in a fishery) and rules that regulate how much it is to be used. This distinction in turn is closely related to the difference between input and output rules, and these two are sometimes conflated. A quantitative input rule, for example, is found in the Maine Lobster fishery that limits the number of lobster traps that can be used. Finally, we need to ask about the potential role of use entitlements, which creates a connection to market-based policies in Chapter 9. The most prominent policy example of use entitlements that we have discussed are PES policies.

The first part of Chapter 5 shows us the importance of asking about the role of exchange entitlements. Here we were introduced to a new model, the patron–client relationship, which encourages us to ask about the distribution of exchange entitlements, and whether market intermediaries are acting predatorily or not. This relationship reminds us that, even if we are dealing with a familiar tragedy of the commons scenario, say the depletion of a local fishery, we need to consider not only the incentives and behaviours of resource users.

The chapter also introduces the principles of efficiency and equity. We often want to promote these outcomes in our prescriptions, but we need to be aware of how difficult it can be to use them meaningfully. We need to also consider the impacts of policy and culture on multiple outcomes and ask whether there are trade-offs or synergies among these outcomes. Because of the multiple ways such outcomes can be used, they can have different relationships with each other in different cases. I questioned, for example, the assumption that efficiency and equity are necessarily negatively related, but such a negative association forms part of an important critique of catch share policy. Finally, Chapter 5 introduced us to the concept of transaction costs, or the costs of developing and enforcing exchange agreements. Here we emphasized that while traditionally we would want to minimize these, they also can represent a more holistic accounting of the costs and benefits of exchange. We saw an example of this in the limitations that some communities impose on individual exchange rights.

Part III: Property regimes and panaceas

Chapter 6 transitions us to policy solutions. It tells us that we should be asking about the types of prescriptions we want to make to solve a problem, and why we want to make them. We might be confident in making a very specific prescription, but in complex real-world systems it is often more responsible to make broader prescriptions that allow local implementers more flexibility in their implementation. Ostrom's design principles stand out here as an effective way to do this, with her first principle being about boundaries. We know that any system needs boundaries, but without knowing the specifics of a case we should be wary of prescribing a certain type of boundaries, referring to our discussion in Chapter 2.

The formalism of expertise can open us up to other traps as well. We should ask if we are unrealistically framing a policy prescription as politically neutral, and if we are avoiding the underlying drivers of a problem in our prescriptions. We also need to ask if we are forcing a case to fit our preferred framework and thereby be legible to us as an outside actor. This chapter also encourages us to ask about our group affiliations and if these affect our assessment of the best response to a problem (here's a hint: they do).

Based on Chapter 7, we should ask about the role of individual and common property and understand that they have a close relationship in most systems. In asking about the role of each type of property, we should be open to how each might be the result of local users adapting to their local context, as is the case with common property adapting to resource scarcity. We should also ask ourselves if we are being naively adaptationist in how we interpret local institutions, and discounting the possibility that an adaptation for some can impose costs on others, as we saw in the case of the bovine mystique in Lesotho. Relatedly, we shouldn't treat communities or even individuals as unitary actors with a single identity and interest. Communities are always somewhat heterogenous, and individuals have multiple motivations that often compete with each other. Just as we need to know who the powerful actors in a community are, we need to know what contexts will activate different psychological motivations.

Chapter 8 reveals the need to recognize that we may be overemphasizing the importance of broad categories like property regimes in our analysis. How such regimes are implemented matters just as much as their classification, and there is much variation within regime types as well. And we need to understand the complexity of how property regimes are combined in complex cases to create hybrid regimes. In this chapter we also further explore reasons to support or question common property and community-based governance. An important conclusion here is that, even if we are wary of the problems caused by top-down, command-and-control governance, we shouldn't assume that all local communities are created equal in terms of their impact on their environment. Finally, the rights of nature movement represents a new option to formalize the intrinsic value of nature introduced in Chapter 3, although it must confront Western norms which dismiss this perspective.

In Chapter 9, we return to the topic of exchange through market policies, which we defined as hybrid property regimes. These have an important role to play but have also been given the panacea treatment by many of their supporters. This chapter showed us the trap of being unthinkingly supportive or dismissive of market policies. The real world is complex and as always we shouldn't assume that all market policies are the same. Policies like catch shares and carbon markets may be associated with positive outcomes, but those outcomes can also be a result of a combination of many different rules that are not part of the core theory of the policy, leading to an exaggeration of the importance of this core theory.

A new kind of expertise

Policy is not just about rules, it is also about the people who design and implement them, because "personnel is policy". As such, when we think about our role in helping to promote better outcomes for people and the environment, we need to look inward as well as outward. This topic also builds on our discussion of human nature throughout this book. We are all collective actors with different parts, and our success as experts and leaders depends on the other actors we can interact with, but also on how our internal parts relate to each other. We all have basic needs as highlighted by self-determination theory, and we can try to meet these needs or cope with their absence in ways that don't help ourselves or others, for example by imposing our authority onto a situation to establish a sense of agency that we feel we are lacking inside. In this final section I explore the attributes of effective experts and leaders, building on the work of Matson, Clark and Andersson (2016). These authors argue that the following attributes characterize successful "sustainability leaders": (1) systems thinking; (2) reflective and adaptive thinking; (3) self-awareness; and (4) creativity.

Systems thinking

In Chapter 3, I discussed Vaughan's (2018) book, *Kaiāulu: Gathering Tides* in my discussion of kinship, reciprocity and our relationship with nature. One of the aspects of this book that I particularly admire is how Vaughan describes the interconnectivity of the terms that she uses from the Hawaiian language. Vaughan describes a dense network of meaning; the meaning of any one concept is relational, dependent on its connections to other ideas. This is what systems thinking mostly means to me: the ability to travel a network of associations between related issues and ideas, so that you know what questions to ask based on where you are in the network. I call this associative expertise. This is different from a more linear expertise, which plots out a theory of change from inputs to outputs. It is about knowing the right questions to ask based on what you know so far. It is about knowing when you should stay in one dense cluster of a network, and when you should jump to another set of concerns.

This is what I have tried to accomplish with this book as well, and one of the main challenges I have experienced is deciding how to fit a network of knowledge into the linear format of language and writing. I don't think there is a beginning and an end to systemic expertise, as you are always being led to something else. We can't understand property regimes without also understanding the different types of rights that actors might have. This also reflects one of the main points I have tried to make in this book, that to be an expert in environmental property rights requires that the knowledge network extends between what are normally considered separate areas of activity. We have needed to explore the nature of humanity; we need to understand how we act collectively and sometimes with a single purpose but also how we tend to form in-groups and out-groups; how we extend our psychologies of kinship and reciprocity to scale up the in-group to include more people and potentially much of nature as well; how we have basic needs and biases that constantly influence our thinking. We also need to consider the nature of the environment itself, from how "ownable" it is to whether we can think at least parts of it as a unified whole.

Reflective and adaptive thinking

Matson, Clark and Andersson argue that good leaders are able to contemplate uncertainty and update their thinking. They think about how they think. And while we might say we subscribe to this point of view, it is hard to maintain in practice, as we are often more rewarded for having strong opinions and for standing by our principles. Like social influence, I think we are all more dependent on confirmation bias and extending our opinions beyond the available evidence than we are ready to admit. We all have our sacred ideas, whether these are about the sanctity of Indigenous relationships with the environment or the potential of market policies to solve our problems. And I don't mean to imply a false equivalence here: I believe more in the power intrinsic value to cure what ails us than in the promise of continued commodification of common resources. But I am aware that my commitment here also says something about my own social influences.

I agree with Clancy and Davis (2019: 177) when they argue that we "should also ask about the trope of the detached scientist whose perspective of those he studies is the most valuable and objective". The kind of expertise we need is one that entertains seemingly contradictory interpretations of a concept. Too often, expertise is signalled by the confidence and simplicity of our assertations and committing to seeming contradictions is seen as a sign of muddled and incomplete thinking. But boundaries can be both rigid and contextual; panacea promoters can earnestly want to help, and sometimes they may, and sometimes they may not; property can be both adaptive and unequal; alienation can be both empowering to individuals and crippling to communities, and we can care about both of these outcomes at once.

I set out to help the reader understand the complexity of property rights in this book, and having written it, I now believe this also means that we must learn to tolerate ambiguity. My thoughts on the contents of this book are not settled. I used the occasion of writing to sort out what I think, and the connections I have made are the result of a constant deliberation between my head and my hands.

Self-awareness and reflexivity

Self-awareness means an awareness of our integration with other collective selves, and the collectives that are within each of us. Reflexivity is the ability to look within ourselves and question our assumptions and motivations. I think one of the primary challenges to complex, reflexive thinking is our group-based affiliations. Group identity often requires an adherence to one way of thinking or one conclusion, not a messy "on the one hand and on the other". And the greater the external threat is, the stricter the adherence is required, leading competing groups down an arms race of internal rigidity and fragility. I think maintaining reflexiveness then requires an ability to sit within and at the boundary of one's group affiliations, even if this can feel like it means that one is rejected by competing groups. An identity that we haven't discussed much in this book is the boundary actor, who is perceived as legitimate in multiple groups. But many of the goals that I have described are a function of how these boundary actors are able to communicate across groups. Milne (2022), for example, attributes some of the challenges of the CAM programme in Cambodia to how knowledge was translated by such actors across boundaries, in a way that concealed what was happening on the ground to more central actors.

I also believe that many of the arguments we have made should encourage us to consider our own thought processes. We are not unitary actors ourselves, but collections of different motivations and interests. Which of these takes hold of us and when, and why? Do we understand our own collective nature, and how context changes what parts of us emerge into our experience and behaviour? Can we be a leader in one situation and a follower in another, while holding on to an essential sense of self? How does this impact our ability to engage with others in ways that help us and them? Collective outcomes will be achieved as much through the character of those involved as by the formal categories they are trying to implement, even if such character is harder to measure.

Creativity

Part of the importance of documenting institutional diversity is that it helps us better understand the range of opportunities available to us. But this is not nearly as useful if we cannot think creatively about how we might create new institutional solutions to our problems based on what has developed before us. This has often gone by the very academic-sounding term of "institutional bricolage", which sounds a lot like institutional evolution. Building incrementally from what is available may sound limiting, and not disruptive enough maybe for the change we need to address environmental problems. But I think we under-appreciate just how cumulative progress is, in part because the collective efforts behind supposed individual moments of genius are much less visible from the outside.

Future directions

I wouldn't argue that the language and tools of property rights are sufficient in addressing our environmental problems. But I do believe that it is a necessary part. And I hope that I have shown the importance of interdisciplinary synthesis in understanding the sources and possible solutions to our environmental problems. At the same time, we need to keep in mind that the goal of interdisciplinary work is not to entirely remove barriers from disciplines and do away forever with intergroup disciplinary conflict. We all need to belong to a group, and we aren't going to simply remove our tendency to establish boundaries between in-groups and out-groups. But we can be more aware of how to construct and police these boundaries, and how we respond to people who are not in our own group, making sure to not overly homogenize them in our imaginations and interactions.

Being more interdisciplinary also requires different incentives. Learning new approaches takes time and effort that is not immediately legible to reward systems. If we decide to systematically capture the complexity of hybrid property regimes around the world, this requires cooperation and overcoming the temptation for participants to free-ride. The current way that academia is individualistically "gamified" (Nguyen 2020), incentivizing each academic researcher to become the centre of their own academic personality cult, exacerbates this challenge, once again reflecting the trade-off between cooperation at one level of social organization and cooperation at successive levels.

We also need to find a way to muddle through complexity. Writing this book was partly a response to reductionist discourses about the best way to manage the environment, some of which I have described. But it is also a response to reactions to reductionism that I have not found helpful because of how abstract they often are. In such reactions we face a new barrage of jargon, with words like complexity, non-linearity, adaptability, relationality, dynamics, and the list goes on. I think the most valuable approach is to find a middle ground between these two poles. This can feel less glamorous because it affords less confident policy pronouncements. But muddling through the details and slowly making connections between ideas and cases is the way forward.

Glossary

Access rights   The right to physically access a part of the environment. A type of *use right*.

Adaptationism   An approach that assumes that long-lasting traits are adaptive. Can help uncover the meaning of certain traits but can also crowd out competing interpretations of these traits based on power and politics.

Alienation rights   The right to sell one's rights to a *resource system* and the stream of benefits it confers. A type of *exchange right*.

Asymmetry   A description of a relationship between two actors. The asymmetry can be informational, where one knows more than the other, or in terms of incentives in an upstream versus downstream relationship, where an upstream actor can impact the welfare of a downstream actor but not vice versa. Moderates the presence of a collective interest by separating upstream versus downstream interests.

Autonomy   The *basic need*, as identified by self-determination theory, to see one's actions match one's values and sense of self. Also a justification for *bottom-up governance*.

Balancing rights   An approach to resolve competing rights claims by weighing the interests of different parties to achieve a balance. Contrasted with *hierarchical rights*.

Basic needs   Identified by self-determination theory as critical to human welfare and intrinsic motivation. See *autonomy*, *efficacy* and *belonging*.

Belonging   The *basic need*, as identified by self-determination theory, to belong to a social group and feel valued within it.

Bias   Describes a way in which human cognition steers human attention and decision-making.

Bottom-up governance   Governance that places authority primarily in the hands of individuals and communities and is not very hierarchical. Contrasted with *top-down governance*.

Boundaries   The combination of social and biophysical boundaries are the defining feature of environmental property rights. Types of boundaries include *rigid* versus *contextual*.

Bundle of rights   Expresses the idea that there are multiple ways to own the environment, as an owner can have one or more of a bundle of rights.

Capital inputs principle   A principle for allocating rights based on the input of capital (e.g., labour, time).

Catch shares   An example of a *shared resource market* applied to the fisheries sector.

Collective action   The label for individuals incurring personal costs to contribute to a public good for a group they belong to. Synonymous with cooperation.

Collective action problem   A divergence between the interests of a group and the individual interests of its members. One of the primary motivations for governance and property rights.

Collective property   A *property regime* that allocates ownership to a collective entity rather than to individuals. Includes *common property*, *corporate property* and *public property*.

Co-management   A hybrid *property regime* that grants rights to both resource users as well as governmental actors. Often reserves more powerful control rights for governmental actors.

Commons   A shared resource.

Common-pool resource   A shared resource, or *commons*, that can be used up through use, (also referred to as subtractability or exhaustability).

Common property   A *property regime* that allocates resource rights primarily to a group of resource users. A type of *collective property*.

Community-based natural resource management   An approach to resource governance where communities of users are granted environmental rights. As a formal approach it has been criticized as a *policy panacea*.

Confirmation bias   Describes how humans pay more attention to evidence that supports their previously held views and dismiss contradictory evidence.

Conformity bias   The tendency to conform to the norms of one's in-group. A type of *in-group bias* and related to the basic need of *belonging*.

Contextual boundaries   Boundaries that change over time, space and context. Contrasted with *rigid boundaries*.

Control rights   The right to design, allocate and enforce the rules associated with other rights.

Coproduction   Collaborative service provision by service providers and receivers.

Cumulative advantage   Occurs when actors with wealth and other resources leverage these resources to further extend their social advantages. A form of *path dependence*.

Direct reciprocity   The direct exchange of goods and resources between two actors, with each being incentivized by the other's contribution. Contrasted with *indirect reciprocity*.

Direct rights   The right to engage in a concrete action with respect to the environment through use or exchange. Contrasted with *entitlements*.

Distributive justice   The pursuit of *equity* via equal allocations of resources and benefits.

Dominant institutional design   A set of institutions that become entrenched in a system and force future actions to adapt to their dominance, creating *path dependence*.

Ecological fallacy The assumption that we can use aggregated measures of a group (e.g., household income) to make inferences about its members.

Efficacy The *basic need*, as identified by self-determination theory, to influence one's social and biophysical environment in accordance with one's goals.

Efficiency The maximization of a ratio of outputs over inputs. Arguably the most popular policy goal in Western societies.

Elite capture The capturing of public benefits by the elites of a community. A common criticism of policies that confer benefits or rights to local communities.

Entitlements The right to indirectly benefit from the use of the environment or the exchange of rights. Contrasted with *direct rights*.

Environmental property right A social claim by an actor that they can take an action that impacts the environment.

Essentialism A perspective that views the attributes of a concept, person or object as being inherent in them and not a function of their relationships with others. Contrasted with *holism*.

Equality An equal distribution. Often thought of as a type of *equity*.

Equity The fairness of a procedure or outcome.

Evolution Occurs through the generation of diversity, selection on this diversity, and the inheritance of selected traits. Evolution can occur at the level of individuals and groups, and can occur genetically or culturally. Sometimes used loosely to mean some form of development. Also associated with arguments that there is one "best way" for society to organize itself and develop.

Exaptation Occurs when an existing adaptation is applied to a new context and for a new function. Cultural kinship is an example. Also represents a form of *path dependence*.

Exchange rights The right to exchange other rights to a resource or to otherwise benefit from such exchanges.

Exclusion rights Grants authority to deny access rights to other actors. Traditionally seen as the most fundamental environmental property right. A type of *control right*.

Externality A social cost or benefit that is unaccounted for by the actor that produces it.

Extrinsic value and motivation Values and motivation that come from the outside, and are important instrumentally, or insofar as they satisfy some other goal. Contrasted with *intrinsic value and motivation*.

False positive bias The tendency to look for patterns in a piece of evidence that show that a preferred policy had a positive effect, even when it may not have.

Formality Formal rights, and institutions more generally, are those that are written down or otherwise codified in a way that is interpretable by a third party. Contrasted with *informal rights and institutions*.

Formal legibility A type of *legibility* that describes an agreement between two actors when it is legible to a third actor, who can then understand this agreement and enforce it.

Fortress conservation A label of some conservation efforts that criticizes them for being excessively exclusionary, particularly to traditional resource users. Most often associated with *protected areas*.

Gamification   The application of values and principles from the world of games to real life. See also *Goodhart's law*.

Goodhart's law   A claim that once a variable becomes a metric used to measure performance, it stops being a good metric because of the strategic behaviour that it incentivizes.

Hierarchical rights   An approach to resolve competing rights claims by prioritizing some claims over others without weighing competing interests. A popular example is the prior appropriation regime for water use in the western United States. Contrasted with *balancing rights*.

Historical right   A right that is established based on who started to use the environment first, also known as the *priority principle*.

Holism   A perspective that emphasizes how the identities of concepts and objects are a function of their relationships with others. Associated with *intrinsic value and motivation*. Contrasted with *essentialism*.

Hybrid property regime   A combination of multiple *property regimes* with competing claims by different actor groups. *Co-management* is an example of a hybrid regime.

Indirect reciprocity   The exchange of goods and resources among multiple actors, with no direct reciprocal tie between any two actors. Creates social cohesion through collective exchange.

Individual property   A type of *property regime* that refers to ownership by individuals or households. Often loosely referred to with the term *private property*, but this includes other regimes as well, including *common property*.

Informality   Informal rights, and institutions more generally, are those that are expressed through social norms and common understandings. Contrasted with *formal rights and institutions*.

In-group bias   The tendencies to identify with members of one's own group, to search for markers of belonging among others, and to treat non-members poorly in comparison. Associated with several other biases.

Input rules   A type of rule associated mostly with *stock and flow rights* that describes the inputs that may go into an activity to achieve on output or outcome. Associated with the *capital inputs principle*. See also *output rules* and *outcome rules*.

Intrinsic value and motivation   Values and motivation that come from the inside, and are important inherently, without the need to satisfy some other goal. Contrasted with *extrinsic value and motivation*.

Kinship psychology   A state of mind that supports the treatment of others, including non-genetically related humans, non-humans and the environment, with *intrinsic value and motivation*.

Legibility   Describes the extent to which an object is visually perceivable and can be interpreted by an actor through an analytical framework. See also *formal legibility*.

Management rights   Rights that confer authority over the expression of *stock and flow* and *physical development* rights. A type of *control right*.

Market-based policies   Policies that involve a *hybrid property regime* and which allocate *exchange rights* to resource users. Primary examples include *public good markets* and *tradeable environmental allowances*.

Moralistic bias The tendency in storytelling to label a group as the cause of the main problem in the story, thereby establishing a "heroes versus villains" framing. A type of *in-group bias*.

Motivational crowding The crowding out of *intrinsic motivation* by *extrinsic motivation*. A common concern expressed with respect to *payment for ecosystem service* policies.

Naturalistic fallacy The assumption that if something is natural, it must be good.

Negativity bias The tendency to pay much more attention to negative trends than positive ones.

Open access property regime Supposedly a type of *property regime*, but really represents the absence of any property regime and associated limitations on resource use. Associated with the *tragedy of the commons*.

Outcome rules A type of rule that applies mostly to stock and flow rights, specifying how much of a stock must be present (e.g., how many lobsters should remain after harvest or what the concentration of a pollutant should be in a body of air or water). See also *input rules* and *output rules*.

Out-group homogeneity bias The tendency to downplay the diversity of individuals in groups that one does not belong to. A type of *in-group bias*.

Output rules A type of rule that applies mostly to *stock and flow rights*, specifying how much of a stock can be added or removed in a given period of time (e.g., how many lobsters can be caught in a year in a fishery). See also *input rules* and *outcome rules*.

Paper rights Rights that exist formally (on paper) but not informally (in fact). When applied to *protected areas* this is referred to as a paper park.

Path dependence The tendency for a system to stay on the particular path that it is on through self-reinforcing processes.

Patron–client relationship A relationship in which a wealthier patron gives resources to a client who then repays the patron with loyalty and economic goods. A common example is the relationship between a natural resource user (client) and a market intermediary (patron).

Payment for ecosystem services A policy in which payments are made to natural resource users to incentivize them to provide ecosystem services. This payment establishes a *direct use entitlement* for resource users. A type of *public good market*.

Physical development rights A type of *use right* related to the physical alteration of the environment.

Place attachment The application of *intrinsic value and motivation* to a geographic location.

Policy panacea A policy that is implemented across a range of contexts without sufficient concern for how such contexts, and the politics and power relationships within them, will influence outcomes achieved by the policy.

Principal–agent relationship A relationship in which a principal hires an agent to conduct certain activities or achieve certain outcomes. From the principal's perspective such relationships are challenging because of an asymmetry between their interests and information and those of the agent.

Priority principle   One of the primary principles for allocating rights, prioritizing claims that were established earlier than others. A popular example is the doctrine of prior appropriation that is used to allocate water rights in the western United States. Establishes a *historical right*.

Private property   A type of *property regime* that loosely refers to ownership by anyone other than a governmental actor, including individuals, communities or corporations. Often used to refer to individual property specifically but without making this explicit.

Procedural justice   The pursuit of *equity* through *equality* of participation in political processes.

Protected area   A common conservation policy that specifies a certain area to be protected, and often sub-areas to be governed by additional restrictions.

Property regime   Describes what type of actor owns the environment. Common types include *public, private, common, individual, rights of nature* and *open access*.

Proximity principle   A principle for allocating rights to a resource based on ownership to nearby resources.

Public good   A type of *commons*, or shared resource. It is further defined by its lack of exhaustability, unlike *common-pool resources*, which are exhaustible. The most common example are property rights arrangements themselves if they benefit a group.

Public good market   A type of *market-based policy* that involves the payment for a *public good*. A common example is *payment for ecosystem services* policies.

Public property   A type of *property regime* in which rights are primarily owned by a state government or agency, supposedly with the public interest in mind.

Qualitative rules   Rules that prescribe how the environment can be used. Contrasted with *quantitative rules*.

Quantitative rules   Rules that prescribe how much of the environment can be used or how many inputs can be used to obtain benefits from the environment. Contrasted with *qualitative rules*.

Reciprocity   The tendency to reciprocate the behaviour that we receive from others. Can be extended to non-humans and the environment.

Regulatory markets   A policy for managing environmental pollution. Commonly referred to as cap-and-trade. A type of *tradeable environmental allowance*, itself a type of *market-based policy*.

Resource system   a set of interconnected parts that work together to support a stream of benefits to resource users, often through the provision of *resource units*.

Resource unit   A physical object that is provided by a *resource system*, such as a fish or tree.

Rigid boundaries   Boundaries that do not change much over time, space and context. Contrasted with *contextual boundaries*.

Rights of nature   A type of *property regime* in which nature itself is granted ownership rights.

Roving banditry   A type of pernicious resource use by highly mobile actors who are motivated by the demands of long-distance markets to *serially deplete* natural resources.

Serial resource depletion　A type of resource depletion that is caused in part by the lack of stewardship incentives for a given resource due to the availability of additional resources that can be used after a given resource is depleted. A component of *roving banditry.*

Shared resource markets　A policy for managing a natural resource system that involves exchange rights. The most common example is catch shares in the fisheries sector. A type of *tradeable environmental allowance,* itself a type of *market-based policy.*

Shifting the burden　Refers to the process of coping with the symptoms of a problem rather than adapting by dealing with its underlying drivers. Treating underlying drivers can get to the root of a problem and ultimately resolve it, but this is more costly and takes more time.

Stewardship　An expression of care for the environment through *intrinsic value.* Can also be thought of as a *use right* that entails a sense of obligation for the environment.

Stock and flow rights　A type of *use right* associated with the removal of resource units from or the addition of pollutants to the environment.

Theory of environmental reciprocity　Argues that property rights incentivize environmental investment (*development* or *stewardship*) in the environment by conferring benefits back to those who make the investments. The most common justification for environmental property rights.

Top-down governance　Governance that places authority primarily with large, hierarchical organizations such as states and corporations. Contrasted with *bottom-up governance.*

Tradeable environmental allowances　A type of *market-based policy* that starts with a cap on resource use (an *output rule*) and then distributes exchangeable use rights. The two primary examples are *shared resource markets* (e.g., catch shares for fisheries) and *regulatory markets* (e.g., cap-and-trade for air pollution).

Tragedy of the anticommons　Represents the possibility that the environment and other resources may be underused and underprovided as a result of an excess of property rights that thwart such use and provision.

Tragedy of the commons　The degradation of a resource that results from an unresolved *collective action problem.* Associated with *open access* property conditions.

Transaction costs　The costs of developing and enforcing social agreements, including property rights arrangements.

Unitary actor assumption　The assumption that we can meaningfully talk about an actor at any scale as if they had a single identity and interest, rather than multiple sub-identities and conflicting interests.

Usufruct rights　The right to use a part of the environment that is owned by someone else for a specific purpose.

Appendix: Ostrom's design principles

Number and name	Statement
1A: Social boundaries	Boundaries between legitimate users and nonusers must be clearly defined.
1B: Physical boundaries	The boundaries of the shared resource must be well defined
2A: Fit	Congruence between local rules and local environmental conditions
2B: Proportionality	Congruence between provision of costs and benefits
3: Collective-choice	Most individuals affected by operational rules can participate in modifying these rules
4A: Social monitoring	Monitors actively audit behaviour of resource users
4B: Environmental monitoring	Monitors actively audit resource conditions
5: Graduated sanctions	Sanctions are proportional to the severity of an offense, or to the number of times it has been committed.
4 and 5: Accountability	Individuals who monitor and sanction are accountable to community members
6: Conflict resolution	Low-cost mechanisms to resolve conflict exist
7: Rights to organize	External governmental authorities recognize the rights of local users to self-organize
8: Co-management	Governance is expressed in multiple layers of nested institutions

Source: Based on Cox, Arnold and Villamayor-Tomas (2010).

References

99% Invisible 2015. "Devil's rope". Podcast. https://99percentinvisible.org/episode/devils-rope/.

Abrams, R. 2019. "Prior appropriation and the commons". *UCLA Journal of Environmental Law and Policy* 37(2): 141–89.

Acheson, J. 2003. *Capturing the Commons: Devising Institutions to Manage the Maine Lobster Industry*. Lebanon, NH: UPNE.

Acheson, J., S. Apollonio & J. Wilson 2015. "Individual transferable quotas and conservation: a critical assessment". *Ecology and Society* 20(4): 7–16.

Acheson, J. & J. Wilson 1996. "Order out of chaos: the case for parametric fisheries management". *American Anthropologist* 98(3): 579–94.

Agrawal, A. 1993. "Mobility and cooperation among nomadic shepherds: the case of the Raikas". *Human Ecology: An Interdisciplinary Journal* 21(3): 261–79.

Agrawal, A. 1998. "Profits on the move: the economics of collective migration among the Raika Shepherds in India". *Human Organization* 57(4): 469–79.

Agrawal, A. 2007. "Forests, governance, and sustainability: common property theory and its contributions". *International Journal of the Commons* 1(1): 111.

Agrawal, A. & C. Gibson 1999. "Enchantment and disenchantment: the role of community in natural resource conservation". *World Development* 27(4): 629–49.

Agrawal, A. & G. Yadama 1997. "How do local institutions mediate market and population pressures on resources? Forest Panchayats in Kumaon, India". *Development and Change* 28(3): 435–65.

Akers, J. & M. Yasué 2019. "Motivational crowding in payments for ecosystem service schemes". *Conservation & Society* 17(4): 377–89.

Albertus, M. 2021. *Property without Rights: Origins and Consequences of the Property Rights Gap*. Cambridge: Cambridge University Press.

Alchian, A. & H. Demsetz 1973. "The property right paradigm". *Journal of Economic History* 33(1): 16–27.

Anderson, S. *et al.* 2011. "Serial exploitation of global sea cucumber fisheries". *Fish and Fisheries* 12(3): 317–39.

Anderson, T. & G. Libecap 2014. *Environmental Markets: A Property Rights Approach*. Cambridge: Cambridge University Press.

Armborst, T. *et al.* 2017. *The Arsenal of Exclusion and Inclusion.* Barcelona: Actar Publishers.

Badgley, G. *et al.* 2022. "Systematic over-crediting in California's forest carbon offsets program". *Global Change Biology* 28(4): 1433–45.

Bagley, N. 2019. "The procedure fetish". *Michigan Law Review* 118(3): 345–402.

Bahuchet, S. 1990. "Food sharing among the pygmies of Central Africa". African Study Monographs, HAL Open Science. https://hal.science/hal-00361817/.

Baland, J.-M. & J.-P. Platteau 1996. *Halting Degradation of Natural Resources: Is There a Role for Rural Communities?* Oxford: Oxford University Press.

Ban, N. *et al.* 2017. "Social and ecological effectiveness of large marine protected areas". *Global Environmental Change* 43: 82–91.

Bastin, J.-F. *et al.* 2019. "The global tree restoration potential". *Science* 365(6448): 76–9.

Basurto, X. 2005. "How locally designed access and use controls can prevent the tragedy of the commons in a Mexican small-scale fishing community". *Society & Natural Resources* 18(7): 643–59.

Basurto, X. *et al.* 2012. "The emergence of access controls in small-scale fishing commons: a comparative analysis of individual licenses and common property-rights in two Mexican communities". *Human Ecology* 40(4): 597–609.

Basurto, X. *et al.* 2020. "Governing the commons beyond harvesting: an empirical illustration from fishing". *PloS One* 15(4): e0231575.

Berkes, F. 1986. "Local-level management and the commons problem: a comparative study of Turkish coastal fisheries". *Marine Policy* 10(3): 215–29.

Berkes, F. 2018. *Sacred Ecology: Traditional Ecological Knowledge and Resource Management.* Philadelphia, PA: Taylor & Francis.

Berkes, F. *et al.* 2006. "Globalization, roving bandits, and marine resources". Science 311(5767): 1557–8.

Berman, E. 2022. *Thinking Like an Economist: How Efficiency Replaced Equality in US Public Policy.* Princeton, NJ: Princeton University Press.

Birkenbach, A., D. Kaczan & M. Smith 2017. "Catch shares slow the race to fish". *Nature* 544(7649): 223–6.

Bollier, D. & S. Helfrich 2019. *Free, Fair, and Alive: The Insurgent Power of the Commons.* Gabriola Island, BC: New Society Publishers.

Bowles, S. 2016. *The Moral Economy.* New Haven, CT: Yale University Press.

Bowles, S. & S. Polania-Reyes 2012. "Economic incentives and social preferences: substitutes or complements?". *Journal of Economic Literature* 50(2): 368–425.

Boyd, D. 2017. *The Rights of Nature: A Legal Revolution That Could Save the World.* Toronto: ECW Press.

Bray, D. 2020. *Mexico's Community Forest Enterprises: Success on the Commons and the Seeds of a Good Anthropocene.* Tucson, AZ: University of Arizona Press.

Brewer, J. 2012. "Don't fence me in: boundaries, policy, and deliberation in Maine's lobster commons". *Annals of the Association of American Geographers* 102(2): 383–402.

Brockington, D. 2002. *Fortress Conservation: The Preservation of the Mkomazi Game Reserve, Tanzania.* Bloomington, IN: Indiana University Press.

Brockington, D., R. Duffy & J. Igoe 2008. *Nature Unbound: Conservation, Capitalism and the Future of Protected Areas.* London: Routledge.

Bromley, D. 1991. "Environment and economy: property rights and public policy." www.cabdirect.org/cabdirect/abstract/19921898862.

Bromley, D. 1992. "The commons, common property, and environmental policy". *Environmental & Resource Economics* 2(1): 1–17.

Bromley, D. & I. Hodge 1990. "Private property rights and presumptive policy entitlements: reconsidering the premises of rural policy". *European Review of Agricultural Economics* 17(2): 197–214.

Brown, D. 1991. *Human Universals*. New York: McGraw Hill.

Callahan, C. & J. Mankin 2022. "National attribution of historical climate damages". *Climatic Change* 172(3): 40.

Carlsson, L. & F. Berkes 2005. "Co-management: concepts and methodological implications". *Journal of Environmental Management* 75(1): 65–76.

Carothers, C. & C. Chambers 2012. "Fisheries privatization and the remaking of fishery systems". *Environment and Society* 3(1): 39–59.

Carothers, C. *et al.* 2021. "Indigenous peoples and salmon stewardship: a critical relationship". *Ecology and Society* 26(1); doi:10.5751/ES-11972-260116.

Cerasoli, C., J. Nicklin & M. Ford 2014. "Intrinsic motivation and extrinsic incentives jointly predict performance: a 40-year meta-analysis". *Psychological Bulletin* 140(4): 980–1008.

Chinigò, D. 2015. "The politics of land registration in Ethiopia: territorialising state power in the rural milieu". *Review of African Political Economy* 42(144): 174–89.

Christakis, N. 2019. *Blueprint: The Evolutionary Origins of a Good Society*. London: Hachette.

Christy, F. 1996. "The death rattle of open access and the advent of property rights regimes in fisheries". *Marine Resource Economics* 11(4): 287–304.

Cinner, J. *et al.* 2013. "Global effects of local human population density and distance to markets on the condition of coral reef fisheries". *Conservation Biology* 27(3): 453–58.

Clancy, K. & J. Davis 2019. "Soylent is people, and WEIRD is white: biological anthropology, whiteness, and the limits of the WEIRD". *Annual Review of Anthropology* 48(1): 169–86.

Cleaver, F. 1999. "Paradoxes of participation: questioning participatory approaches to development". *Journal of International Development* 11(4): 597–612.

Cody, K. *et al.* 2015. "Emergence of collective action in a groundwater commons: irrigators in the San Luis Valley of Colorado". *Society & Natural Resources* 28(4): 405–22.

Cohen, M., J. March & J. Olsen 1972. "A garbage can model of organizational choice". *Administrative Science Quarterly* 17(1): 1–25.

Collins, J. 2015. "Please, not another bias! An evolutionary take on behavioural economics". Blog post; www.jasoncollins.blog/please-not-another-bias-an-evolutionary-take-on-behavioural-economics/.

Cox, M. 2008. "Balancing accuracy and meaning in common-pool resource theory". *Ecology and Society* 13(2): 44.

Cox, M. 2014. "Understanding large social-ecological systems: introducing the SESMAD project". *International Journal of the Commons* 8(2): 265–76.

Cox, M., G. Arnold & S. Villamayor-Tomas 2010. "A review of design principles for community-based natural resource management". *Ecology and Society* 15(4): 38.

Cox, M., F. Payton & L. Pimentel 2019. "A gilded trap in Dominican rice farming". *Land Use Policy* 80: 10–20.

Cox, M. & M. Schoon 2020. "The academic arms race". Common Podcast blog. www.incommonpodcast.org/the-academic-arms-race/.

Cox, M., S. Villamayor-Tomas & Y. Hartberg 2014. "The role of religion in community-based natural resource management". *World Development* 54: 46–55.

Cox, M. *et al.* 2018. "The Dominican fishery of Manzanillo: a coastal system in transition". *Ocean & Coastal Management* 162: 170–80.

Cox, M. *et al.* 2021. "Lessons learned from synthetic research projects based on the Ostrom Workshop frameworks". *Ecology and Society* 26(1): 17.

Cronon, W. 2011. *Changes in the Land: Indians, Colonists, and the Ecology of New England*. London: Macmillan.

Cullenward, D. & D. Victor 2020. *Making Climate Policy Work*. Cambridge: Polity.

Cundill, G. *et al.* 2013. "Land claims and the pursuit of co-management on four protected areas in South Africa". *Land Use Policy* 35: 171–8.

Dagan, H. 2011. *Property: Values and Institutions*. Oxford: Oxford University Press.

Daigneault, A., S. Greenhalgh & O. Samarasinghe 2017. "Equitably slicing the pie: water policy and allocation". *Ecological Economics* 131: 449–59.

Daintith, T. 2010. *Finders Keepers: How the Law of Capture Has Shaped the World Oil Industry*. London: Routledge.

De Vos, A. *et al.* 2019. "The dynamics of proclaimed privately protected areas in South Africa over 83 years". *Conservation Letters* 12(6): e12644.

DeCaro, D., M. Janssen & A. Lee 2015. "Synergistic effects of voting and enforcement on internalized motivation to cooperate in a resource dilemma". *Judgment and Decision Making* 10(6): 511–37.

DeCaro, D., M. Janssen & A. Lee 2021. "Motivational foundations of communication, voluntary cooperation, and self-governance in a common-pool resource dilemma". *Current Research in Ecological and Social Psychology* 2: 100016.

DeCaro, D. & M. Stokes 2013. "Public participation and institutional fit: a social-psychological perspective". *Ecology and Society* 18(4): 40–61.

Degens, P. 2021. "Towards sustainable property? Exploring the entanglement of ownership and sustainability". *Social Sciences Information* 60(2): 209–29.

Degnbol, P. *et al.* 2006. "Painting the floor with a hammer: technical fixes in fisheries management". *Marine Policy* 30(5): 534–43.

Dell'Angelo, J. *et al.* 2017. "The tragedy of the grabbed commons: coercion and dispossession in the global land rush". *World Development* 92: 1–12.

Dell'Angelo, J. *et al.* 2021. "Commons grabbing and agribusiness: violence, resistance and social mobilization". *Ecological Economics* 184: 107004.

Dennett, D. 2013. *Intuition Pumps and Other Tools for Thinking*. Illustrated edition. New York: Norton.

DiGirolamo, M. 2021. "Carbon cowboys' and illegal logging, Mongabay". Mongabay Explores Podcast. https://news.mongabay.com/2022/02/podcast-carbon-cowboys-and-illegal-logging/.

Drury O'Neill, E. & B. Crona 2017. "Assistance networks in seafood trade: a means to assess benefit distribution in small-scale fisheries". *Marine Policy* 78: 196–205.

Duflo, E. & A. Banerjee 2011. *Poor Economics*. New York: Public Affairs.

Dunn, M. 2000. "Privatization, land reform, and property rights: the Mexican experience". *Constitutional Political Economy* 11(3): 215–30.

Duthu, N. 2008. *American Indians and the Law*. London: Penguin.

Easterly, W. 2008. "Institutions: top down or bottom up?". *American Economic Review* 98(2): 95–9.

Eger, J. *et al.* 2022. "Does evidence matter? The impact of evidence regarding aid effectiveness on attitudes towards aid". *European Journal of Development Research*; doi:10.1057/s41287-022-00570-w.

Ellenberg, J. 2014. *How Not to be Wrong: The Power of Mathematical Thinking*. London: Penguin.

Ellickson, R. 1991. *Order Without Law: How Neighbors Settle Disputes*. Cambridge, MA: Harvard University Press.

Ellickson, R. 1993. "Property in land". *Yale Law Journal* 102: 1315–400.

Emery, T. *et al.* 2012. "Are input controls required in individual transferable quota fisheries to address ecosystem based fisheries management objectives?". *Marine Policy* 36(1): 122–31.

Ferguson, C. *et al.* 2022. "The tragedy of the commodity is not inevitable: Indigenous resistance prevents high-value fisheries collapse in the Pacific islands". *Global Environmental Change* 73: 102477.

Ferguson, J. 1994. *The Anti-Politics Machine: Development, Depoliticization and Bureaucratic Power in Lesotho*. Minneapolis, MN: University of Minnesota Press.

Ferguson, J. 2005. "Seeing like an oil company: space, security, and global capital in neoliberal Africa". *American Anthropologist* 107(3): 377–82.

Fernald, S., T. Baker & S. Guldan 2007. "Hydrologic, riparian, and agroecosystem functions of traditional acequia irrigation systems". *Journal of Sustainable Agriculture* 30(2): 147–71.

Fernald, S. & S. Guldan 2006. "Surface-groundwater interactions between irrigation ditches, alluvial aquifers, and streams". *Reviews in Fisheries Science* 14: 79–89.

Ferraro, P. 2008. "Asymmetric information and contract design for payments for environmental services". *Ecological Economics* 65(4): 810–21.

Field, E. 2004. "Fertility responses to land titling: the roles of ownership security and the distribution of household assets". https://scholar.harvard.edu/field/files/field_fertility_05.pdf.

Fischel, W. 2015. *Zoning Rules! The Economics of Land Use Regulation*. Cambridge, MA: Lincoln Institute of Land Policy.

Fleischman, F. & C. Solorzano 2018. "Institutional supply, public demand, and citizen capabilities to participate in environmental programs in Mexico and India". *International Journal of the Commons* 12(2): 162–90.

Fletcher, R. & J. Breitling 2012. "Market mechanism or subsidy in disguise? Governing payment for environmental services in Costa Rica". *Geoforum* 43(3): 402–11.

Fortmann, L. 1995. "Talking claims: discursive strategies in contesting property". *World Development* 23(6): 1053–63.

Freitas, F. 2021. *Nationalizing Nature*. Cambridge: Cambridge University Press.

Frey, U. 2020. *Sustainable Governance of Natural Resources: Uncovering Success Patterns with Machine Learning*. Oxford: Oxford University Press.

Furth-Matzkin, M. & C. Sunstein 2018. "Social influences on policy preferences: conformity and reactance". *Minnesota Law Review* 102(3): 1339–80.

Gadgil, M. 2018. "Sacred groves: an ancient tradition of nature conservation". *Scientific American* 319(6); doi:10.1038/scientificamerican1218-48.

Galaty, J. 2016. "Reasserting the commons: pastoral contestations of private and state lands in East Africa". *International Journal of the Commons* 10(2): 709–27.

Galik, C. & P. Jagger 2015. "Bundles, duties, and rights: a revised framework for analysis of natural resource property rights regimes". *Land Economics* 91(1): 76–90.

Gazzaniga, M. 2012. *Who's in Charge? Free Will and the Science of the Brain*. London: HarperCollins.

Gelfand, M. 2018. *Rule Makers, Rule Breakers: How Tight and Loose Cultures Wire Our World*. Reprint edition. New York: Scribner.

Giridharadas, A. 2018. *Winners Take All: The Elite Charade of Changing the World*. New York: Alfred A. Knopf.

Goldstein, J. & M. Childs 2020. "Negative oil". Planet Money, podcast. www.npr.org/2020/04/22/842095406/episode-993-negative-oil.

Goode, A. *et al.* 2019. "The brighter side of climate change: how local oceanography amplified a lobster boom in the Gulf of Maine". *Global Change Biology* 25(11): 3906–17.

Gottschall, J. 2021. *The Story Paradox: How Our Love of Storytelling Builds Societies and Tears them Down*. New York: Basic Books.

Gould, C. & J. Urpelainen 2020. "The gendered nature of liquefied petroleum gas stove adoption and use in rural India". *Journal of Development Studies* 56(7): 1309–29.

Gould, S. & R. Lewontin 1979. "The spandrels of San Marco and the Panglossian paradigm: a critique of the adaptationist programme". *Proceedings of the Royal Society of London, Series B* 205(1161): 581–98.

Goulder, L. & A. Schein 2013. "Carbon taxes versus cap and trade: a critical review". *Climate Change Economics* 4(3): 1350010.

Greene, J. 2013. *Moral Tribes: Emotion, Reason, and the Gap Between Us and Them*. New York: Penguin.

Greenleaf, M. 2020. "The value of the untenured forest: land rights, green labor, and forest carbon in the Brazilian Amazon". *Journal of Peasant Studies* 47(2): 286–305.

Gunnoe, A., C. Bailey & L. Ameyaw 2018. "Millions of acres, billions of trees: Socioecological impacts of shifting timberland ownership". *Rural Sociology* 83(4): 799–822.

Hamilton, W. 1964. "The genetical evolution of social behaviour 1". *Journal of Theoretical Biology* 7(1): 1–16.

Harden-Davies, H. *et al.* 2020. "Rights of nature: perspectives for global ocean stewardship". *Marine Policy* 122: 104059.

Hardin, G. 1968. "The tragedy of the commons". *Science* 162(3859): 1243–8.

Hardin, G. 1974. "Commentary: living on a lifeboat". *Bioscience* 24(10): 561–8.

Harvey, H., R. Orvis & J. Rissman 2018. *Designing Climate Solutions: A Policy Guide for Low-Carbon Energy*. Washington, DC: Island Press.

Havice, E. 2013. "Rights-based management in the Western and Central Pacific Ocean tuna fishery: economic and environmental change under the Vessel Day Scheme". *Marine Policy* 42: 259–67.

Heller, M. 1998. "The tragedy of the anticommons: property in the transition from Marx to markets". *Harvard Law Review* 111(3): 621–88.

Heller, M. & J. Salzman 2021. *Mine! How the Hidden Rules of Ownership Control Our Lives*. New York: Knopf Doubleday.

Hēnare, M. 2018. " 'Ko te hau tēnā o tō taonga …': the words of Ranapiri on the spirit of gift exchange and economy". *Journal of the Polynesian Society* 127(4): 451–63.

Henrich, J. 2015. *The Secret of Our Success: How Culture is Driving Human Evolution, Domesticating Our Species, and Making Us Smarter*. Princeton, NJ: Princeton University Press.

Henrich, J. 2020. *The WEIRDest People in the World: How the West Became Psychologically Peculiar and Particularly Prosperous*. New York: Farrar, Straus & Giroux.

Henrich, J. & R. McElreath 2002. "Are peasants risk-averse decision makers?" *Current Anthropology* 43(1): 172–81.

Hinkel, J. *et al.* 2015. "A diagnostic procedure for applying the social-ecological systems framework in diverse cases". *Ecology and Society* 20(1): 32–45.

Holland, D. 2018. "Collective rights-based fishery management: a path to ecosystem-based fishery management". *Annual Review of Resource Economics* 10(1): 469–85.

Holland, D. 2022. "111: Fisheries policy and catch shares with Dan Holland". In *Common Podcast*. www.incommonpodcast.org/podcast/111-fisheries-policy-and-catch-shares-with-dan-holland/.

Holland, D. *et al.* 2017. "Impact of catch shares on diversification of fishers' income and risk". *Proceedings of the National Academy of Sciences* 114(35): 9302–7.

Holling, C. & G. Meffe 1996. "Command and control and the pathology of natural resource management". *Conservation Biology* 10(2): 328–37.

Holm, P. & K. Nielsen 2007. "Framing fish, making markets: the construction of individual transferable quotas (ITQs)". *Sociological Review* 55(2 suppl): 173–95.

Høst, J. 2015. *Market-Based Fisheries Management: Private Fish and Captains of Finance*. Berlin: Springer.

Howe, B. 2022. "It's public land. But the public can't reach it". *New York Times*, 26 November. www.nytimes.com/2022/11/26/business/hunting-wyoming-elk-mountain-access.html.

Hyde, L. 2019. *The Gift: How the Creative Spirit Transforms the World*. London: Vintage.

Ichikawa, M. 1981. "Ecological and sociological importance of honey to the Mbuti net hunters, Eastern Zaire". African Study Monographs 1: 55–68.

James, W. 1970. "Why the Uduk won't pay bridewealth". *Sudan Notes and Records* 51: 75–84.

Janssen, M., J. Anderies & J.-C. Cardenas 2011. "Head-enders as stationary bandits in asymmetric commons: comparing irrigation experiments in the laboratory and the field". *Ecological Economics* 70(9): 1590–8.

Jepson, P. *et al.* 2001. "Essays on science and society: the end for Indonesia's lowland forests?". *Science* 292(5518): 859–61.

Johnson, D. 2010. "Institutional adaptation as a governability problem in fisheries: patron–client relations in the Junagadh fishery, India". *Fish and Fisheries* 11(3): 264–77.

Kahneman, D. 2011. *Thinking, Fast and Slow*. New York: Farrar, Straus & Giroux.

Kashwan, P. *et al.* 2021. "From racialized neocolonial global conservation to an inclusive and regenerative conservation". *Environment: Science and Policy for Sustainable Development* 63(4): 4–19.

Kaur, K., K. Chang & K. Andersson 2023. "Collective forest land rights facilitate cooperative behavior". *Conservation Letters* 16; doi:10.1111/conl.12950.

Kieran, C. *et al.* 2017. "Gender gaps in landownership across and within households in four Asian countries". *Land Economics* 93(2): 342–70.

Kilgore, M. *et al.* 2018. "Private forest owners and property tax incentive programs in the United States: a national review and analysis of ecosystem services promoted, landowner participation, forestland area enrolled, and magnitude of tax benefits provided". *Forest Policy and Economics* 97: 33–40.

Kilic, T., H. Moylan & G. Koolwal 2021. "Getting the (gender-disaggregated) lay of the land: impact of survey respondent selection on measuring land ownership and rights". *World Development* 146: 105545.

Knight, J. 1992. *Institutions and Social Conflict*. Cambridge: Cambridge University Press.

Koeppel, D. 2008. *Banana: The Fate of the Fruit that Changed the World*. London: Penguin.

Kuhn, T. 2012. *The Structure of Scientific Revolutions*. Chicago, IL: University of Chicago Press.

Kurlansky, M. 2011. *Cod: A Biography of the Fish That Changed the World*. Toronto: Knopf Canada.

Kurzban, R. 2012. *Why Everyone (Else) Is a Hypocrite: Evolution and the Modular Mind*. Princeton, NJ: Princeton University Press.

Kurzban, R., M. Burton-Chellew & S. West 2015. "The evolution of altruism in humans". *Annual Review of Psychology* 66(1): 575–99.

Lahsen, M. & J. Ribot 2022. "Politics of attributing extreme events and disasters to climate change". *Wiley Interdisciplinary Reviews: Climate Change* 13(1): e750.

Landon, A. *et al.* 2021. "Psychological needs satisfaction and attachment to natural landscapes". *Environment and Behavior* 53(6): 661–83.

Langdon, S. 2007. "Sustaining a relationship: inquiry into the emergence of a logic of engagement with salmon among the southern Tlingits". In M. Harkin & D. Lewis (eds), *Native Americans and the Environment: Perspectives on the Ecological Indian*, 233–73. Lincoln, NE: University of Nebraska Press.

Lansing, J. 2012. *Perfect Order: Recognizing Complexity in Bali*. Princeton, NJ: Princeton University Press.

Leach, M., R. Mearns & I. Scoones 1999. "Environmental entitlements: dynamics and institutions in community-based natural resource management". *World Development* 27(2): 225–47.

Lehavi, A. 2008. "Mixing property". *Seton Hall Law Review* 38(1): 137–212.

Lemos, M. & A. Agrawal 2006. "Environmental governance". *Annual Review of Environment and Resources* 31(1): 297–325.

Leopold, A. 2020. *A Sand County Almanac: And Sketches Here and There*. Oxford: Oxford University Press.

Levin, S. 2000. *Fragile Dominion*. New York: Basic Books.

Lewicka, M. 2011. "Place attachment: how far have we come in the last 40 years?". *Journal of Environmental Psychology* 31(3): 207–30.

Libecap, G. 2007. "Assigning property rights in the common pool: implications of the prevalence of first-possession rules for ITQs in fisheries". *Marine Resource Economics* 22(4): 407–23.

Liscow, Z. 2013. "Do property rights promote investment but cause deforestation? Quasi-experimental evidence from Nicaragua". *Journal of Environmental Economics and Management* 65(2): 241–61.

List, J. 2022. *The Voltage Effect*. London: Penguin.

Lockhart, J. 1992. "Three experiences of culture contact: Nahua, Maya, and Quechua". *Mester* 21(2). https://escholarship.org/content/qt5m36v2x5/qt5m36v2x5.pdf.

Lubell, M. 2013. "Governing institutional complexity: the ecology of games framework". *Policy Studies Journal* 41(3): 537–59.

Lund, J. 2015. "Paradoxes of participation: The logic of professionalization in participatory forestry". Forest Policy and Economics 60: 1–6.

Lynham, J. 2014. "How have catch shares been allocated?". *Marine Policy* 44: 42–8.

Mabey, R. 1980. *The Common Ground: A Place for Nature in Britain's Future?* London: Hutchinson.

Matson, P., W. Clark & K. Andersson 2016. *Pursuing Sustainability: A Guide to the Science and Practice*. Princeton, NJ: Princeton University Press.

Mauss, M. 2016. *The Gift*. Chicago, IL: University of Chicago Press.

McGreavy, B. *et al.* 2018. "Enhancing adaptive capacities in coastal communities through engaged communication research: insights from a statewide study of shellfish co-management". *Ocean & Coastal Management* 163: 240–53.

Meadows, D. 1999. *Leverage Points: Places to Intervene in a System*. The Sustainability Institute. https://donellameadows.org/archives/leverage-points-places-to-intervene-in-a-system/.

Mesa-Lago, C. & M. González-Corzo 2021. "Agrarian reform and usufruct farming in socialist Cuba". *Journal of Economic Policy Reform* 24(2): 119–33.

Mildenberger, M. 2019. "The tragedy of the tragedy of the commons". *Scientific American*. https://blogs.scientificamerican.com/voices/the-tragedy-of-the-tragedy-of-the-commons/.

Milne, S. 2022. *Corporate Nature: An Insider's Ethnography of Global Conservation*. Tucson, AZ: University of Arizona Press.

Milne, S. & B. Adams 2012. "Market masquerades: uncovering the politics of community-level payments for environmental services in Cambodia". *Development and Change* 43(1): 133–58.

Miñarro, S. *et al.* 2016. "The role of patron-client relations on the fishing behaviour of artisanal fishermen in the Spermonde Archipelago (Indonesia)". *Marine Policy* 69: 73–83.

Monterroso, I. & D. Barry 2012. "The underpinnings of the forest tenure reform in the protected areas of Petén, Guatemala". *Conservation and Society* 10(2): 136–50.

Moritz, M. *et al.* 2018. "Emergent sustainability in open property regimes". *Proceedings of the National Academy of Sciences of the United States of America* 115(51): 12859–67.

Muller, J. 2018. *The Tyranny of Metrics*. Princeton, NJ: Princeton University Press.

Nagendra, H. 2007. "Drivers of reforestation in human-dominated forests". *Proceedings of the National Academy of Sciences of the United States of America* 104(39): 15218–23.

Netting, R. 1976. "What Alpine peasants have in common: observations on communal tenure in a Swiss village". *Human Ecology* 4(2): 135–46.

Newig, J. *et al.* 2018. "The environmental performance of participatory and collaborative governance: A framework of causal mechanisms". *Policy Studies Journal* 46(2): 269–97.

Nguyen, C. 2020. *Games: Agency As Art*. Oxford: Oxford University Press.

Niamir-Fuller, M. 1999. "Managing mobility in African rangelands". In N. McCarthy *et al.* (eds), *Property Rights, Risk, and Livestock Development in Africa*, 102–32. Washington, DC: International Food Policy Research Institute.

Nicholson, A. 2019. "Hau: giving voices to the ancestors". *Journal of the Polynesian Society* 128(2): 137–62.

Nockur, L. *et al.* 2020. "Collective choice fosters sustainable resource management in the presence of asymmetric opportunities". *Scientific Reports* 10(1): 10724.

Nowak, M. 2006. "Five rules for the evolution of cooperation". *Science* 314(5805): 1560–3.

O'Donnell, E. 2018. *Legal Rights for Rivers: Competition, Collaboration and Water Governance*. Abingdon: Routledge.

Ojanen, M. *et al.* 2017. "What are the environmental impacts of property rights regimes in forests, fisheries and rangelands?". *Environmental Evidence* 6(1): 1–23.

Olson, M. 1965. *The Logic of Collective Action*. Cambridge, MA: Harvard University Press.

Ostrom, E. 1990. *Governing the Commons: The Evolution of Institutions for Collective Action*. Cambridge: Cambridge University Press.

Ostrom, E. 1996. "Crossing the great divide: coproduction, synergy, and development". *World Development* 24(6): 1073–87.

Ostrom, E. 2007a. "A diagnostic approach for going beyond panaceas". *Proceedings of the National Academy of Sciences of the United States of America* 104(39): 15181–7.

Ostrom, E. 2007b. "Collective action theory". In C. Stokes (ed.), *Oxford Handbook of Comparative Politics*, 186–210. Oxford: Oxford University Press.

Ostrom, E. 2011. "Reflections on 'some unsettled problems of irrigation'". *American Economic Review* 101(1): 49–63.

Ostrom, E. & D. Cole 2012. "The variety of property systems in rights in natural resources". In D. Cole & E. Ostrom (eds), *Property in Land and Other Resources*, 37–64. Lincoln: Institute for Land Policy.

Ostrom, E., R. Gardner & J. Walker 1994. *Rules, Games, and Common-Pool Resources*. Ann Arbor, MI: University of Michigan Press.

Pacheco-Vega, R. 2020. "039: Water, waste, Covid, and the invisibility of life support systems with Raul Pacheco-Vega". In Common Podcast. www.incommonpodcast. org/podcast/039-water-waste-covid-and-the-invisibility-of-life-support-systems-with-raul-pacheco-vega/.

Perez, C. 2019. *Invisible Women: Data Bias in a World Designed for Men*. New York: Abrams Press.

Persha, L. & K. Andersson 2014. "Elite capture risk and mitigation in decentralized forest governance regimes". *Global Environmental Change* 24: 265–76.

Pink, D. 2011. *Drive: The Surprising Truth About What Motivates Us*. London: Penguin.

Popkin, G. 2022. "Are trees talking underground? For scientists, it's in dispute". *New York Times*, 7 November. www.nytimes.com/2022/11/07/science/trees-fungi-talking.html.

Poteete, A., M. Janssen & E. Ostrom 2010. *Working Together: Collective Action, the Commons, and Multiple Methods in Practice*. Princeton, NJ: Princeton University Press.

Reisner, M. 1986. *Cadillac Desert: The American West and Its Disappearing Water*. New York: Penguin.

Ribot, J. 1998. "Theorizing access: forest profits along Senegal's charcoal commodity chain". *Development and Change* 29(2): 307–41.

Ribot, J. & N. Peluso 2003. "A theory of access". *Rural Sociology* 68(2): 153–81.

Rode, J., E. Gómez-Baggethun & T. Krause 2015. "Motivation crowding by economic incentives in conservation policy: a review of the empirical evidence". *Ecological Economics* 117: 270–82.

Rodriguez, C. 2016. "To protect nature and boost economy, Cambodia must follow Costa Rica's lead". www.conservation.org/blog/to-protect-nature-and-boost-economy-cambodia-must-follow-costa-ricas-lead.

Rose, C. 2019. *Property and Persuasion: Essays on the History, Theory, and Rhetoric of Ownership*. Abingdon: Routledge.

Ryan, R. & E. Deci 2018. *Self-Determination Theory: Basic Psychological Needs in Motivation, Development, and Wellness*. New York: Guilford Press.

Sahlins, M. 2011. "What kinship is (part one)". *Journal of the Royal Anthropological Institute* 17(1): 2–19.

Sauls, L., F. Galeana & S. Lawry 2022. "Indigenous and customary land tenure security: history, trends, and challenges in the Latin American context". In M. Holland, Y. Masuda & B. Robinson (eds), *Land Tenure Security and Sustainable Development*, 57–79. London: Palgrave Macmillan.

Schlager, E., W. Blomquist & S. Tang 1994. "Mobile flows, storage, and self-organized institutions for governing common-pool resources". *Land Economics* 70(3): 294–317.

Schlager, E. & E. Ostrom 1992. "Property-rights regimes and natural resources: a conceptual analysis". *Land Economics* 68(3): 249–62.

Schlüter, M. *et al.* 2021. "Synthesis and emerging frontiers in social-ecological systems research methods". In R. Biggs *et al.* (eds), *Routledge Handbook of Research Methods for Social-Ecological Systems*, 453–79. Abingdon: Routledge.

Scott, J. 1977. *The Moral Economy of the Peasant: Rebellion and Subsistence in Southeast Asia*. New Haven, CT: Yale University Press.

Scott, J. 1998. *Seeing Like a State: How Certain Schemes to Improve the Human Condition Have Failed*. New Haven, CT: Yale University Press.

Scott, J. 2009. *The Art of Not Being Governed: An Anarchist History of Upland Southeast Asia*. New Haven, CT: Yale University Press.

Sen, A. 1982. *Poverty and Famines: An Essay on Entitlement and Deprivation*. Oxford: Oxford University Press.

Senge, P. 2010. *The Fifth Discipline: The Art and Practice of the Learning Organization*. London: Crown Publishing.

Shipton, P. 1988. "The Kenyan land tenure reform: misunderstanding in the public creation of private property". In R. Reyna (ed.), *Land and Society in Contemporary Africa*, 91–138. Lebanon, NH: University Press of New England.

Shipton, P. 2009. *Mortgaging the Ancestors: Ideologies of Attachment in Africa*. New Haven, CT: Yale University Press.

Shivakoti, G. & E. Ostrom 2002. *Improving Irrigation Governance and Management in Nepal*. San Francisco, CA: ICS Press.

Shrubsole, G. 2019. *Who Owns England? How We Lost Our Green and Pleasant Land, and How to Take It Back*. London William Collins.

Sikor, T., J. He & G. Lestrelin 2017. "Property rights regimes and natural resources: a conceptual analysis revisited". *World Development* 93: 337–49.

Sikor, T. & C. Lund 2009. "Access and property: a question of power and authority". *Development and Change* 40(1): 1–22.

Simard, S. 2021. *Finding the Mother Tree*. London: Penguin.

Smith, S. 2019. "Instream flow rights within the prior appropriation doctrine: insights from Colorado". *Natural Resources Journal* 59: 181.

Smith, S. *et al.* 2017. "Responding to a groundwater crisis: the effects of self-imposed economic incentives". *Journal of the Association of Environmental and Resource Economists* 4(4): 985–1023.

Snorek, J., F. Renaud & J. Kloos 2014. "Divergent adaptation to climate variability: a case study of pastoral and agricultural societies in Niger". *Global Environmental Change* 29: 371–86.

Steneck, R. *et al.* 2011. "Creation of a gilded trap by the high economic value of the Maine lobster fishery". *Conservation Biology* 25(5): 904–12.

Stoll, J. *et al.* 2019. "Evaluating aquaculture as a diversification strategy for Maine's commercial fishing sector in the face of change". *Marine Policy* 107: 103583.

Stone, C. 2010. *Should Trees Have Standing? Law, Morality, and the Environment*. Oxford: Oxford University Press.

Stone, D. 1997. *Policy Paradox: The Art of Political Decision Making*. New York: Norton.

Talbot-Jones, J. 2017. "The institutional economics of granting a river legal standing". https://openresearch-repository.anu.edu.au/handle/1885/132935.

Thaler, R. & C. Sunstein 2009. *Nudge: Improving Decisions about Health, Wealth, and Happiness*. London: Penguin.

Thompson, D. 2023. "Why there is so much bullshit in science". Plain English podcast, The Ringer. www.theringer.com/2023/1/11/23550859/why-there-is-so-much-bullshit-in-science.

Tolentino, J. 2019. *Trick Mirror: Reflections on Self-Delusion*. London: Random House.

Tooby, J. & L. Cosmides 1996. "Friendship and the banker's paradox: other pathways to the evolution of adaptations for altruism". *Proceedings of the British Academy* 88: 119–43.

Torres-Mazuera, G. 2022. "Dispossession through land titling: legal loopholes and shadow procedures to urbanized forestlands in the Yucatán Peninsula". *Journal of Agrarian Change* 23(2): 346–64.

Trimbach, D., W. Fleming & K. Biedenweg 2022. "Whose Puget Sound? Examining place attachment, residency, and stewardship in the Puget Sound region". *Geographical Review* 112(1): 46–65.

Trzeciak, S. & A. Mazzarelli 2019. *Compassionomics (The Revolutionary Scientific Evidence that Caring Makes a Difference)*. Pensacola, FL: Studer Group.

Van der Kolk, B. 2015. *The Body Keeps the Score: Brain, Mind, and Body in the Healing of Trauma*. London: Penguin.

van der Voo, L. 2016. *The Fish Market: Inside the Big-Money Battle for the Ocean and Your Dinner Plate*. New York: St Martin's.

van Kooten, G., S. Shaikh & P. Suchánek 2002. "Mitigating climate change by planting trees: the transaction costs trap". *Land Economics* 78(4): 559–72.

van Prooijen, J.-W. 2009. "Procedural justice as autonomy regulation". *Journal of Personality and Social Psychology* 96(6): 1166–80.

van Putten, I. *et al.* 2014. "Individual transferable quota contribution to environmental stewardship: a theory in need of validation". *Ecology and Society* 19(2): 35–48.

Vaughan, M. 2018. *Kaiāulu: Gathering Tides*. Corvallis, OR: Oregon State University Press.

Veldman, J. *et al.* 2019. "Comment on 'The global tree restoration potential'". *Science* 36(6463); doi:10.1126/science.aay7976.

Verkuyten, M. & B. Martinovic 2017. "Collective psychological ownership and inter-group relations". *Perspectives on Psychological Science* 12(6): 1021–39.

Vollan, B. 2008. "Socio-ecological explanations for crowding-out effects from economic field experiments in southern Africa". *Ecological Economics* 67(4): 560–73.

Wang, X., K. Fielding & A. Dean 2022. "Psychological ownership of nature: a conceptual elaboration and research agenda". *Biological Conservation* 267: 109477.

Webster, D. 2015. *Beyond the Tragedy in Global Fisheries*. Cambridge, MA: MIT Press.

Wheeler, S. *et al.* 2013. "Evaluating water market products to acquire water for the environment in Australia". *Land Use Policy* 30(1): 427–36.

Wilson, C. & C. Tisdell 2001. "Why farmers continue to use pesticides despite environmental, health and sustainability costs". *Ecological Economics* 39(3): 449–62.

Wilson, D. 2016. *Does Altruism Exist? Culture, Genes, and the Welfare of Others*. New Haven, CT: Yale University Press.

Wilson, D., E. Ostrom & M. Cox 2013. "Generalizing the core design principles for the efficacy of groups". *Journal of Economic Behavior & Organization* 90: S21–32.

Wilson, E. 1999. *Consilience: The Unity of Knowledge*. New York: Vintage.

Wilson, M., T. Pavlowich & M. Cox 2015. "Studying common-pool resources over time: a longitudinal case study of the Buen Hombre fishery in the Dominican Republic". *Ambio* 45(2): 215–29.

Young, O. 2002. *The Institutional Dimensions of Environmental Change: Fit, Interplay, and Scale*. Cambridge, MA: MIT Press.

Zückert, H. 2014. "The commons: a historical concept of property rights". In D. Bollier & S. Helfrich (eds), *The Wealth of the Commons: A World Beyond Market and State*. Amherst, MA: Levellers Press.

Index